Psychology's Sanction for Selfishness

A Series of Books in Psychology

Editors: Richard C. Atkinson
Gardner Lindzey
Richard F. Thompson

Psychology's Sanction for Selfishness

THE ERROR OF EGOISM
IN THEORY AND THERAPY

Michael A. Wallach
and Lise Wallach

Duke University

W. H. Freeman and Company

San Francisco

Project Editor: Pearl C. Vapnek
Copy Editor: Pat Tompkins
Designer: Eric Jungerman
Production Coordinator: Linda Jupiter
Compositor: Vera Allen Composition
Printer and Binder: The Maple-Vail Book Manufacturing Group

Library of Congress Cataloging in Publication Data

Wallach, Michael A.
    Psychology's sanction for selfishness.

    (A Series of books in psychology)
    Bibliography: p.
    Includes indexes.
    1. Psychology—Philosophy. 2. Self-interest.
3. Egoism. 4. Psychoanalysis. 5. Humanistic psychology.
6. Behaviorism (Psychology) I. Wallach, Lise.
II. Title. III. Series. [DNLM: 1. Defense mechanisms.
2. Motivation. 3. Psychological theory. WM 193 W195p]
BF38.W35   1983   150   82-18391
ISBN 0-7167-1465-5
ISBN 0-7167-1466-3   (pbk.)

Printed in the United States of America

1 2 3 4 5 6 7 8 9 0   MP   1 0 8 9 8 7 6 5 4 3

BF
38
.W35
1983

Contents

Preface   *ix*

**1   Should We Be "Looking Out
for Number One"?**   1

Concern for Others   *2*
Celebration of Self   *9*
The Role of Psychology   *17*
Notes   *29*

**2   Freud and the Selfishness Legacy:
Freud's Basic Ideas**   31

Freudian Beliefs About Motivation   *31*
Freud's Assumption and Encouragement
   of Egoism   *39*
Notes   *44*

**3   Freud and the Selfishness Legacy:
Why Did Freud Think This Way?**   46

The Wish to Unmask Illusion   *47*
"Naturalistic" Explanation
   Instead of Mysterious Forces   *50*

Observational Evidence 55
Notes 60

**4 Freud and the Selfishness Legacy:
Other Forms of Motivation**   61

Primary Energies of the Ego 63
Social Motivation 69
Implications 75
Notes 78

**5 Sullivan, Horney, and Fromm:
The Significance of the Social**   79

Sullivan 80
Horney 90
Fromm 99
Notes 108

**6 Sullivan, Horney, and Fromm:
Opposing Prescriptions and Restraints,
Promoting Self-Realization**   109

Self-Realization and the Attack
  on Restraints 111
Can the General Good Be Served
  Without Restraints? 115
Do Restraints Necessarily Oppose the Interests
  of the Individual? 118
Recapitulating the Argument 125
Notes 126

**7 Maslow and Rogers:
Further Calls to Actualize and Be Oneself**   127

Maslow 130
Rogers 140
Notes 150

8   Maslow and Rogers:
    Determination from Within Ourselves,
    Not from Outside   151

    No Determination from Outside the Self   152
    Can Freedom from External Determination
        Serve the General Welfare?   158
    Is Freedom from External Determination
        Best for the Individual?   165
    Freud's Opposing Principles Revisited   169
    Notes   172

9   Current Academic Psychology
    on Human Conduct   173

    A Sampling of "Conservative" Academic
        Trends   176
    A Sampling of "Liberal" Academic
        Trends   186
    Notes   194

10 Must Psychology Promote Selfishness?
    The Assumption of Egoism   196

    Isn't Egoism the Only Possibility?   199
    Psychological Theories of Motivation,
        Past and Present   204
    Motivation Not Based on Needs   217
    Notes   225

11 Must Psychology Promote Selfishness?
    Therapeutic Benefits from Turning Outward   227

    Detaching from Self-Oriented Experiences   233
    Furthering Something Beyond Oneself   244
    Notes   258

12 The Place of Ethics   260

  Are Ethical Values Irrational? *264*
  An Alternative View *270*
  Notes *274*

References *275*

Index of Names *297*

Index of Topics *303*

Preface

There is currently in our society an enormous emphasis upon the self, widely recognized in books and articles on narcissism, self-concern, and preoccupation with "me." In this book we consider the contributions of psychology to this trend. A surprisingly broad and influential range of psychological theory turns out to legitimize selfishness. Although this is usually far from what is intended, support is lent by academic thinkers as well as clinicians, by Freudians as well as anti-Freudians, by behaviorists as well as contenders against behaviorism, and by psychologists who investigate altruism as well as by those who deny its existence. Support is lent even by psychologists who themselves deplore the adverse moral impact of psychology's teachings.

In what follows, we examine the historical points of departure that have played such a pervasive and enduring role—sometimes explicit, sometimes implicit—in the panoply of current clinical and academic work. Our analysis suggests that the roots of psychology's ubiquitous sanction for selfishness lie in fundamental assumptions about motivation that almost all psychologists have come to take for granted. We attempt to demonstrate that these assumptions constitute holdovers from a time when they possessed a scientific plausibility that they now lack. The directions taken by psychological theorizing that serve to support and encourage selfishness do not, we find, seem justified in the light of current knowledge and evidence. Counter to the thrust of most thinking about motivation, a different picture may be emerging, suggesting that we can be genuinely motivated by ends outside of ourselves and that this may in fact be therapeutic for the individual as well as beneficial for the group.

While the book carries out a scholarly undertaking, we have tried to write it in a way that will be meaningful for the generally educated reader and for students as well as for clinical and academic professionals interested in the questions it raises. Thus, we include brief summaries of particular theorists' major ideas insofar as they are relevant to the topic of concern, and we avoid specialized terminologies. In this way our argument can be discerned whether or not the reader comes to this book with an articulated background in psychology. We have found that the notions expressed in this book lead to lively, sometimes very intense, discussions with graduate and undergraduate students of psychology, professionals, and other interested people whose formal acquaintance with psychology is minimal. We hope the book will have something to say that matters to each of these several audiences.

We owe much to more people than can be thanked individually, as well as to the heritage of concerns associated with the departments where we studied psychology: Swarthmore, Harvard, and Kansas. Roger Brown and M. Brewster Smith made helpful comments. Our colleagues at Duke University have been generous in their intellectual support. So have our students; we are especially grateful to Marianne Celano, Lisa Heimann, Daniel Doernberg, and Marcia Mandel. We would also like to thank Rachel Wallach, who was a discerning sounding board, and Verble Roberts, who handled all secretarial aspects of this work with excellent judgment, unfailing accuracy, and good cheer.

December 1982   Michael A. Wallach
                                                  Lise Wallach

1
Should We Be "Looking Out for Number One"?

This is a book about selfishness and psychology's role in promoting it. It is also a book about what could happen instead. In the name of scientific honesty and candor, psychological theorizing about human nature has become a significant force supporting what many view as a contemporary malady: preoccupation with self. To what extent is such support in fact a warranted inference from psychology? To what extent may it be ideological rather than thrust upon us by scientific necessity? What, in light of the concepts and evidence of psychology, are we really in a position to say about human tendencies toward egoism and selfishness?

These are the questions with which we deal in this book. In the course of trying to answer them, it will be necessary to examine, for their implications about selfishness, views that have been influential from psychology about what motivates us and what significance others have for us. Embedded in these views are assumptions running so deep that they can color a whole society's mode of construing what is natural, what is desirable, what is healthy, and what is appropriate in the human enterprise. Such presuppositions need to be laid bare and given a close look. In this first chapter, however, we want to illustrate the kinds of phenomena we seek to understand and glimpse something of the urgency of the issues raised.

Concern for Others

Apparent concern for the welfare of others can be found in humble as well as heroic contexts and at ages stretching from the cradle to the grave. What is this concern like? Is it no more than apparent, reducing to concern for self, or might it be real? It certainly starts young enough not to seem devious:

> Recently, two mothers whose 15- and 13-month-old sons frequently play together related how the 15-month-old inadvertently knocked down his 13-month-old playmate to get a toy. When the younger child began to howl, the 15-month-old first hugged him to get him to stop. He then tried to pick him up. Finally, everything else having failed, he located the younger child's bottle and handed it to him.[1]

Trying to alleviate his friend's distress, this young child seeks one way after another to make him feel better, tries to undo the damage by setting him back on his feet, and shows overall a considerable understanding of what might comfort him. Indeed, infants as young as one year already appear to take others into account in the sense of wanting to show and to give them what they themselves find of interest.[2]

Other people matter even for the infant. Children matter for their parents and friends for one another. A whole group can emphasize concern for others and devotion to their well-being as a strong part of its way of life. A 105-

year-old Amish woman in Pennsylvania describes this concern within her group: "Times change, and styles and ways of doing things change for us Amish. But the thing that has never changed is the way we help and care for each other. That never changes."[3]

However mundane it is, people can find significance in what they do because of its meaning for others. A retired tailor of 80 is proud of the role played by the neighborhood tailor working in America, believing that such tailors made it possible for poor people to wear coats. No matter how inexpensively it must be done, he points out, the tailor must remember that how well he cuts and sews the garment will mean the difference between whether a poor person can keep warm or not: "A coat is not a piece of cloth only. The tailor is connected to the one who wears it and he should not forget it."[4] His wife of 74 works to help striking Mexican-American migrant laborers by trying to get passersby to sign petitions in support of their strike. She doesn't like having to stand outside in the cold, and she doesn't like having to argue with people. Why then does she do this? "You don't do these things to enjoy. It has to be done, that's all."[5]

And those others to whom one feels connected can be animals as well as human beings. Myerhoff describes how another retiree takes it upon himself to make sure the stray neighborhood cats get fed. One day he gets beaten about the head by a psychotic woman; rather than wait for medical attention, he goes home to see to it that the stray cats on his street get their dinner. An elderly woman, no matter how bad the weather, goes out every day to feed the pigeons with huge bags of crumbs that she gathers from neighbors, stores, and restaurants, knowing that the pigeons are there waiting for her.[6]

People will do for the sake of someone else what they will not do for themselves. An older woman who is going blind refuses an operation that will save her vision, raging to herself at the doctors for their meddlesomeness, just wanting to be left as she is. "Then suddenly she realized what she might be doing to her children and grandchildren if she went blind. A blind old grandmother was the last thing she wanted to impose on them. Her torment ceased. She entered hospital without a further qualm. She had found someone to have her operation *for*."[7]

A person may volunteer, sometimes repeatedly, to donate blood for strangers—despite potential unpleasantness for the donor, no clear sanctions against not giving blood, no expressions of thanks from the unknown recipient, and the possibility that one might find the recipient's beliefs, character, and way of life totally repugnant. Titmuss[8] asked more than 3000 voluntary blood donors in Britain to indicate confidentially why they first decided to give blood. Nearly 80 percent of those surveyed—in a nation that, unlike ours, obtains most of its blood through strictly voluntary donation—gave reasons suggesting a high sense of concern for the needs of others.

One donor wrote: "You cant get blood from supermarkets and chaine stores. People them selves must come forword, sick people cant get out of bed to ask you for a pint to save thier life so I cam forword in hope to help somebody who needs blood."[9] This person made four donations. Another, who made 23 donations, writes: "Anonymously, without financial reward to help others."[10] Another, who made 10 donations: "Knowing I mite be saving somebody life."[11] Another person, who donated three times, noted: "Being in the construction side of building you see many people hurt and it makes you feel as though you have done a little bit to help."[12] "Sense of duty to the community and nation as a whole" was the reason supplied by a person who donated seven times.[13] People seem to want to be generous, indeed will give up a part of themselves, and find a certain fulfillment in doing so. They receive no pay or promise of future benefits. They may even be embarrassed when asked for an explanation, leading to a response like the following, from someone who made 19 donations—not counted in the high-concern 80 percent, although probably belonging there: "No money to spare. Plenty of blood to spare."[14]

The part of themselves a person gives up to another may represent a greater gift than blood. Those who donate one of their kidneys to save another's life see the act, when interviewed later on, as a triumph of what is good in themselves over what is bad.[15] For most people, it is something they knew they wanted to do as soon as the issue was broached, rather than something they backed into. Looking back after the operation, many see it as the most important act of their lives, this act by which they undertook in a heroic way to contribute to another's welfare. They feel they have done something to respect themselves for, become a better person. This feeling seems more than just a transitory phenomenon, since some interviews took place long after the operation. One donor, interviewed a year later, said: "The whole of my life is different. I've done something with my life."[16] Another person, interviewed 15 months after, explained: "It gives me inner satisfaction. When I have moments of depression, I think of my sister. I am happy."[17] Indeed, donors interviewed a second time nine years later still reported feeling much the same way.[18] Choosing to make these "sacrifices" of blood donations and kidney donations lets the person feel he is doing something of value—in the case of the kidney donors, of surpassing value.

Of course, people can accept still greater risks to themselves in pursuit of service to others. Civil rights activists working in the South through 1961 were largely committed to nonviolence, were often stigmatized as crackpots, and, working on long-term projects such as voter registration of Blacks, were often in serious danger for their lives. Interviewed later, those who had continuously worked a year or more on such projects were more likely than others who were less active to have parents who were themselves fully committed to sustained activities of social concern during their children's formative years.[19] For example, one person had a father who fought on the side of the Loyalists in the Spanish Civil War. Another activist's father was so outraged at Hitler that he managed to join the army during World War II even though he was overage.

A similar picture emerges of the parents of Christians who rescued Jews from the Nazis in Europe during World War II.[20] These rescuers' parents also acted in ways that strongly reflected what they believed in, despite personal costs, and their children had witnessed this. When the children grew up, they tended to do the same. For example, one such rescuer, interviewed after the end of the war, is a Seventh Day Adventist minister from the Netherlands who had organized a very effective large-scale operation for saving Dutch Jews from Nazi death camps. A nation where almost everyone is either Calvinist or Catholic, Holland did not always treat its Seventh Day Adventists kindly. His father had also been a minister in this marginal religious minority group, and had been forced to spend considerable time in jail. The son saw the father standing up for his beliefs even though it meant imprisonment. Why did the son, who even described himself as mildly anti-Semitic, carry out his rescue work? The reason he gave was a simple one: it is a Christian's duty.

By the time a whole village has generations of its inhabitants withstanding persecution by the religious majority, the kind of rescue work by the people of Le Chambon in southern France during World War II becomes more likely.[21] France is largely Catholic, but most of Le Chambon's approximately 3000 residents are Protestant. For hundreds of years the French Protestant minority had been persecuted for their faith, and Le Chambon already had a history of assimilating Protestants seeking sanctuary from elsewhere in France. The Chambonnais knew about death at the hands of the king's forces for refusing to abjure their Protestantism. The response of these mountain people had been the nonviolent one of secrecy, silence, and cunning—quietly refusing to give up their beliefs, using a portable pulpit for secretly conducting their religious services in the forests. With the Nazi occupation of France in World War II, this was a village ready to be led by its pastor in providing a haven for new victims of persecution—Jews from France and other nations.

Elaborate arrangements were worked out, virtually under the noses of the Vichy police and the Nazi Gestapo, for harboring Jewish refugees in the townspeople's homes, along with forging the necessary identification and ration cards—extremely dangerous activities. Hallie recounts, for instance, how a standing plan was devised for the "disappearance of the Jews" whenever a police raid was imminent. If the police tried to round up Jewish refugees for deportation, the Boy Scouts of the town were sent out as unobtrusively as possible to the houses harboring Jews to give warning that they should disperse into the surrounding woods.[22] Boy Scouts and young leaders of Bible classes functioned as crucial messengers in this plan, which worked smoothly enough that the Vichy police once spent the night sleeping on empty buses brought for removing the Jews the next day, while all around them in the houses and outlying farms the Jews were receiving their warnings and were quietly slipping into the woods.

Decades after these events, Hallie interviewed the Chambonnais about their hiding of Jewish refugees from the authorities; their basic explanation of why they took these risks, which could have resulted in extermination of the whole village, resembled that of the woman mentioned earlier who spent her time getting petitions signed to support migrant laborers. The Chambonnais said: "We were doing what had to be done. Who else could help them?"[23] "Things had to be done, that's all, and we happened to be there to do them."[24] "Who else would have taken care of them if we didn't?"[25] As with the Dutch minister, what comes through is a felt imperative to meet another person's need. They resisted being called "good" for what they did, since it "had to be done."

The Boy Scouts of Le Chambon played an important role as trusted messengers under dangerous circumstances. It seems ironic that talk of the Boy Scouts today is as likely to bring sneers as approval. Being a Boy Scout connotes someone who is *too* good and therefore not really what he purports to be, but a phony. Yet the Boy Scouts of Le Chambon during the Occupation were no more insincere than the rest of the town. They were living by the recommendations that are still to be found in the *Official Boy Scout Handbook*, which, as Fussell[26] points out, remains a best-seller. Fussell comments on what is to be found in this book: "The constant moral theme is the benefits of looking objectively outward and losing consciousness of self in the work to be done. To its young audience vulnerable to future invitations to . . . anxious self-absorption, the book calmly says, 'Forget yourself.' "[27]

Perhaps many are inspired by this kind of goal. The difficulty of its attainment needn't automatically make us view behavior in line with it as dishonest or self-deceptive. Even the pastor of Le Chambon, who courageously guided the townspeople in the complex arrangements necessary for hiding refugees, saw himself as constantly having to struggle to act unselfishly. He recounts in his memoirs how he realized, when his wife lay in danger of dying from loss of blood during the birth of their first child, that despite his deep love for her, part of himself was glad of his own health.[28] Unselfishness need not be a likely occurrence for it to be a possible one. At best, acting unselfishly may take constant struggle. Although unlikely, perhaps it is a possibility that is available to us.

Celebration of Self

What is most visible on the current scene is otherwise. As many have noted, self-gratification abounds, not only as fact but also as recommended ideal. The point can be illustrated by comparing two American films separated by 37 years, each containing a moral protagonist whom the audience is expected to admire: *Manhattan* (1979), with Woody Allen, and *Casablanca* (1942), with Humphrey Bogart. When the Humphrey Bogart character in *Casablanca*, a "tough-guy" night-club owner, talks of only looking out for himself, this cynicism turns out to be a cover for really caring about the welfare of others. For instance, he fixes things so that a young husband wins at the club's roulette table the money he and his wife need to leave wartime Casablanca, thereby saving the wife from her desperate resolve to arrange for their passage by selling herself. Most importantly, he gives up to another man the woman he loves, because he feels this renunciation and sacrifice on

his part will work out best for the others. The film's poign-
ancy turns on the fact that, when push comes to shove,
the Humphrey Bogart character, for all his talk, is anything
but selfish.

The Woody Allen character in *Manhattan*, on the other
hand, is accused by his friends of trying to play God—
leading to his defense at one point that, after all, he has
to model himself on someone. But the magnitude of his
own sacrifices for principle seem to be on the order of
moving to a smaller but still attractive apartment when,
after years of making money at it, he finally quits his job
as a writer for television. When a new girl friend becomes
available, the Woody Allen character drops the teenager
with whom he has been having an affair. After the new
lover in turn then abandons him, he has no qualms about
interfering with the teenager's career plans—she is on her
way to London to study acting—by trying to talk her out
of going. Earlier, when it suited his interests in getting her
out of the way, he had been only too glad to encourage
her to go. When push comes to shove for him, his basic
concern seems to lie in his own gratifications and what
they dictate, an attitude given its justification in terms of
the supreme value of being in touch with one's feelings.
As Kauffmann notes, what is missing under Allen's characteristic self-deprecation "is any true sense of dissatisfaction. Allen's mode . . . is basically a version of self-love."[29]

Even in someone proposed as a moral protagonist, the
height of wisdom seems to be understanding one's feelings
so that one can gratify them. Where in *Casablanca* cynicism
hid idealism, in *Manhattan* scratching the idealistic rhetoric
seems to bring us to a cynical core, which is legitimated
as psychological truth. Such a view of human nature is
hardly new; Hobbes enunciated it centuries ago when he
wrote, "All society . . . is either for gain, or for glory; that

is, not so much for love of our fellows, as for the love of ourselves."[30] What may be new, however, is the degree to which it currently stands in favor as an accurate account. Hobbes drew strong denials from religious circles,[31] but contemporary psychology seems to lend its support. Demurrals based on religion today tend to be readily dismissed as unscientific. A college teacher of literature has recently commented, in describing class discussions about characters, that her students are clear that the right actions for the characters, as for themselves, are the ones contributing to "their own personal and immediate well-being."[32] Even if this personal well-being must be at another's expense, any other way of proceeding is seen as pointless. What happens to the other person may be regretted, but where one owes one's primary obligation and allegiance is clear.

By now, the ramifications of self-concern as a dominant cultural theme have been chronicled in various ways. As Goodwin puts it, "The ideology of individualism is so powerful that we . . . look on bonds as restraints; values as opinions or prejudices; customs as impositions."[33] The self, Goodwin points out, is seen as a fully autonomous unit that should be responsible to no authority in the forming of its relationships beyond the exercise of its own volition—what it voluntarily wills and wishes to do. The social arrangements remaining that would permit a sense of community or shared social purpose "are assaulted as unjust restraints on liberty, impediments to the free assertion of the self."[34] The proper mode of living is to be oneself—to find out who one is and let no one and nothing interfere with one's self-realization.

Our society seems to promote as an ideal the ability to contain within ourselves all that matters to us. On a material level, this is reflected in the assumption that each of our household units should replicate all of the products and appliances that might contribute to our comfort, even if they could be shared among households. And on a psychological level, we should not lack any attributes that would enable us to stand alone. "The self-contained person is one who does not require or desire others for his or her completion or life; self-contained persons either are or hope to be entire unto themselves."[35] This seeking and affirmation of self-sufficiency implies a denial that others have any claims upon us, that there is an outside world of other people contributing to whatever sense of self we possess. It is a denial of the retired tailor's understanding that a human connection exists between the person who wears a coat and the one who made it. "What disappears in this view of things is the ground of community, the felt sense of collective responsibility for the fate of each separate other."[36]

An interesting example of self-sufficiency as a cultural ideal is the current approval and support in progressive circles for "psychological androgyny." The androgynous individual is one who is not sex-typed but rather contains within himself or herself both masculine and feminine characteristics.[37] Such a person would be more self-contained and independent of others than a person who is sex-typed as masculine or feminine. Perhaps ironically, support by liberals or progressives for the goal of psychological androgyny is support for a kind of person who does not need others to gain completeness. The effect would seem to reduce the extent to which we live through one another. Sampson questions the wisdom of such a goal: "If anything, to reinforce [androgyny] as the ideal seems to contribute to further human isolation and alienation and to thwart necessary cooperative ventures that build upon and recognize the needs of interdependence for their solution."[38]

In various ways, our society seems to value assertion or expression of self as an ultimate good. Ironically once again, the expression of self is pushed vigorously these days in just that therapeutic context in which one might most expect social values to be recognized: the encounter group or sensitivity-training group of the human potential movement. Other people are present in group therapy sessions, but not to encourage each other to find completion through serving specific others or contributing to their welfare. Rather, each group member is there to engage in the search for the true me, to improve her or his self-expression.

> The greatest good is individual self-expression; the group and the culture are seen as the evils that thwart freedom and independence. What has happened to the concept of interdependence in such settings? Persons are helped to separate themselves even further from others. Although much of this work takes place within a group context, it appears to be more a case of parallel play than of real interdependence.[39]

The encounter group's function, as a transitory, intensive social experience, is to advance the fulfillment of the individual; the individual, Smith points out, is defined as free from commitments to others.[40] Such concentration on personal will and wish as the proper guide to conduct and the appropriate definition of one's responsibilities may reach its extreme in something like Werner Erhard's form of group instruction—Erhard Seminars Training, or "est"—but leaves its mark, as Marin notes, on most of the group therapies of the human-potential movement.[41]

Celebration of self can be seen, in one form or another, exercising its effects across a wide spectrum of beliefs and practices—from personal relationships among adults, to parents' outlooks on child rearing, to what should take place in schools, in business, and in sports. In their personal relationships, men and women are frequently advised that it is legitimate to express their wants and desires without reserve and seek to have them gratified. However, their stance toward others should be one of detachment, of minimized commitments and dependencies. One has the right to assert oneself and seek gratification, but one should avoid entangling commitments and preserve one's freedom to move on without regrets or a sense of loss. As Lasch[42] points out, this posture of trying to get without giving was described years ago by Willard Waller[43] in his sociological study of the life style of recently divorced bohemians in the 1920s. The difference is the extent to which this outlook has gained ground as not only defensible but appropriate. Today, it is quite pervasive rather than more or less confined to a self-styled avant-garde. The role of another person is, insofar as one can manage it, to serve as a means for fulfilling one's own emotional requirements. One should not be losing oneself in that other person, subordinating oneself as a part that seeks completion and meaning through another person—or through a cause or tradition outside oneself. Such superordinate loyalties tend to be viewed as an unacceptable limitation on one's personal freedom. Rather, one should cultivate a posture of detachment and make "nonbinding commitments."

In parent–child relations, it is frequently emphasized that both parties—child and parent—have the right to self-expression and that what they should do is communicate their personal wishes to each other and use this as a basis for some sort of negotiation process.[44] Parents are in effect advised that they should not guide their children in terms of the values they hold and the nature of reality, that they should not identify with their children or encourage the children to identify with them or with the family as a whole, but rather that the parents should view their interactions entirely as adversaries. The goal for parents is to minimize friction and limitations of autonomy; child and parent are alien entities rightfully engaged in pursuing their own gratifications. Enlightenment comes with admitting that one's child is a rival to be dealt with respectfully. One should expect to feel jealous of displacement by the young rather than finding the possibility of fulfillment and continuity through them. An obvious solution, if one is sufficiently foresightful, is not having children at all.

Views of how teachers should interact with students similarly tend to see the main task as arbitration between what everyone wants for themselves. Again ironically, it is especially in progressive educational circles that children are encouraged toward individual self-expression, in the interests of fostering personal creativity, freedom, and spontaneity. Submergence of self in the fulfillment of larger loyalties and responsibilities is viewed with suspicion; the rest of the world is less important, if not downright oppressive. As Cagan notes, the educational progressives emphasize individual autonomy and self-fulfillment as the child's rights, reflecting in this the general society's individualism even as they claim to pose an alternative to that society's values.[45] The teacher, like the parent, is an equal to the child with little right to interfere. Since invoking of larger values and priorities is suspect, the major possibility that remains is a standoff based on mutual tolerance for the legitimacy of each person's self-interests, child or adult.

Even in the realms of business and sports, commitments to the firm or team of which one is a member seem increasingly eclipsed by the pursuit of advantage of an entirely personal kind. The notion of dedication to some higher purpose or larger goal represented by advancement of the team or the firm as a whole seems increasingly quaint and out of date. Instead, the team or firm constitutes an arena within which the individual strives to enhance personal success or reputation, feeling free to use the larger organization toward that end. The organization is to be manipulated for one's personal advancement, while at the same time one's luggage is packed for pursuit of the next offer. Lasch puts it this way: "In sport as in business, group loyalties no longer temper competition. Individuals seek to exploit the organization to their own advantage and to advance their interests not merely against rival organizations but against their own teammates. The team player, like the organization man, has become an anachronism."[46]

The legitimacy of expression and assertion of self as a ground for our conduct reaches a kind of reductio ad absurdum when it is invoked as an explanation, if not exoneration, of terrorist attacks on civilians. Krauthammer points out that this seems to be happening in press and television accounts of the reasons for terrorist actions that can't be explained in terms of clear military or propaganda objectives. For example, he notes that the "ABC Evening News" of April 2, 1979, rather blandly explained an attack by the Palestine Liberation Organization on the U.S. Embassy in Beirut using rocket-propelled grenades as serving "perhaps as an expression of frustration and resentment" over the peace treaty between Egypt and Israel. In the "casually matter-of-fact explanation" in terms of emotional self-expression given by the mass media in their recent coverage of such terrorist attacks, Krauthammer sees an example of the widespread acceptance that expressive freedom has won as a justification for what people do.[47] We almost seem to respect terrorists for a kind of honesty of self-expression while we question the motivation of Boy

Scouts for the helpfulness and concern for others that they may show.

The Role of Psychology

What about the impact of psychology on this situation? First, we need to make some points concerning current outlooks about clinical and therapeutic practice. Then we shall consider what seems to come across most vividly in texts and teaching. In regard to clinicians' and therapists' outlooks, their beliefs and values were once thought to have little direct effect on their clients. The clinician was understood to be a kind of horticulturist engaged in bringing out the true nature of each client by encouraging a process of unfolding along predetermined lines. More recently, the outlooks of a clinician or therapist have been recognized to be anything but irrelevant.[48] The clinician is acknowledged as not so much a horticulturist as a teacher who, implicitly if not explicitly, guides and influences the client in ways affected by the clinician's view of psychological truth. Indeed, the conflict that can exist between the values the clinician may believe in and seek to implement and the values of many clients has been increasingly called to attention.[49]

If we look at the titles of self-help books on the popular psychology bookshelves, what gets offered as advice presumably coming from psychology for our conduct is clear. Provided without apology or diffidence are titles like *Looking Out for Number One*, *The Art of Being Selfish*, and *How to Be Your Own Best Friend*. If we consider the content of Erhard's est, what we find is similar. But is it fair to take this emphasis in popular psychology as a reflection, even if in caricature, of the psychological mainstream? The answer appears to be yes. Asserting oneself seems quite broadly accepted as a sign of mental health; guilt seems readily viewed as a form of oppression from which we are entitled to deliver ourselves in the interests of psychological soundness. To view personal gratification as the primary basis of our functioning is taken as necessary if we are not to be crippled psychologically. As commentators like Cagan[50] and Hogan[51] have pointed out, the current psychological consensus emphasizes, as the requirement of a healthy personality, that we act and judge ourselves in terms of achievement of the satisfaction of our personal needs and desires.

This consensus appears despite considerable differences in other respects. We can find a Fromm or a Rogers or a Maslow believing we should trust self-expression because human nature, left to its own devices, is essentially wholesome. Troubles are viewed as coming from the outside society, whose constraints and coercions oppress us. The task therefore is to find a mode of living that is truly expressive of, and really satisfying to, the individual in question. Let the person's nature rise up and manifest itself; it is to be trusted. But we can also find a Freud arguing that too much attempted goodness goes against our less-than-wholesome nature and therefore bespeaks neurosis. Therapy must act to relieve the pangs of conscience that otherwise are marshaled against the pleasures we seek for ourselves; it must free us to pursue our satisfactions with more impunity. Thus, hardly an optimist about human nature, Freud ends up at a similar place: the necessity of expressing and gratifying ourselves. Different outlooks all tend to see particular others or society in general as inhibitors of our nature, as sources of bondage. Their therapies all seek to further the client's mental health by bringing about greater self-acceptance and self-fulfillment, along with the recognition that one's troubles may be induced by the impact of others—one's parents or spouse, society's pressures and expectations.

The push toward selfishness inherent in these sentiments has not entirely escaped the notice of those psychologists who ponder the implications of therapy. Some, although they seem to be in the minority, see a problem with such views. Two examples of how psychologists who sense a problem here seek to define it and cope with it will serve to illustrate something of the extent to which psychology itself—the nature of its guiding assumptions and modes of thought—seems part of what is problematical. At one extreme stands a psychologist like Vitz, who finds psychology so tied up with celebration of self that the only alternative is to move outside it and embrace the Christian doctrines of sin and salvation. Vitz seems to feel that human nature as such cannot offer a sufficient basis for hope, because that nature is tainted with evil. He writes, "The efforts that parents and teachers put into helping children to share, to play together, to cooperate, and so forth are tributes to the natural negative capacity of children."[52] Apparently ignoring the kinds of observations of infants' positive concern for one another that we sampled at the beginning of this chapter, Vitz concludes that we must transcend our nature by accepting the beliefs of Christianity. The answer, by emphasizing the Christian virtues of humility, curbing of pride, and service to others, is to lose the self—to let it become "an object in the love and the service of God."[53] Religious commitment is the necessary corrective to psychology.

Just as unhappy as Vitz is with psychology's support of selfishness is Kanfer, a psychologist who nevertheless tries to offer a remedy from within psychology. He proposes that what is to be done is to train people in altruistic behavior. They can be provided with social approval and recognition for helping behavior and led to reinforce themselves by praising themselves for their competence when they behave unselfishly. The incentives for helping others, in this conception, continue to be one's experiences of social reward and one's feelings of competence, not the well-being of the other person or group. As Kanfer puts it, "The task . . . is to train persons to act for the benefits of another because it is in their own self-interest."[54] If the only way to arrive at concern for others is through linking it in some arbitrary fashion to egocentric gratifications, we can understand how a psychologist like Vitz might throw up his hands and feel he must seek his answers from religion. For all his genuine worry over the support that current psychological beliefs provide for selfishness, Kanfer illustrates, ironically enough, that his own outlooks are part of the problem he deplores.

What of the impact of psychological texts and teaching? The perspective that gets communicated in the teaching of psychology is hardly a trivial matter, since, as Campbell points out, it reaches a substantial proportion of the students who attend college, not to mention increasing numbers of high school students. Understandably, the subject matter dealt with by psychology matters a great deal to students, concerned as they are with choices affecting how they will live their lives. A psychologist who has taught for many years, Campbell gives this account of the perspective that gets communicated in the teaching of psychology:

> Psychology and psychiatry . . . not only describe man as selfishly motivated, but implicitly or explicitly teach that he ought to be so. They tend to see repression and inhibition of individual impulse as undesirable, and see all guilt as a dysfunctional neurotic blight created by cruel child rearing and a needlessly repressive society. They further recommend that we accept our biological and psychological im-

pulses as good and seek pleasure rather than enchain ourselves with duty.[55]

A decade earlier, Campbell had already noted that psychology's teaching about human interaction—"social psychology"—explains our relations with one another in terms of "the self-centered concern of the actors as to 'What's there in it for me?'—a mutual back scratching on the part of fundamentally selfish organisms."[56]

However tentatively textbooks may put forth generalizations of these kinds—and often the mode of presentation is anything but tentative—the qualifications tend to get lost, and what remain are presumptive formulations about human nature invested with an aura of scientific necessity. What the students carry away with them are, in their view, scientific laws or necessary truths about how we act. These tend to be taken, as Sampson points out, to have universality of application and broad generality, rather than reflecting some of what may go on in a particular culture at a given time with particular values such as individualism.[57] Do we work hard and persistently at pursuing achievements? If we do, the reason is a personal wish to excel and win in competition.[58] Another possible reason for working hard in this way—seeking to further values one holds to be important independent of one's self—tends to be ignored. Do we try to fight for the rights of people who are oppressed? The place to look for an explanation is in the channeling and conversion of aggression originally felt for other reasons, thus giving this otherwise unacceptable feeling a permissible discharge.[59] Psychology in such ways seems to be recommending that when we see striving or persistence, whether in others or in ourselves, we should approach it cynically and ask what is in it for the person.

Believing these generalizations to be universal and immutable can, of course, have an element of self-fulfilling prophecy. Students, as consumers of psychological knowledge, can draw the conclusion that they have no choice but to behave in selfish ways, since that is what people are like—themselves included. The result, ironically, can be students feeling guilty if caught doing something altruistic, as if this violates some higher ethic that they should be looking out for themselves, and doing anything other than that means they are being taken advantage of, or behaving like a sucker.[60] The appropriate posture becomes a debunking attitude toward one's own motives as well as those of others. One needn't try to act altruistically since one cannot do so anyway; all such action can produce is insincerity. Especially in a secular society like ours, which has tended to replace religion with "scientific knowledge" about people as a guide to conduct, students can be expected to use what they learn from psychology to interpret their own and others' lives. Berger and Luckmann[61] argue that such doctrines readily take on considerable power for us—they have a quality of requiredness about them, defining what we are really like. To the extent that we believe them, they can influence us to act accordingly.

As illustrations of what can come across in the teaching, we take as examples two books: one general (an introductory text); the other more specific (a text on social psychology). They are both books aiming to be quite scientific rather than popular treatments—high-level texts intending to provide serious accounts of the subject for sophisticated students.

Consider first the highly regarded introductory text written by Brown and Herrnstein. Human desire is understood as basically antisocial; there is a "tension between desire and society."[62] Society manages to get its demands met and to maintain complex institutions and values such as marriage, parenthood, scholarship, loyalty to friends and fam-

ily, faith in one's country, and integrity essentially by gear-
ing into and making use of individual selfishness: "A person
who has learned to accept some social values will be re-
warded, or not punished, by serving them. He is still acting selfishly . . . but the selfishness will have been har-
nessed to some part of the collective judgment."[63] Brown
and Herrnstein put quotes around "social" when giving
an account of why people engage in social acts, reminding
the reader thereby that while the acts may look social, the
explanation for these acts really involves individual gains
and losses. Again we see the kind of outlook that Kanfer
represented—the idea that you will get people to be altruistic to the extent that you harness altruism to serving
their own selfish interests. The possibility of direct concern
for others or for the furthering of what one believes in and
values is given little consideration. The implications of this
view are borne out in Brown and Herrnstein's conception
of morality as something that is likely to be a lot of talk
with little substance. They suggest that one should not be
"so naive as to think that what a person says has anything
to do with how he behaves. . . . We may act to maximize
our tangible selfish rewards, and talk in a way that credits
us with greater altruism."[64]

As an example of the use of research evidence, consider
Brown and Herrnstein's discussion of what bystanders do
in emergencies. The authors emphasize the theme of bystander unresponsiveness. Thus, they describe a study by
Latané and Darley[65] in which 96 shopliftings were staged
at a discount beer store. In the staged shoplifting, two
would-be customers make off with a case of beer, saying
"They'll never miss this," while the store clerk is in the
back. Rate of spontaneous reporting of the occurrence by
genuine customers when the clerk returned was only 20
percent, which Brown and Herrnstein seem to treat as

striking evidence of not caring. Yet, as they themselves also indicate, the meaning of the low level of reporting is not clear, since some customers may have viewed reporting as a kind of squealing. Brown and Herrnstein ignore a study published in 1969 that could have been cited as evidence for an opposite point of view. Piliavin, Rodin, and Piliavin[66] staged 103 emergencies in New York City subway trains. About a minute into an express train's run of some seven and one-half minutes between two stations on the subway line, a man in the subway car staggered forward and collapsed on the floor. Spontaneous help by subway riders was provided on 81 of the 103 trials—a very high rate. The bystander would drag the victim to a seat or to an upright position. In almost all the instances in which spontaneous help was not forthcoming, the victim had been made to seem like a drunk. But even under those conditions, he often was helped anyway.

Our aim is not to pit one study against another, but to indicate that hard evidence does not inexorably draw one to a cynical outlook. The strength of the cynicism seems to come from elsewhere. This attitude becomes all the more clear when we note that the investigators who carried out the subway study themselves explained their findings cynically, writing: "Note that the major motivation implied in the model is not a positive 'altruistic' one, but rather a selfish desire to rid oneself of an unpleasant emotional state."[67] (The model has since been revised in a somewhat less egoistic direction, but it is still essentially the same.[68])

What happens when we turn to a text that concentrates on social psychology in particular? The recent one by Harrison again aims at a scientific treatment for the intelligent student, rather than being "easy" or a popularization. In this text, dating and marriage are understood as a marketplace phenomenon involving the exchange of commodities—you barter some commodity in your possession for another commodity in someone else's possession. Thus, Harrison argues, "The choice of a partner represents a trade-off in which both persons get the best they can with what they have to offer."[69] An example of one such exchange would be "a trade of sexual prowess and good looks for money and prestige, as when a handsome but penniless young man is drawn to a rich but elderly dowager."[70] This might have been called a form of prostitution, but seems to be viewed by Harrison as structurally like other dating and mating; it all involves bartering assets.

The message to the student appears to be that you fool yourself if you think dating and marriage, including your own, are other than a marketplace phenomenon. Cynicism is encouraged in the name of scientific accuracy, which is called for if we are to honestly face the realities of our own nature. The possibility of concern for and commitment to another person's welfare as an end in itself, rather than as a presumptive means to some personal benefit, seems not to be taken seriously. It should be no surprise if a market-place orientation to dating and mating had a hand in driving divorce rates up. Such an orientation would make it only natural, after all, to stay on the lookout for some better deal obtainable by dropping a present partner for a new one—a chance to trade upward.

In this text, too, cynicism seems to have a strength that goes beyond the evidence adduced in its behalf. For example, Harrison points out that help to a stranded motorist with a flat is more likely to be offered by someone who has expertise at changing flat tires than by someone without it and that emergency medical help is more likely to be offered by someone trained in first aid than by someone lacking training. The explanation he gives is this: "When a person feels competent, he or she is likely to offer assistance because the costs of helping (in terms of effort, risk, and danger) will tend to be low."[71] But the same events can be understood in a different, less cynical way. If you are more competent, you can expect to do more actual good. Here is a direct reason for the person of greater competence to be more likely to offer help, yet Harrison ignores it. The impression is left that the explanation based on reducing personal costs is the scientific view of the matter.

These are not isolated illustrations. They could be multiplied, and they seem typical. A cynical outlook is, by and large, believed to be the objective, scientific one. Most psychologists, furthermore, seem to be quite open about it. Thus, Aronfreed[72] views the child's attempts to reduce another's distress as coming entirely from an arbitrary hooking of that distress to distress in oneself. The child is in fact trying to reduce his or her own distress. But note that if the real goal is minimizing distress in oneself, rather than helping another, an obvious alternative becomes learning to ignore others. In a text intended to present a scientific treatment of the self, Arkin informs his readers that persons who have unfairly profited at another's expense put on a public display of unhappiness and guilt but really feel happy.[73] Schopler, in turn, provides an analysis that suggests that, if people only understood what was really going on, they would hardly ever help one another except in the context of specific role requirements.[74] He considers that a recipient of help will want to reciprocate only if the help seems given with no strings attached—from the goodness of the donor's heart. The recipient will feel gratitude and affection and will be concerned to repay the donor to the degree that the help seems offered with no expectation of reciprocation. Schopler's suggestion is that donors in fact conceal strings that really are there. They will give help seemingly without thought of reward while covertly relying upon the reciprocity norm to operate. In reality, then, there is no legitimate basis for the recipient to feel gratitude and affection toward the donor or to be motivated to reciprocate. And without expectation of return, the donor would no longer be motivated to help. As Hatfield, Walster, and Piliavin sum up the situation, "The majority of scientists . . . are fairly cynical."[75] Including themselves in this majority, they feel that, "most often . . . scientists attribute apparent altruism to more selfish motives."[76]

Cynicism influences what a psychologist will choose to study about people, which in turn can give more grounds for cynicism. Thus, in the study described earlier of an emergency in the subway, Piliavin, Rodin, and Piliavin[77] manipulated cost to the bystander by varying whether the victim who collapsed on the subway car floor looked drunk—and hence disagreeable—or sober. Because spontaneous help was less likely (although still often given) if the victim appeared drunk, the investigators make the essentially cynical point that bystanders are more likely to help if potential costs to themselves are smaller. Instead, they could have done a different kind of study—one manipulating the costs to the victim of not receiving help— and seen whether bystanders are more likely to help if potential costs to the victim of not receiving help are greater. Shotland and Huston did just this, finding that drivers in a campus parking lot were more likely to give someone a ride to a town five miles away if the situation seemed to be an emergency (64 percent helped) than if it did not (45 percent helped).[78] Here is evidence against cynicism. Yet, psychologists have been much more interested in manipulations that would document cynicism rather than its opposite. Note too that, just as some bystanders helped the subway victim even if he was made to seem like a drunk, some people provided the requested lift in their car even if the situation was not an emergency. The cynicism of most psychological experiments seems to go beyond the data, suggesting that prior commitment of an ideological kind has taken place. This commitment then affects what is chosen for study and what aspects of the results receive emphasis.

It is not just popular psychology, with its self-help books and its est sessions, that promotes acceptance of selfishness and cynicism. The popular psychology claims a scientific basis that appears to be granted to it. Psychology at its most scientific seems tied up with promoting cynicism and selfishness.

Having suggested the impact of psychology on students, we close this chapter with some statements by students and recent graduates who not only are familiar with psychology but also have been seriously involved in providing crisis-intervention or peer-counseling services. They have acted to help others. What do they think of their motives? One said: "Doing something for other people is gratifying needs in yourself, otherwise you wouldn't do it." Another observed: "There is a part of me that needs to believe that altruism is alive and well, especially in me. But there's also a cynicism—something like altruism can't exist." These sentiments were expressed by another student: "I think there's always a payoff. You always get something back. . . . Often it looks as if it's altruistic, but there's always a reason. . . . You always get things back and if you say you don't, then I think you're kidding yourself."

Recall that in their introductory psychology text Brown and Herrnstein offered the expectation that people would act selfishly but in their talk would credit themselves with altruism.[79] What we find in the statements just quoted, however, suggests the opposite: people engaged in activities aimed at helping others, but, in their talk, tending to view themselves as selfish. They seem skeptical about altruism, confused about understanding what they do in other than cynical terms. This seems to be where the psychology they have learned has gotten them.

It may be unavoidable for psychology to foster cynicism and encourage self-centeredness, if recognition of the egoism of motivation and the dependence of mental health on expression and gratification of self follows from objective consideration of the evidence and the issues. But is this really where objective consideration takes us? Let us now look more closely at how these views developed, the reasons for their acceptance, and some possible alternatives.

Notes

1. Borke, 1972, p. 108.
2. Hay, 1979.
3. Bryer, 1979, pp. 260–261.
4. Myerhoff, 1978, p. 44.
5. Myerhoff, 1978, p. 49.
6. Myerhoff, 1978.
7. de Castillejo, 1974, p. 155.
8. Titmuss, 1971.
9. Titmuss, 1971, p. 227.
10. Titmuss, 1971, p. 227.
11. Titmuss, 1971, p. 227.
12. Titmuss, 1971, p. 229.
13. Titmuss, 1971, p. 230.
14. Titmuss, 1971, p. 234.
15. Fellner and Marshall, 1970.
16. Fellner and Marshall, 1970, p. 276.
17. Fellner and Marshall, 1970, p. 277.
18. Fellner and Marshall, 1981.
19. Rosenhan, 1970.
20. London, 1970.
21. Hallie, 1979.
22. Hallie, 1979.
23. Hallie, 1979, p. 20.
24. Hallie, 1979, p. 21.
25. Hallic, 1979, p. 127.
26. Fussell, 1979.
27. Fussell, 1979, p. 21.
28. Hallie, 1979.
29. Kauffmann, 1979, p. 23.
30. Hobbes, 1642/1973, p. 20.
31. See, for example, Butler, 1726/1973.
32. Parr, 1977, p. 40.
33. Goodwin, 1974, p. 75.
34. Goodwin, 1974, p. 75.
35. Sampson, 1977, p. 770.
36. Marin, 1975, p. 48.
37. See, for example, Bem, 1974.
38. Sampson, 1977, p. 774.
39. Sampson, 1977, p. 777.
40. Smith, 1978.
41. Marin, 1975.
42. Lasch, 1978.
43. Waller, 1930.
44. See, for example, Gordon, 1976.
45. Cagan, 1978.
46. Lasch, 1978, p. 116.

30   Looking Out for Number One?

47. Krauthammer, 1979, p. 16E.
48. Carson, 1969.
49. Bergin, 1980.
50. Cagan, 1978.
51. Hogan, 1975.
52. Vitz, 1977, p. 87.
53. Vitz, 1977, p. 127.
54. Kanfer, 1979, p. 237.
55. Campbell, 1975, p. 1104.
56. Campbell, 1965, p. 285.
57. Sampson, 1978.
58. McClelland and Winter, 1971; McClelland, 1978.
59. Vaillant, 1977.
60. Campbell, 1965.
61. Berger and Luckmann, 1966.
62. Brown and Herrnstein, 1975, p. 185.
63. Brown and Herrnstein, 1975, p. 174.
64. Brown and Herrnstein, 1975, p. 289.
65. Latané and Darley, 1970.
66. Piliavin, Rodin, and Piliavin, 1969.
67. Piliavin, Rodin, and Piliavin, 1969, p. 298.
68. Piliavin, Dovidio, Gaertner, and Clark, 1981.
69. Harrison, 1976, p. 284.
70. Harrison, 1976, p. 284.
71. Harrison, 1976, p. 321.
72. Aronfreed, 1970.
73. Arkin, 1980.
74. Schopler, 1970.
75. Hatfield, Walster, and Piliavin, 1978, p. 128.
76. Hatfield, Walster, and Piliavin, 1978, p. 129.
77. Piliavin, Rodin, and Piliavin, 1969.
78. Shotland and Huston, 1979.
79. Brown and Herrnstein, 1975.

2

Freud and the Selfishness Legacy: Freud's Basic Ideas

Implicitly as well as explicitly, Freud's thinking casts a long shadow across our topic of inquiry. In Chapters 2, 3, and 4, we come to terms with the legacy of selfishness that he bequeathed to psychology's understanding of human motivation. There is, of course, a great deal to Freudian theory—enough to have filled volume after volume of expository as well as critical work. Important to us here are just the major outlines and how they imply a conception of humans as necessarily selfish or egoistic. Although many aspects of Freud's theory have been subjected to serious criticism and are accepted now, when at all, largely in revised form, most students of Freud seem to have continued taking for granted the basic egoism or selfishness that the theory assumes.

Freudian Beliefs About Motivation

Let us then sketch the central features of Freud's view. He believed that all behavior is motivated: nothing we do is a consequence just of chance, or automatic habit, but is always really somehow a function of what we desire or wish. Even slips of the tongue, for example, are not simply mistakes but, rather, reflections of our motives. To cite just one illustration: "A young woman who wore the breeches in her home told me that her sick husband had been to the doctor to ask what diet he ought to follow for his health. The doctor, however, had said that a special diet was not important. She added: 'He can eat and drink what *I* want.' "[1]

The motives or wishes that underlie our actions are, according to Freud, by no means always conscious ones. The woman in this example might well deny that she wants the husband's diet to be her decision rather than his, but we would probably not be convinced. A great deal of our motivation remains unconscious or repressed, Freud says, because in one way or another awareness of it would cause us too much pain. Admitting some things to awareness would mean that we would have to recognize aspects of ourselves we would find abhorrent: wishes to dominate those we love, feelings of hate toward them as well as love, and all manner of other dispositions we do not conceive of as tolerable in a worthy individual.

Crucially important, then, in everything we do, are our wants, our motivations, our wishes—which are sometimes conscious and often not. Where do these come from? They originate, according to Freud, in instinctual drives with which we are born. Freud did not always hold the same position on what instinctual drives were to be found in us. Much of his theory is worked out in terms of a set of life-preserving instincts such as hunger and thirst and another set for preservation of the species—sex; later he added a destructive or death instinct and grouped all the former ones together as Eros, a love or life instinct. (This later version was never so fully developed or so well integrated with the rest of his thinking as the earlier version.) In any case, certain particular instincts were postulated to exist, corresponding to basic biological needs. Our wishes and desires were understood to be ultimately traceable to the operation of these instincts or needs.

The way in which the instincts are conceived of as operating can be illustrated by considering Freud's view of the hunger drive. We become hungry (normally) when we have a physical need for food; this need is somehow represented psychologically—as drive or tension—in such a way as to lead to activity that will tend to satisfy this need. When we have gotten food and eaten it, the drive diminishes again until the next time. The drive or tension is what makes us act; it is unpleasurable, and its reduction is pleasurable.

Freud thought that all activity, like the food-seeking of a hungry organism, essentially results from bodily stimulation or excitation that the activity is designed to diminish. We act to remove stimulation, and it is reduction in stimulation that, in general, is felt as pleasurable. (Freud recognized that there were certain complications in this, as in the case of increase in tension with sexual excitation, but he never gave it up as a general principle.[2])

External stimuli can be reduced by the relatively simple mechanism of withdrawing from them. Because of their origin, internal stimuli cannot be handled in that way. They therefore exert much more complex demands on the nervous system, requiring it to execute intricate maneuvers that manage to change the outside environment in ways that serve to reduce those internal stimuli and thus result in instinctual satisfaction.[3]

The satisfaction of instinctual drives is by no means a simple matter. There are various kinds of problems and dangers. One is the nature of physical reality itself, which does not always make gratification possible. For example, there may simply be no food available when a person is hungry, or the only means to food may involve grave threats.

A second kind of problem for instinctual satisfaction is that society inevitably imposes severe restraints on the direct expression of our instincts, particularly those of sex and destructiveness. If human beings simply had sexual relations with whomever they chose, whenever they chose, if they expressed their destructive urges whenever and wherever they wished, community life would be impossible and all would be chaos. Behavior of this kind is thus severely punished, which means that one's freedoms to express one's instincts are seriously limited not just by physical but also by social reality.

And finally, there is a third source of limitation—oneself. Growing up in society, one internalizes its prohibitions— often in overly restrictive, distorted ways—and imposes them on oneself. Why do we continue to refrain from so much our parents have forbidden when our parents are no longer in a position to punish us or when no one could even find out what we have done? Why do we sometimes demand of ourselves more than anyone else does? We curb and spur ourselves because we have taken in the prohibitions and demands of our parents and other authorities and made them our own, often strengthening and rigidifying them in the process.

Freud graphically described these problems of instinct expression in terms of the id, ego, and superego.[4] He thought of the instincts as belonging to the innately given id, which was the source of all psychic energy. The id is amoral, knowing no distinctions of good and evil. An irrational, primitive chaos, it is "a cauldron full of seething excitations."[5] The id is a reservoir of energy that comes to it from the instincts, but in itself has no structure, organization, or integration. It is subject only to the operation of the "pleasure principle," which is to say that it continually strives for the satisfaction of instinctual needs.

The ego develops to deal with the external world. The task of the ego is to represent the external world to the id. This task is necessary because the id would destroy itself in its blind efforts to satisfy instincts if the nature of reality were not taken into account. The ego carries out this function by observing the external world, recording its characteristics accurately in the memory traces of what it perceives and, by means of "reality-testing," removing from this record of the external world whatever has been added on the basis of encroachments by the instincts. The id by itself would operate solely on the pleasure principle; the ego replaces this by the "reality principle," which increases the likelihood that instinctual gratifications will be achieved. While the id stands for the passions in all their unreasonableness, the ego represents the operation of reason and good judgment.

The ego, however, has no energy of its own. The energies at its disposal are energies borrowed from the id. This puts the ego in the position of essentially having to carry out the id's intentions. The ego's task is to work out ways for most effectively achieving those intentions.

In attempting to serve the id, the ego must take into consideration not only the nature of the external world but also the prohibitions and demands of the society as they have become internalized in the superego. The superego observes and criticizes what one does; it includes one's conscience and one's ideals. The superego is the source in us of every moral prohibition and the champion of whatever strivings toward goodness we have been able to muster. It represents as much as humans are capable of grasping of what would be most worthy in their conduct.

The ego has a difficult task. Cast in the role of mediator between the id and reality, the ego often finds it necessary to disguise and offer rationalizations for the commands of the id, to hide and smooth over the id's conflicts with reality, to claim to be paying proper attention to the nature of reality despite stubborn refusals of cooperation from the id. At the same time, it is accountable to the ever-watchful superego, which prescribes strict standards for the ego's conduct and has no sympathy for the difficulties it faces in trying to cope, on the one hand, with the demands of the id and, on the other hand, with the demands of reality. Furthermore, if the superego's standards are not obeyed by the ego, punishment is meted out to it in the form of feelings of guilt and a sense of inferiority. In sum, the ego is locked in a struggle with the instinctual pressures of the id, the unyielding nature of reality, and the strictures of the superego. Somehow it must arbitrate among these forces and bring them into sufficient harmony to keep the enterprise going.

According to Freud's theory, the ego and superego, which come into such tremendous conflicts with the id, are ultimately still derived from it. When a child is born, only the id exists. The ego begins to develop out of the id soon thereafter, essentially to take account of the external world in the satisfaction of the instincts. The ego remains very weak for a long time. But there are already strong sexual instincts in the early period of life. These instincts typically become focused on the mother, who is the child's first "love object." The boy (for whom Freud worked this all out more fully than for the girl) "becomes his mother's lover . . . , wishes to possess her physically . . . , [and] seeks to take his father's place with her."—the Oedipus complex.[6] This development is, however, prohibited by the parents, who put an end to such possibilities by the anxiety-producing threat of castration. The sexual instincts are then forced, for the time being, into repression, the desires toward the mother are given up, and the boy comes to identify with the father and to internalize his rules and prohibitions. This is the formation of the superego. There follows a period of relative calm, until the arrival of adolescence, when the sex instincts become strengthened and demand satisfaction.

Throughout development, what goes on for a person psychologically is largely conceived to be a matter of what happens to the person's instincts, particularly the sex instincts. We have seen how much stands in the way of their direct expression. Faced with the restraints of society and then the superego, they are repressed, displaced, and transformed. Thus, for instance, at a particular stage in the young child's "psychosexual" development, the character traits of stubbornness, parsimony, and orderliness manifest themselves as an "anal triad" derived from the imposition of toilet training—the first two as an expression of resistance to timely performance on the toilet, the third as a "reaction formation" against wishes for being messy. Some of the energy of the instincts can be "sublimated" or diverted toward more socially valuable ends. It is upon a base of instinctual repression, according to Freud, that everything of greatest value in human civilization is erected.[7] Sublimation of instinct is crucial to the development of culture, making possible the wide array of cultural achievements, ranging across the arts, sciences, and humanities, and the important role they play in human affairs. For civilized values to exist, instinctual renunciation must take place. Whether by means of repression, suppression, or in some other way, there must be insufficient satisfaction of instincts.[8]

Thus, it is the inhibition of the instincts that makes possible all that we cherish in civilization. But too great an inhibition of the instincts is what leads to neurosis. Direct satisfaction should be granted to some portion of the repressed instinctual impulses. Civilized life is altogether too hard on most people in this regard, imposing standards of libidinal renunciation, the attempted fulfillment of which leads to neuroses without achieving anything culturally useful in the process. The sexual devil inside us must be given his due:

> We ought not to exalt ourselves so high as completely to neglect what was originally animal in our nature. Nor should we forget that the satisfaction of the individual's happiness cannot be erased from among the aims of our civilization. The plasticity of the components of sexuality, shown by their capacity for sublimation, may indeed offer a great temptation to strive for still greater cultural achievements by still further sublimation. But, just as we do not count on our machines converting more than a certain fraction of the heat consumed into useful mechanical work, we ought not to seek to alienate the whole amount of the energy of the sexual instinct from its proper ends.[9]

Attempts to do so will fail anyway, producing neurosis and retreat from reality in their wake. Excessive repression of sexuality is like robbing the soil of its necessary nutrients.

The ego of a neurotic patient has failed in its function of mediating the demands of external reality, id, and superego. Too much of what it experiences is lost to it, the traces in its store of memories unavailable and inaccessible. Its range of activity is severely constrained by the injunctions of the superego, and it uses up its energy in fruitless attempts to cope with pressures from the id. The constant stress of the id's demands upon it has impaired its synthesizing ability—its power to organize and integrate the disputing forces that impinge on it from various quarters.

Instead, it is pulled apart by the contradictory impulses to which it is subject, beset by uncertainties and paralyzed by conflicts.[10]

Psychoanalytic therapy proceeds, in essence, by attempting to undo the inappropriate defenses that have been erected against the instinctual impulses of the id because of the stern superego and to bring them under more adequate ego control. The aim of such therapy is to make the ego stronger and to augment its organizational ability to assimilate what the id thrusts up. Therapy is designed to give the ego greater independence from the superego's overly harsh restraints upon the id's urges.[11]

Freud's Assumption and Encouragement of Egoism

Freud's theory has been subject to a great deal of criticism. Many have argued against the overriding significance attributed to what is unconscious, to early childhood, and to sex. Almost every aspect of his theory, large and small, has been subject to much debate and is often regarded as dubious, at best. However, the assumption and encouragement of egoism—in the sense of selfishness, not Freud's "ego"—that is implicit in psychoanalysis is widely taken for granted.

Let us see how this egoism is assumed. Consider how the theory says our actions can be affected by the external world. There are only two ways for this to happen:

1. The environment can directly stimulate us in a way that leads to withdrawal (the relatively simple mechanism by which we can reduce external, though not internal, stimuli).
2. The environment can provide for the possibility of satisfying our internal needs through certain actions. Or if what is needed is not available or if sanctions exist

against the necessary actions, the environment can fail to provide for this possibility.

Except for stimulation we seek to avoid, and for providing or not providing ways to satisfy our internal needs, the external world is not supposed to have any relevance for our behavior.

All our actions represent either an attempt to ward off stimulation from the environment or to get rid of stimulation produced by our needs. *All we can be motivated to do about anything outside ourselves is either to make use of it to satisfy our needs or to rid ourselves of it.* Note that this is an egoism of a very different order from the harmless and tautological statement, "Everything one wants, one wants because of one's own motives." This egoism rules out the possibility of having any motives toward anything other than escape from unpleasant stimulation or the satisfaction of one's internal needs, or what is expected to lead to such escape or satisfaction.

Note also that the selfishness implicitly assumed in psychoanalysis is not the same as "narcissism." Freud did not imply that people could only love themselves and not one another. They can take another person as the object of their instinct—that is, "cathect" that person. But there is no room in his theory for any kind of motivation related to other people except as it derives from one's own needs.

Concern for, positive feelings toward, and love of other people are usually seen as dependent on our sex instincts. Freud's conception of the Oedipus complex, for example, makes clear the role he attributed to sex in the child's attachment to its parents. Early in his work he said explicitly:

> There may perhaps be an inclination to dispute the possibility of identifying a child's affection and esteem for those who look after him with sexual love. I think, however, that a closer psychological examination may make it possible to establish this identity beyond any doubt. A child's inter-

course with anyone responsible for his care affords him an unending source of sexual excitation and satisfaction from his erotogenic zones. This is especially so since the person in charge of him, who, after all, is as a rule his mother, herself regards him with feelings that are derived from her own sexual life: she strokes him, kisses him, rocks him and quite clearly treats him as a substitute for a complete sexual object.[12]

The dependence of positive relations with others on sex is stated quite generally in Freud's assertion that "all the emotional relations of sympathy, friendship, trust, and the like, which can be turned to good account in our lives, are genetically linked with sexuality and have developed from purely sexual desires through a softening of their sexual aim, however pure and unsensual they may appear to our conscious self-perception."[13]

Freud did sometimes discuss the existence of positive feelings for people that were not directly related to sexual desires toward them—but such feelings were inevitably still viewed as a function of one's own needs. An important example is his derivation of brotherly or group feeling from the rivalry and envy among siblings and different members of a group, in relation to the father or leader. Each wishes to have the father's or leader's special love and preferential treatment, but since this is impossible, they insist upon equality and develop social feeling by reversing the hostility they first felt into an identification with the others.[14]

As with positive feelings for others, moral aspirations too are inevitably viewed as derivative from more fundamental needs. The origin of the desire for social justice is thought to be this same insistence on equality among members of the group so that none can have preference over oneself:

> Social justice means that we deny ourselves many things
> so that others may have to do without them as well, or,
> what is the same thing, may not be able to ask for them.
> This demand for equality is the root of social conscience and
> the sense of duty. It reveals itself unexpectedly in the syph-
> ilitic's dread of infecting other people, which psychoanalysis
> has taught us to understand. The dread exhibited by these
> poor wretches corresponds to their violent struggles against
> the unconscious wish to spread their infection on to other
> people; for why should they alone be infected and cut off
> from so much? why not other people as well?[15]

The way Freud wrote about the syphilitic here strikingly
illustrates the impossibility, in his view, of people directly
caring about the good of others and wanting to avoid causing them harm. Such concern is not even conceived of as
a possibility in accounting for the dread of spreading an
infection of whose horror syphilitics are fully aware. Instead, it must be accounted for in terms of an opposite
wish to cause others misery equal to one's own.

We have already seen how the superego, which guides
a person's obedience to moral principles, develops from
the internalization of parental restrictions at the time of
the Oedipus complex. The morality of young children is
motivated by fear of punishment from their parents; the
morality of persons who are older stems from similar fear
of punishment from their superegos. Such fear always remains as the only motivational basis for ethical behavior.
Freudian theory never allows for any direct motivations
toward what is right or good, just as it never allows for
direct motivations toward other people. What is outside
ourselves can only matter to us—unless it is unpleasant or
gets in our way—if we can make use of it to satisfy our
own internal needs.

Despite the way Freudian theory views relations among
people and moral behavior, Freud personally cared deeply
about these matters himself. Of course, he was a human

being rather than a saint and not above feelings of intellectual rivalry, as in his relationship with Wilhelm Fliess.[16] Still, when Freud's friend and biographer Ernest Jones, who certainly knew him well, brings together a range of material that testifies to what Freud was like,[17] it is hard not to be impressed with Freud's personal as well as scientific qualities. Even allowing for hyperbole from someone who obviously was closely attached to Freud, that he was a considerate and principled person there can be little doubt. The enormous value Freud placed on friendship and concern for others—"aim-inhibited love"—and on putting one's energies to work for the higher things of civilization and for the common good—"sublimation"—is also evident again and again in his writings. Quite simply, he saw his ultimate aims as not fundamentally different from those of religion, with which he otherwise so strongly disagreed—namely, to further people's concern for one another and to decrease suffering.[18]

But, much as Freud himself so strongly wished to promote and contribute to the concern of human beings for one another and for their highest values, the theory he formulated inevitably pushes in the opposite direction. If ultimately all we can be motivated toward in the world must serve the satisfaction of our own internal needs, if love for others and for what is good can only represent an indirect attempt at such satisfaction or a kind of instinct displacement, then such love hardly finds itself encouraged. As Philip Rieff has put it: " 'Displaced' differs by only one small letter from 'misplaced.' "[19] To act in the service of others or of ethical values is never the alternative of choice; direct gratification of one's internal needs, if it were possible, would always be the preferred path.

Further, as we have seen, insufficient direct satisfaction of needs always is the cause that Freud believes lies at the root of neurosis. His therapy inevitably tends to counter the ethical forces in the individual that inhibit this direct satisfaction. Thus, he is led by his views of the therapy required for neurosis to reproach the patient's superego. According to Freud, the superego, in its harsh demands for the ego's obedience to its strictures, neglects the problems faced by the ego on two fronts: from the instinctual pressures of the id and from the nature of the outside world. What is very often necessary therapeutically, therefore, is that the psychoanalyst oppose the demands of the superego and try to weaken them.[20] Or, as Freud expresses it in one striking sentence: "All who wish to be more noble-minded than their constitution allows fall victims to neurosis; they would have been more healthy if it could have been possible for them to be less good."[21]

In his striving to decrease suffering, to promote concern for others, and to advance the common good, Freud thus ends up making such striving look like at best a kind of compromise and often an outright mistake. It is only an attempt at indirect and partial gratification because of the impossibility of gratification that is direct and full. We would be better off—"more healthy"—if we could only be "less good."

Notes

1. Freud, 1901/1960, vol. 6, p. 70.

2. See Freud, 1905/1953, vol. 7, p. 209; Freud, 1924/1961b, vol. 19, p. 160; and Freud, 1940/1964b, vol. 23, p. 146.

3. Freud, 1915/1957b, vol. 14, p. 120.

4. Freud, 1933/1964a, vol. 22.

5. Freud, 1933/1964a, vol. 22, p. 73.

6. Freud, 1940/1964b, vol. 23, p. 189.

7. Freud, 1920/1955b, vol. 18, p. 42.

8. Freud, 1930/1961d, vol. 21, p. 97.

9. Freud, 1910/1957a, vol. 11, p. 54.

10. Freud, 1940/1964b, vol. 23, pp. 180–181.
11. Freud, 1933/1964a, vol. 22, p. 80.
12. Freud, 1905/1953, vol. 7, p. 223.
13. Freud, 1912/1958, vol. 12, p. 105.
14. Freud, 1921/1955c, vol. 18, p. 121.
15. Freud, 1921/1955c, vol. 18, p. 121.

16. Sulloway, 1979, p. 231.
17. Jones, 1955, vol. 2, chap. 16.
18. Freud, 1927/1961c, vol. 21, p. 53.
19. Rieff, 1959, p. 241.
20. Freud, 1930/1961d, vol. 21, pp. 142–143.
21. Freud, 1908/1959, vol. 9, p. 191.

3

Freud and the Selfishness Legacy: Why Did Freud Think This Way?

There seem to be three major reasons for Freud's view of human motivation and the assumption of selfishness inherent in that view: (1) his wish to unmask illusion and combat false pieties about human conduct, (2) his commitment to what he viewed as "naturalistic" forms of explanation in contrast to occultism and the positing of mysterious forces, and (3) his clinical observations of patients in therapy, including the forcefulness or peremptory quality with which some motivations manifest themselves. It is not difficult to agree with Freud that illusions are to be fought against, that explanations should be naturalistic, and that clinical observations must be accounted for. But in light of what we know today, these points do not by any means imply that human motivation is as Freud thought of it or that humans are necessarily selfish beings. Let us consider each of the reasons in turn.

The Wish to Unmask Illusion

Freud was deeply committed to facing the facts about people, fighting hypocrisy, and avoiding false pieties. His misgivings about religion were tied up with his conviction that it promoted illusions about human motivation, and even if such illusions afforded temporary security and comfort, they ultimately contributed to suffering by making demands that could not be met. The ethical precept to love thy neighbor as thyself is a case in point.[1] Such a commandment is impossible to fulfill. In Freud's view, it is a reaction formation against the aggressiveness we really feel toward our neighbor and can cause as much grief and misery as the aggressiveness itself. Thus, when the apostle Paul took the assumption of universal love as the basis for Christianity, it was inevitable that the result would be hostility on the part of Christians toward those outside the Christian community. The illusion of brotherly love ends up promoting human hatred and strife.

We will be more humane toward one another if we accept the reality of people as they are, rather than pretend to a degree of virtue that could only be purchased at the price of neurosis. By the same token, Freud maintained, building such religious or ethical precepts into education does young people great harm by deceiving them about what they will encounter from others. "In sending the young out into life with such a false psychological orientation, education is behaving as though one were to equip people starting on a Polar expedition with summer clothing and maps of the Italian Lakes."[2] It is no service to our children to raise them with idealistic stars in their eyes when they are about to be devoured by wolves. Because ethical precepts are defenses against opposite urges rather than something to be accepted at face value, unmasking them is not cynicism; it is necessary for human welfare.

Freud saw human beings as historically enmeshed in a fabric of illusion that had to be torn away if real betterment of the human condition was to occur. First, science had shattered the illusion that the earth is the stationary center of the universe; next, it had dispelled the belief that human beings were discontinuous from the rest of the animal kingdom; and now it had to destroy the myth that people were masters of their own minds.[3] Of these three successive blows to human vanity, Freud viewed the third as perhaps most wounding of all. Since instincts cannot be fully tamed and there will always be unconscious mental processes, we cannot be expected to know in rational fashion the contents of our minds. What we know about ourselves must always be incomplete, partial, and untrustworthy.

Freud has probably irrevocably heightened our awareness of the enormous self-deceptions of which we are capable. There can no longer be any doubt that all kinds of selfish intentions can parade as altruism or morality. No one today will accept claims to nobler and higher feelings at face value. Behavior that looks as if it is motivated by concern for others or by ethical considerations may really be selfish; however, this does not mean that it always is selfish.

In order to reveal the illusoriness of the traditional view that morality is something planted deeply and stably within us, Freud called attention to the vicissitudes that moral feelings undergo in patients who are depressed. Morality seems to wax and wane. Freud pointed out how such patients may be overcome with feelings of guilt and unworthiness about actions that, only a little while later, when the "attack" of morality is over, no longer bother them in the slightest.[4] That there can be times when we are particularly ready to denounce ourselves and other times when we are likely to defend our virtue against all attack does mean that our feelings of morality cannot automatically be relied upon. But it does not mean that we never have genuine moral concerns.

A commitment to combat illusion about ourselves does not carry the implication that concern for others or for ethical principles must be illusory or at best always derivative from one's own needs. Such an implication follows only from Freud's theoretical commitment to biological drives as the only real wellsprings of human action. His views of small children as notoriously amoral fit in with this conception. Young children, he believed, are totally ruled by pressures toward immediate gratification of their biological needs, such as those reflecting hunger and early forms of sexuality. Little else matters to them. But there now is extensive evidence that infants and young children seem strongly directed toward other people; from an early age they share things with others, help and take care of others, cooperate, take turns, and express friendliness, affection, empathy, and sympathy toward others.[5] The view of small children as caring only about their own biological needs thus is not supported by observation.

We can agree with Freud that human conduct should be seen for what it really is, and sentimentalism about morality should be exposed as illusion when it is that. But concern for others and morality in one's dealings with other people may be more basic than Freud understood. It is widely accepted that much of what passes as altruistic or caring has been shown by Freud only to seem so, that we delude ourselves and one another in the interests of appearing better than we really are. Although such deception occurs, this in no way establishes that goodness is always illusion. Even Freud seemed to have difficulty maintaining that, since he also believed humans to be capable of great good: "The normal man is not only far more immoral than he believes but also far more moral than he knows."[6] Freud's wish to unmask illusion and combat hypocrisy may have led him to a more extreme position in most of his pronouncements about the nature of human beings than the facts justify.

"Naturalistic" Explanation
Instead of Mysterious Forces

Freud was part of a wave of science that, since Darwin, saw itself as seeking to understand human behavior in terms of natural processes rather than through appeals to teleology, "élan vital," or the supernaturalism of religious belief. While mostly writing as if psychoanalysis were fully an induction from empirical facts, Freud actually was heavily influenced by the biology of his times, and, indeed, he eagerly sought biological underpinnings for his work.[7] Not only from his teachers in medical school,[8] but from a wider range of German, French, and English scientists as well,[9] Freud absorbed a new outlook that, by viewing the human being as a biological machine, sought to slay the dragons of vitalism and occultism.

A broad consensus had arisen about the properties of such a machine. The nervous system was conceived of as a passive instrument whose function was to rid itself of physical energies that could intrude from sources in the outside world or from sources within the body. These energies goaded the otherwise quiescent organism into activity, which ceased in turn when the noxious input of energy had been eliminated. Interest in the environment and its objects came about only in the service of divesting the nervous system of excitation and restoring quiescence. In this growing scientific consensus, which had gained momentum after Darwin's *On the Origin of Species* appeared in 1859, "it was widely assumed . . . that all aspects of mental functioning had developed out of primitive processes geared to the satisfaction of biological needs and had evolved as devices for more effectively achieving that satisfaction. From this perspective, observers commonly concluded that the ultimate motivation for all mental functioning continues to be the gratification of biological drives."[10]

Freud's views about the essential nature of sex and hunger motivation thus were rather straightforward applications of this paradigm. Sexual motivation in the male, for example, was understood to originate in an accumulation of somatic tension that floods the organism with stimulation, which it seeks to reduce by appropriate action. Or in the case of hunger, a buildup of internal stimulation causes discomfort and restlessness, eventuating in eating, which serves to discharge the accumulated excitation. An appropriate external object—a female in the first case, food in the second—becomes attractive only by virtue of its function as a means to help the organism rid itself of excitation. Positive tendencies toward persons and things in the external world arise only secondarily, as a result of discovering their role in reducing somatic tensions.

As Holt[11] has pointed out, however, the ideas about human motivation adopted by Freud because of their apparent basis in naturalistic explanation no longer can be justified in those terms. The neurophysiological views current at that time are no longer tenable. They have been replaced by biological concepts that suggest quite different outlooks on motivation. First of all, the nervous system is not a passive reflex mechanism; we now know from electroencephalographic data that it is always active, even in deep sleep or in coma. It is not set up to rid itself of stimulation imposed by the body or the external world. Rather, it contains tiny amounts of energy different in kind from those of impinging stimuli, quantitatively negligible, with no relation between the amount of such energies and the person's motivational state. Further, stimulus input does not seem to be inherently and originally offensive to the nervous system, flooding it with unwanted excitation. To the contrary, stimulation is necessary for the nervous system's proper functioning. Minimizing stimulation in restricted environments leads to boredom and restlessness and, when kept up long enough, to deterioration of cognitive processes and hallucinations.[12] And as we shall discuss in more detail later, animals and human infants often seem to act in ways that will bring about novel spectacles and experiences.

If the nervous system doesn't function in the manner believed in Freud's time, what of the physiology of sex and hunger, which provided such influential models for Freud? Here, too, the conceptions of an earlier day have been superseded by evidence for different processes. It turns out that sexual motivation in the male seems minimally influenced by a cumulative buildup of tension goading the organism to activity that will serve to reduce it. Critical for sexual arousal and activity in many species seems to be the social factor—the presence of a suitable sexual partner. For example, when a male of a variety of species has copulated with a female to the point of apparent sexual exhaustion and shows no further interest in her, offering the male a new mate can have the effect of restoring his capacity for sexual performance.[13] Evidence such as this suggests that, rather than thinking of it as a drive, sexual motivation may be better understood as an appetite.

In regard to hunger, we now know, for example, that eating depends heavily on preferences for particular kinds of substances, some of which, such as saccharine, may be nonnutritive. In research by Sheffield and Roby, saccharine strongly maintained its reward value for rats despite "ingestion of thousands of ccs. of saccharine solution and no doubt millions of instrumental tongue movements."[14] The rats seemed for all the world simply to like what was sweet and to keep on liking what was sweet even in the face of mounting experience that it did not nourish them. Reduction of bodily "tension" or need doesn't have to occur as a support for the behavior of eating. What the environment has to offer can be of value for the organism quite apart from somatic tension or need. Again, appetite seems a more relevant term than drive.

The desire for naturalistic explanation led Freud to embrace the biological ideas of his time as the basis for understanding human motivation. This same desire also made him receptive to philosophers who gave maximum credit to the biological in human nature. A good example was Nietzsche, who insisted that the instinctual side of humans is neglected at one's peril. The importance his ideas had for Freud can be gauged from the following passages in Nietzsche's *The Genealogy of Morals,* published in 1887: "All instincts which do not find a vent without *turn inwards.* . . . The whole inner world burst apart when man's external outlet became *obstructed.*" This obstruction, caused by social organization, has the effect of turning the instincts inward against the person, bringing about "that most grave and sinister illness from which mankind has not yet recovered, the suffering of man from the disease called man as the result of a violent breaking from his animal past . . . the result of a declaration of war against the old instincts."[15] As Sulloway points out, Freud belonged for five years as a university student to a reading society that avidly digested and discussed Nietzsche's views and that even corresponded with him.[16]

The desire for a naturalistic explanation is often associated with the view that naturalism—what is biologically natural to the organism—should be accepted as good. Thus, we find criticism of the restrictiveness of society in the passages just quoted from Nietzsche, and it is present in Freud also. For Nietzsche and Freud, as well as for other thinkers such as Rousseau, human society—in blocking the expression of what is natural to human beings—is responsible for much of human misery. But, as we have seen, our understanding of what is natural to the person has been changing. Current conceptions of neurophysiology no longer support Freud's view of motivation.

A different line of defense of Freud from biology might be offered to the effect that the nature of evolution supports the idea of inevitable human selfishness. Human beings must have evolved by natural selection, and it is sometimes believed that natural selection must favor the evolution of selfish genetic factors over altruistic ones. When evolution is regarded in terms of what is advantageous for the survival of a group or species, one could expect selection of some altruistic factors that would be beneficial to the group. But it has recently come to be thought that, because of the relatively long time that would be involved, group or species advantage is unlikely to play a significant role in natural selection.[17] Thus, natural selection appears to favor only the development of selfishness. Individuals who are selfish—so the argument would run—will have a better chance of surviving and passing on their genes than individuals who are not.

However, natural selection should favor the evolution of factors that benefit an individual's *genes*, rather than factors that benefit an individual in terms of personal needs or interests. This is a distinction readily lost sight of in evolutionary discussions of altruism, where the main concern is usually to provide an account in terms of natural selection for animals behaving in such ways that they seem to be benefiting others at their own expense. The propagation of an individual's genes is often favored by behavior that is attuned to others' needs or interests as against one's own—the most obvious example being a mother's care for her own children. An extreme example of self-sacrificial behavior is provided by bees who defend their colonies by suicidal stings that cause their own insides to be pulled out. Such bees can have no offspring; by their suicidal action, they are promoting the survival of closely related bees who can pass on the genes that they themselves cannot.

That the self-sacrificing bees are a sterile caste and therefore have no genetic competition with other bees clearly is critical in the evolution of such extreme altruism. The absence of comparable conditions among us humans occasionally leads to skepticism concerning the evolution of altruism in human beings.[18] But that we cannot expect such extreme self-sacrifice to be genetically programmed in human beings hardly means that natural selection favors our being concerned only with ourselves. The role of parental care in the propagation of one's own genes is one clear way in which concern and care for at least some other human beings would seem to be extremely likely to have evolved by natural selection. Some further ways they may have evolved will also be discussed later.

Thus, while Freud's view of motivation was very much in line with certain trends in the biological thinking of his time, this view and the idea that all human motivation is inherently selfish do not seem warranted by current neurophysiology or evolutionary theory.

Observational Evidence

What Freud himself probably felt was the most important basis for his theories was observation, particularly, clinical observation of his patients. One of the factors leading him to the ways he adopted for explaining human motivation may well have been the forcefulness with which some motivations manifest themselves to the person experiencing them. Phenomenologically, these motivations have a peremptory quality. They brook no interference—there is no stopping them. Clearly, there is strong clinical evidence that inexorable urges can govern people's thoughts, feelings, and actions despite their better judgment. They can be dominated by wild sexual passions and overtaken by fits of rage. These events can seem to function as alien forces impervious to the person's attempts to control them. It is understandable that motivational phenomena of this kind could have encouraged Freud to think in terms of energies arising from within the body and pressing for discharge.

That motivations can be pressing, however, doesn't necessarily tell us how best to understand them. For one thing, motivations may be very forceful or peremptory without in any apparent way concerning the content areas of sex, life preservation, or aggression to which Freudian theory attributes overriding significance. The sense of urgency and absolute involvement can issue from intense devotion to duty, as when a lifeguard saves the life of a swimmer and almost dies in the process, or from intense devotion to an idea, as when a physician, surmounting many obstacles, sets up a hospital in a jungle to fight malaria. Parents may go to great lengths of personal hardship and danger to care for their children or save them from a disaster. These motivations are very forceful and yet do not seem to fit Freudian theory, on their face.

Also, apart from the issue of content, the peremptoriness of motivations by no means compels explanation in terms of internal forces pressing for release or discharge.

Holt has pointed out that it is at least as plausible to interpret such phenomena as resulting from defects in the controlling mechanisms for stopping behaviors. The story of the sorcerer's apprentice strikes Holt as a relevant analogy for what may occur: "Surely, when the obliging broom kept bringing water beyond the point where it was wanted, when it indeed began to be a threat to the hapless apprentice's life, its behavior appeared as inexorable and peremptory as one could imagine. Yet all that was involved was the necessary signal to halt the mechanism that had been started: the magic word that would serve as a negative feedback or switch-off."[19] An automobile with a stuck throttle and no one in the driver's seat is another illustration that Holt offers. He also mentions the example of a cat whose interpeduncular nucleus has been cauterized. Not unlike the car with the stuck accelerator, such a cat will walk ahead inexorably regardless of barriers until it knocks itself out from crashing into obstacles or uses up its supply of energy. Behavior may proceed in a peremptory and inexorable fashion, then, because the controls for stopping or modulating it have gone awry, rather than because of biological urges pressing for an outlet. There is no doubt that Freud was right in recognizing that motivated behavior may be peremptory, but there is plenty of doubt that Freud's explanation is correct.

Clinical observations of his patients clearly were also of crucial significance to Freud's motivational theories apart from peremptoriness. By extensive talking with patients who were encouraged not to withhold anything, it became possible to understand behaviors and symptoms that at first seemed utterly "crazy" and senseless; these conversations convinced him of the reality of unconscious motivation. And that the problems of his patients always seemed to come down to sex—later, to sex or aggression—convinced him that, apart from the directly life-sustaining needs such as hunger and thirst, these were the ultimate motives.

There are several well-known problems with the role accorded by Freud to these clinical observations. For one thing, the interpretations that Freud gave of his patients' difficulties were not necessarily always the correct ones. Apparent corroboratory evidence, like the patients' bringing up more and more sexual material in their dreams and free associations, could well have come about because the patients knew what Freud thought was relevant and said the sort of thing he expected to hear. Also, patients didn't always agree with Freud or say things that fit his theories; such inconsistencies were perhaps a little too easily explained away in terms of resistance. Furthermore, even when a patient clearly did have problems of a sexual nature, these were not necessarily the primary problems. Interpersonal disturbances may have come first and brought sexual difficulties in their wake.

Even if one were to assume that Freud was right about the underlying problems of the people who came to him for help, this still would hardly provide strong support for sex and aggression as the only motivational bases for behavior besides directly life-preserving needs. Sex and aggression may be areas in which people are particularly likely to get into difficulties, but this does not mean that there cannot be other bases for behavior as well.

It may be felt that, quite apart from observations in the clinic, the great evils to be observed in the world, the enormity of suffering, and the degree to which human beings themselves are responsible for the suffering of their fellows offer little hope that human nature is any better than Freud thought it was. But we are not attempting to argue that human beings are by nature good or that we do not have to muster all the forces of which we are capable to fight the evil that can be found within us. Our aim here is simply to point out that there is nothing to warrant the idea that only motivation of the kind Freud recognized is to be found in people—only sex and aggression and motives like hunger and thirst, only motivation to satisfy our own internal needs.

The reader may wonder if we are forgetting how easily selfish motivation may masquerade as virtue. One may perform an act of apparent altruism, for example, because one expects a favor or praise in return, or to feel superior to the person one is helping, or to rid oneself of some feeling of guilt, or to make oneself feel good about oneself as a virtuous individual. No matter what people do, it is always possible to explain their actions as ultimately motivated in terms of benefits accruing to themselves. How can we say, then, that there is nothing to warrant the idea that our own needs are always at the bottom of motivated behavior?

That a piece of behavior can be interpreted in a given way by no means demonstrates that it should be interpreted in that way. Any behavior will inevitably be open to multiple interpretations. One cannot show that a given interpretation is likely to be correct without considering the alternative possibilities. Although some behavior that appears to be motivated by a concern for others or for moral principles no doubt does only appear that way while in reality being otherwise, it does not follow that there can never really be genuine concern of this kind. There is no basis for the latter assertion unless one simply assumes it to begin with.

Freud's view that, apart from direct life-preserving needs such as hunger and thirst, only sex and aggression ultimately motivate us and the inherent selfishness that this view implies cannot be accepted as justified on the grounds of observational evidence. Nor is it justifiable on the basis of wishing to combat illusion about ourselves; that would require independent grounds for thinking that any other kind of motivation really is illusory. What does seem most clearly to have supported Freud's motivational theories was the biological thinking of his time. As we have seen, however, that thinking has changed considerably and no longer supports the theoretical scaffolding that he erected. Indeed, in the next chapter we shall find that some strong arguments can be made against Freud's motivational theories. These arguments make it all the more surprising that the Freudian legacy of selfishness has been so long lived and pervasive.

Notes

1. Freud, 1930/1961d, vol. 21.
2. Freud, 1930/1961d, vol. 21, p. 134.
3. Freud, 1917/1955a, vol. 17.
4. Freud, 1933/1964a, vol. 22.
5. See Rheingold and Hay, 1978, for a summary.
6. Freud, 1923/1961a, vol. 19, p. 52.
7. See Sulloway, 1979.
8. See Holt, 1965.
9. See Levin, 1978; Sulloway, 1979.
10. Levin, 1978, p. 253.
11. Holt, 1965, 1976.
12. Bexton, Heron, and Scott, 1954.
13. Dewsbury, 1981.
14. Sheffield and Roby, 1950, p. 479.
15. Nietzsche, 1887/1910, pp. 100–101, as quoted in Jones, 1957, vol. 3, pp. 283–284.
16. Sulloway, 1979, p. 468.
17. See, for example, Campbell, 1972, 1978; Davies and Krebs, 1978; Dawkins, 1976.
18. See Campbell, 1972, 1975, 1978.
19. Holt, 1976, p. 171.

4

Freud and the Selfishness Legacy: Other Forms of Motivation

A great deal of what we want and strive for has always seemed to some psychologists just too remote from essential needs or from sex or aggression to be accounted for in terms of Freudian drives. In the early days of psychoanalysis, Jung felt this way about strivings for religious values, for meaning, and for self-realization; Adler felt this way about strivings for power and superiority. But the majority of psychoanalysts did not find their arguments convincing.

A somewhat later argument made by a number of thinkers, most notably Gordon Allport, was that while primary drives may have been the historical origin of our current motives, many of these motives have become "functionally autonomous" or no longer dependent upon the drives.[1] For instance, Allport suggests, consider the example of a former sailor who originally worked on the sea for his livelihood. He is now a wealthy banker, but still has a craving for the sea. Is not this craving now independent of his basic drives? Similarly, any number of our activities—for example, strolling in a public park, reading novels and short stories, shopping for attractive clothes—may have begun in the interests of the sexual urge. But with time these activities may have become ends in themselves, interests pursued for their own sake, even when they no longer serve the original drive.

Another possible position, most clearly put forth by Asch, is that certain forms of experience and activity—for example, music, dance, and painting—are simply interesting or desirable in their own right from the start.[2] They may be neither currently nor historically dependent upon primary drives, even if the drives recognized by Freud are supplemented with others—for example, with some kinds of drives related to the strivings that concerned Jung or Adler.

In Chapter 3 we argued that Freud's reasons for believing that all motivated behavior has to be a function of basic life-sustaining needs or of sex or aggression do not support this belief. But for many years, few thinkers held that a compelling case could be made against this belief. Most psychoanalysts thought that what Jung and Adler described could still be regarded as indirect expressions of Freudian drives, and they felt the same way about the kinds of examples cited by Allport and Asch. If Allport's former sailor no longer needed the sea for the purpose of making a living, he may still have enjoyed the sensual stimulation of a boat's rocking motion, the (aim-inhibited) fellowship offered by his shipmates, or any number of other drive-related aspects of being at sea. And what was to show that strolling in the park, reading novels, and shopping for clothes were no longer really based upon sex or related to aggression or other needs? As for interests in music, dance, and painting, these were classic instances of Freudian sublimation. (Actually it is not entirely clear that the concept of sublimation itself does not imply something very like a certain degree of functional autonomy. If what a person does is wholly a function of a basic drive, why would it be sublimation? If painting, for example, is fully in the service of an anal urge toward messiness, why is it a sublimation of this urge and not simply an expression of it?)

In any case, most psychoanalytically oriented thinkers seemed to be of the opinion that it was perfectly possible to account for most of the kinds of strivings that Jung or Adler or Allport or Asch or others were concerned with in terms of the basic Freudian drives. But there was one area in which the conviction began to grow that this was not the case, and where there now seems to be fairly wide agreement that some other basis of motivation must be recognized. It has been conceived of in somewhat different ways and has gone by a number of different names. The diverse lines of evidence for it were drawn together in a highly influential article by White, and it is often thought of in the terms he used: "motivation for competence" or "effectance motivation."[3] It is also frequently conceptualized as Hartmann's more definitely psychoanalytic "primary energies of the ego."[4]

Primary Energies of the Ego

Over several decades, as the psychoanalyst Heinz Hartmann examined what he understood as the operations of the ego, he became increasingly impressed with the extent to which its functions appeared to be autonomous of the instincts of the id. Already at the beginning of life, the infant exhibits all manner of adaptive tendencies that seem not to function only in the interests of instinctual needs and are hard to conceive of as arising from them. There are the powerful tendencies for motor developments like grasping, crawling, walking, and making speech sounds. And there are all the cognitive processes of perception, memory, thinking, and learning. These motor and cognitive functions, to be sure, are sometimes used in the service of satisfying basic needs. Frequently, however, they seem to be engaged in without any such role at all. Further, although the postponement of discharge and toleration of displeasure associated with Freud's reality principle are often necessary for need fulfillment to take place, their development can hardly be accounted for in terms of that necessity itself. Without an independent factor that allows development of the capacity to delay gratification in the first place, how could it become available to the organism as a possibility?

For a time, Hartmann was "not prepared to answer" whether all the energy that the ego uses originates in the instinctual drives.[5] He came to believe, however, that "it is likely that part of the energy which the ego uses is not derived . . . from the drives but belongs from the very first to the ego, or to the inborn precursors of what will later be specific ego functions. We may speak of it as primary ego energy."[6]

It came to be generally recognized among psychologists, as is well described in White's article, that the course of development of young children's cognitive and motor abilities and of their interests in their environment could not be accounted for without recognizing some basis independent of the Freudian drives.[7] Sometimes new urges were proposed, for example Hendrick's[8] "instinct to master" or Murphy's[9] activity and sensory drives. The *motivational* aspect of such behaviors as looking, exploring, crawling, and different forms of mastery was clear from such considerations as children's restlessness and anger when the behavior was blocked and their great joy when it succeeded, as well as its directedness and persistence.

Some of Piaget's[10] observations of his own children, as White notes, are excellent examples of the sorts of activities that require some further motivational basis. For instance, there is Laurent's discovery, when he is only a little more than 3 months old, that swinging a chain produces a sound from some rattles that are attached to it. From a gentle swinging he gradually progresses—with concomitant noise on the part of the rattles—to vigorous shaking, laughing uproariously. By 9 months Laurent is found to explore the properties of objects and try out on them the repertoire of actions he knows how to perform, provoking new outcomes as a result. Confronted with a new object, such as a notebook or a purse, he explores it visually, for instance while passing it from hand to hand; he subjects it to tactile exploration, such as by rubbing his hand over it or scratching it; he experiments on it with his repertoire of actions: sucking it, shaking it, swinging it, hitting it. Then from passive experimentation of these kinds, Laurent advances by the age of 10 months, 10 days to active experimentation, for example, now trying to retrieve an object after watching its trajectory when released.

As White points out, "No observant parent will question the fact that babies often act this way during those periods of their waking life when hunger, erotic needs, distresses, and anxiety seem to be exerting no particular pressure. . . . Strong emotion is lacking, but the infant's smiles, gurgles, and occasional peals of laughter strongly suggest the presence of pleasant affect."[11]

It is hard to defend the view that such activity is really based on the primary biological needs. The behavior tends to occur in the midst of times when these needs are in abeyance, and it provides pleasure even though it is clearly not reducing them. Nor does it seem plausible to argue that previous association with need reduction is responsible. Rather, the characteristics of the activities themselves seem to matter. The activities tend to be engaged in and enjoyed precisely when they are just in the process of being mastered or of producing new and interesting effects—circumstances in which they afford more challenge and provocation.

It has sometimes been proposed—for example, by Fenichel—that the exercise and enjoyment of abilities is really a function of the anxiety of not being able to do things, or the result of a fear of what the environment would do if one did not have these abilities.[12] But such behavior is much more likely to occur when anxiety as well as primary needs are low. Further, it seems implausible that fear or anxiety could motivate the *development* of early abilities. These abilities already have to be fairly well perfected before they can serve any extrinsic functions.

In sum, activities like grasping, crawling, walking, perceiving, thinking, manipulating objects, and producing changes in the environment are very hard to account for in terms of the kinds of drives proposed by Freud. Something further seems necessary—whether it is conceived of as some additional specific kind of urge like Hendrick's "instinct to master," or as Hartmann's "primary energies of the ego," or White's "effectance motivation."

Such a further kind of motivation would have an obvious biological function. The development of knowledge of the environment and abilities to interact with it—the development of competence—is clearly advantageous in terms of survival. And experimental research on animals gives further evidence of basic motivation of this kind. Animals of various species seem to possess curiosity about their surroundings and to be motivated to explore, manipulate, and investigate the environment. For example, Butler found that monkeys learned to solve discrimination problems for no reward other than being able to observe what was going on in the laboratory's entrance room through a window.[13] Work by Harlow, Harlow, and Meyer indicates that monkeys solve mechanical problems, such as removing both a hook and a pin in order to raise a hasp, simply to create the stimulus change of getting the hasp raised.[14] It opens nothing and leads to no further discovery; yet monkeys return to the hasp problem and solve it repeatedly when it is available in their cages. Montgomery[15] reported that rats learned to take the path of a maze leading to additional territory that they could explore, and Myers and Miller[16] found that rats learned to press a bar when pressing the bar permitted them to put their heads into a new compartment and sniff around.

There is now wide agreement on the proposition that a further type of motivation exists beyond what Freud was willing to recognize. The kinds of competence-related behavior we have been discussing cannot be accounted for in terms of directly life-sustaining needs or in terms of sex or aggression. What's more, the kind of motivation involved is of quite a different nature than Freud's drives.

Consider again the essentials of Freud's view of motivation. We need food, liquids, sufficient warmth, and so on, in order to survive; we need sex in order to reproduce. Depriving us of food, of liquids, of sex, results in bodily stimulation that we seek to reduce. We will search for and attempt to obtain objects in the environment—food to eat, a sexual partner—that will satisfy our needs and remove this stimulation. Besides the internal stimulation coming from our needs, we are also subject to external stimulation from which we seek to withdraw. Stimulation is always something that is unpleasurable, something we are trying to reduce, and it is always the attempt to reduce it that is the cause of activity.

But the behaviors involved in exploration, interest in novelties, the practice of competencies in the making, and the like, do not depend on bodily needs, and serve to increase rather than to decrease stimulation. Recall 3-month-old Laurent, first gently swinging and then vigorously shaking the chain to which rattles are attached, meanwhile laughing loudly. Laurent's activity does not seem to be a function of any bodily needs, and he is not reducing stimulation—he is causing more of it and apparently enjoying that hugely. The monkeys solving mechanical problems for no extrinsic reason or working so that they will be permitted to look into the entrance room of the laboratory, the rats pressing a bar so that they can sniff around in a new compartment or learning to take the maze path that lets them explore additional territory are all pursuing activities that are unrelated to bodily needs and that increase, instead of reduce, the stimulation they receive. Certain kinds of activities and experiences related to the development of knowledge and abilities seem to be enjoyed, sought, and serve as rewards or positive incentives, without satisfying bodily needs or reducing stimulation.

There is a fair amount of evidence that positive incentives don't necessarily depend on need satisfaction even in the realms of eating and sexual motivation themselves. As Freud realized but never actually was able to integrate into his theory, the rising excitement of sexual activity prior to consummation is not a negative experience but a highly enjoyable one, and not just because of temporal association with orgasm. Sheffield and his collaborators have also shown experimentally that copulation without permitted ejaculation will serve as a reward for male rats.[17] The possibility of a dependence on previous experience with consummation was ruled out by using rats that were sexually inexperienced.

Anyone who has ever been concerned with losing weight knows that foods can be appealing and enjoyed in the absence of a physiological state of hunger. Another experiment by Sheffield and a co-worker shows that for rats, too, food does not have to satisfy hunger in order to be rewarding.[18] As noted in Chapter 3, they will perform responses to obtain saccharine and continue to do so, consuming thousands of cubic centimeters of saccharine solution in the process, despite the fact that saccharine has no nutritional value.

It seems clear—and by this time rather generally accepted[19]—that stimulation can be sought, can serve as a reward or an incentive, without having any relation to reduction of bodily needs. Almost all psychologists recognize that there is some basic motivation underlying exploration, curiosity, manipulation, and the development of competencies generally—whether called "mastery urges," "motivation for competence," "independent energies of the ego," or something else—where stimulation is sought even though it does not reduce bodily needs.

Social Motivation

Now a further question must be addressed: *Is there any reason to suppose that the only other kinds of activities and experiences that can be sought after or rewarding are ones connected to an increase in competence?* In other words, is a relationship to development of competence the only other basis that exists besides need reduction for making something an incentive or reinforcer? We believe there is very little reason to think that is the case and substantial reason to think otherwise.

Consider the classic experiment by Harlow and Zimmermann, in which infant monkeys were reared in isolated cages with artificial mother surrogates.[20] The body of one such surrogate was a wire-mesh cylinder; another surrogate's body was covered with terry cloth. The monkeys came to spend a great deal of time on the terry-cloth "mother." They would cling to her when frightened, and they could be comforted just by the sight of her. None of these things were true of the wire-mesh mother—even when the monkeys had obtained all of their nourishment by sucking the nipple on a bottle of milk attached to this mother. The terry-cloth mother was clearly the one that was positive and rewarding to the infant monkeys, even though the wire-mesh mother was the one associated with hunger reduction.

Perhaps the attachment of the infants to the cloth mother could be accounted for by postulating a need for something like contact comfort. (Possibly this could be related to Freud's sexual instincts, although the ethologist Eibl-Eibesfeldt argues that Freud had things the wrong way around when he thought of the relations between parents and children as based on sexual relations between mates.[21] Eibl-Eibesfeldt presents a fair amount of evidence suggesting rather that behavior patterns expressing affection between mates, such as kissing and caressing, have evolved from patterns of parental caretaking of their young, such as mouth-to-mouth feeding and grooming.) Note, however, that claiming a "need" status for anything like contact comfort is problematic, and that if need reduction is the process responsible for attachment to the cloth mothers, it is hard to explain why contact comfort should be so much more powerful than hunger, on its surface a need of much greater significance.

But in any case, young animals become attached to older ones—even of a different species—in the absence of both direct physical contact and more obvious primary need satisfaction. Cairns and Johnson found that young lambs raised next to adult female collies from whom they were separated by a wire fence—the lamb on one side of the wire fence, its paired collie on the other—developed a strong tendency to approach and follow these collies, even though physical contact was prevented by the fence.[22] Indeed, the wire fence was provided because, without it, the collies had first attacked their lambs. Like separation from a more typical mother figure, subsequent separation from the collie caused strong disturbances in the lambs, such as repeated, vigorous bleating and agitated pacing. All of this was similar to the attraction and the separation-caused disturbances that other lambs showed for adult ewes with whom they had been paired and raised with unrestricted contact.

The young of a species also seem to seek the proximity of, and interaction with, other young, as well as parents and parent surrogates. Harlow has provided an extensive description of such behavior in young rhesus monkeys.[23] Indeed, infant monkeys reared together without their mothers developed strong attachments to one another and also showed very disruptive effects from subsequent separation—hardly what one would expect if positive feelings among peers derive from rivalry and envy in relation to parents or leaders. Describing the observed effects of this infant–infant separation, Suomi, Harlow, and Domek found that the monkeys first behaved in ways suggesting "protest," such as frantic locomotion; then behaved in ways indicating "despair" or depression, such as complete passivity and listlessness; and, after being reunited with their peers, behaved in ways suggesting "recovery," such as clinging and other forms of tactual and oral contact with another monkey.[24] These findings resemble what has been found with separation of infant monkeys from their mothers.

Young monkeys can even act as effective "therapists" when they are put together with monkeys a little older than themselves who have been reared in social isolation:

> The isolates' initial response to their interaction opportunities was to retreat to a corner and rock and huddle . . ., and the therapists' initial response was to follow and cling to the isolates. . . . Soon the isolates were clinging back, and it became only a matter of weeks until isolates and therapists were playing enthusiastically with each other. . . . During this period most of the isolates' previously abnormal behaviors gradually disappeared, and after 6 months recovery was essentially complete.[25]

In the face of the kinds of evidence here sampled, it seems difficult to maintain that competence development is the only other possible basis besides bodily need reduction for something to become rewarding or sought after. Young animals clearly seem to seek the proximity of, and interaction with, parents, parent surrogates, and other young under conditions that do not readily lend themselves to explanation in such terms.

But pursue this a step further. Perhaps *concern* for other individuals also exists without having to be based on the biological needs or competence development of the animal or person showing the concern. Typically, when we are attached to people, we not only want to be near them and to interact with them, but we also seem to care about their welfare. Perhaps such caring also is real and direct, rather than necessarily derivative from one's own needs and welfare.

Very young children frequently show sympathy in response to the suffering of their friends.[26] For example, children barely more than a year old may lead their mother over, bring their teddy bear, or carry a security blanket to a friend who is crying. We may well be predisposed from the beginning to be concerned about others' states. Even newborns cry in response to the cry of another infant.[27] They do so as young as one day of age and seem not to respond as strongly to other stimuli with similar physical properties, such as a synthetic cry or, surprisingly enough, even a recording of their own previous crying.

As we mentioned in Chapter 3, infants and very young children engage in sharing, helping, caretaking, and co-operating. For example, Rheingold, Hay, and West found that 18-month-olds, without prompting, direction, or praise, brought to the attention of others things that they found noteworthy.[28] They would show objects to others or give them objects. Eckerman, Whatley, and Kutz observed children as young as 10 to 12 months old offering toys to a peer.[29] Further, Eckerman, Whatley, and Kutz found the incidence of such positive social responses to be far in excess of such negative social responses as taking a toy from another child who was not offering it. Rheingold and Hay report that 2-year-old boys as well as girls display high frequencies of varying kinds of caretaking activities, such as patting dolls and toy animals, feeding them, giving them baths, brushing and combing their hair, and putting them to bed.[30] Nor are such activities carried out only in play. Thus, Rheingold and Hay also cite observations of a 23-month-old boy putting a sock on a 21-month-old girl, a 24-month-old girl helping a boy out of bed, and a 2-year-old girl kissing and putting a bandage on her mother's hurt finger and covering her with a blanket when she said she was cold. Of course, young children are not always aware of what someone else might or might not appreciate: Eibl-Eibesfeldt describes a 10-month-old repeatedly thrusting her toy into Eibl-Eibesfeldt's mouth.[31]

Numerous instances also have been reported of behavior in animals that looks as if it is motivated by some sort of concern for others. Whales, who need to breathe air to survive, have been observed being rescued by their companions and held up to get air when they were injured and couldn't swim to the surface, as Dawkins describes.[32] Dawkins also states that there is at least one well-authenticated story of a wild dolphin rescuing a human swimmer who was drowning. Hebb reports a dog preventing children from swimming by "rescuing" them despite repeated punishment for doing so, and a chimpanzee who attempted to pull a chimpanzee friend away from a place of risk in the absence of any possible model.[33] Masserman, Wechkin, and Terris found that monkeys who could obtain food by pulling a chain tended to refrain from pulling the chain when that also gave an electric shock to their cage mates.[34] And dwarf mongooses have been reported to assist a sick member of their pack.[35]

Some kind of genetic predisposition among higher animals toward developing attachments to other animals in their species who are in the vicinity—a predisposition to stay in contact with them and sometimes to aid them— seems very likely to have evolved on the basis of natural selection. We discussed in Chapter 3 how the argument that natural selection must favor the evolution of selfishness confounds advantage to an individual's genes with advantage to an individual's needs or interests. Gene advantage is often conferred by behavior that is to the advantage of the needs or interests of others, as in the case of parents' care for their offspring.

There are several reasons why a tendency for an animal to develop such attachments to other nearby animals of its species would seem advantageous to the perpetuation of its own genes. For one thing, since genetic relationship is not readily perceived as such, a tendency of this type could well be a "mechanism" by which an animal could increase the likelihood of survival of its kin, with whom it has close genetic identity. An animal may also develop relationships of mutual benefit, in which that animal is sometimes the helped as well as the helper. In other words, a tendency for a kind of attachment and concern for other animals who are around could mediate the development of "reciprocal altruism"[36]—could get it started and perhaps also help keep it going. Further, a group provides opportunities for protection as well as for learning (and, in some cases, for obtaining food) that are not available to the individual animal by itself. All of these factors seem likely to have played a role in the evolution of human beings as well as other animals of the higher species.

Implications

Let us now recapitulate and draw some implications. In the Freudian view, motivation was seen to be directly dependent on bodily needs, with pleasure or well-being directly tied to "need satisfaction" or "tension reduction." This view implied that an infant would be indifferent to most of what went on in the surrounding environment, with a few exceptions related to physiological needs such as hunger. The infant would gradually develop interest in or positive reactions to other environmental events through their association with satisfaction of these needs.

It has since been realized, in turn, how much lively eager interest young infants display in a wide variety of phenomena. Curiosity, exploration, manipulation, and the like have all been observed among higher animals as well as human infants, and the evolutionary significance of such behaviors has become clear. This has led to a rather broad convergence on the view that the biological needs Freud recognized are *not* the sole basis for motivation. Something on the order of basic effectance motivation or primary energies of the ego is now widely accepted as a necessary addition.

However—and this seems to us crucial—the egoism or selfishness we saw implicit in Freud's theory still typically remains. What the organism does is no longer seen as necessarily aimed at the satisfaction of bodily needs like hunger and sex, but it is still aimed at the organism itself. Hartmann's primary energies of the ego are all aimed at the ego's own development. And the interest in and manipulation of the environment produced by White's effectance motivation are entirely in the service of furthering the organism's own competence. As with Freud, there is still no recognition of any kind of motivation related to anything outside oneself except as derivative. Certainly there is nothing in primary ego autonomy or effectance motivation that would enable one to have genuine concern for another individual.

It is particularly striking that all aims continue to be related to the organism itself even though what originally made that necessary for Freud has now been given up. An organism's activity is necessarily directed toward itself if all activity results from bodily stimulation or excitation, which the activity is designed to diminish, as posited by Freud's instinctual-drives theory. But this is just what Hartmann and White no longer believe is sufficient. To allow for competence motivation or primary ego energy means that all activity does not result from bodily stimulation, which it is aimed at reducing.

Considerations of infant behavior, animal behavior, and evolutionary processes all suggest that we possess basic predispositions to develop attachments to and concern for other individuals, as well as interest in phenomena and activities that will contribute to our own competence. If it seems necessary to add competence motivation or primary energies of the ego to the kinds of basic motivation recognized by Freud, perhaps it is also necessary to add basic social motivation or primary energies of the superego.

We are suggesting, then, that what motivates our actions is not necessarily at bottom always the satisfaction of our own needs or the development of our own competence. The assumption of egoism, which was an integral part of Freud's thinking and, as we shall document, has been implicit in most current psychological approaches as well, seems simply to be unwarranted and untrue. Concern for others does not necessarily have to find its source in egoistic or selfish concerns. It appears rather that concern for others can be direct. Attempting to care for and benefit others does not have to boil down to an indirect attempt at satisfaction of needs of one's own—as it inevitably has to be viewed in Freudian theory. The beaming joy of a child, the comfort of a sick friend, the safety of a comrade can, so we believe, function as goals that are sought after and are rewarding in their own right.

Contributing to the well-being of others or, more generally, furthering what is outside of oneself that one values, may even be crucial for one's own well-being. It may be the lack of such contributions, the very absence of such furthering, that is responsible for the feelings of meaninglessness and anomie currently afflicting so many individuals in our society. Such possibilities will be further discussed later. At this point, we simply note that the encouragement of egoism implicit in Freud's thinking and carried forward by so much of contemporary psychological thinking may well be failing to foster people's happiness and contentment and instead contributing to their widespread dissatisfaction and malaise. Not only may it be without scientific warrant, but it also may be promoting the very dissatisfaction and lack of fulfillment it was designed to cure.

Notes

1. Allport, 1937, 1961.
2. Asch, 1952.
3. White, 1959.
4. Hartmann, 1937/1958, 1950/ 1964a, 1956/1964b.
5. Hartmann, 1950/1964a, p. 130.
6. Hartmann, 1964c, p. xiv.
7. White, 1959.
8. Hendrick, 1942, 1943a, 1943b.
9. Murphy, 1947.
10. Piaget, 1952.
11. White, 1959, p. 320.
12. Fenichel, 1945.
13. Butler, 1953.
14. Harlow, Harlow, and Meyer, 1950.
15. Montgomery, 1954.
16. Myers and Miller, 1954.
17. Sheffield, Wulff, and Backer, 1951.
18. Sheffield and Roby, 1950.
19. See Eisenberger, 1972.
20. Harlow and Zimmermann, 1959.
21. Eibl-Eibesfeldt, 1971.
22. Cairns and Johnson, 1965.
23. Harlow, 1969.
24. Suomi, Harlow, and Domek, 1970.
25. Harlow, Harlow, and Suomi, 1971, p. 548.
26. See, for instance, Hoffman, 1975, 1978.
27. Sagi and Hoffman, 1976; Martin and Clark, 1982.
28. Rheingold, Hay, and West, 1976.
29. Eckerman, Whatley, and Kutz, 1975.
30. Rheingold and Hay, 1978.
31. Eibl-Eibesfeldt, 1971.
32. Dawkins, 1976.
33. Hebb, 1971.
34. Masserman, Wechkin, and Terris, 1964.
35. Bertram, 1978.
36. Trivers, 1971.

5

Sullivan, Horney, and Fromm: The Significance of the Social

Freud based all motivation on biological instincts. Society or other individuals are ultimately relevant to one only insofar as they may contribute to the satisfying of these instincts or may hinder the obtaining of such satisfaction. Although certain psychoanalytic thinkers have suggested adding, within an essentially Freudian framework, some additional bases of motivation for competence-related activities—for example, primary energies of the ego or effectance motivation—these additions do not significantly alter the view of what other people and society mean for a person.

But other thinkers still broadly within the psychoanalytic tradition challenged this view. A number came to feel that Freudian theory gave much too little recognition to interpersonal relationships. These thinkers were impressed by the crucial role that human beings seem to play for one another. They recognized and stressed that there seem to be not only needs for bodily satisfaction and, perhaps, the development of our capacities but also extremely important social or interpersonal needs as well. In Great Britain, Fairbairn formulated a comprehensive theory of personality in which "object relations"—relations with other people—play a central role.[1] In the United States, a group typically referred to as "neo-Freudians" diverged still further from Freud. To them, the society in which we develop as well as the specific interpersonal relations in which we take part looked like decisive factors affecting how we turn out. And we seemed not only to be highly significant for one another but also capable of genuine other-directed concern. Yet, ironically enough, the work of the neo-Freudians in particular—for all its divergence from Freud—played an important role, we believe, in the developing trend toward selfishness. Three of these neo-Freudians—Sullivan, Horney, and Fromm—have been especially significant, and it is to an examination of their views that we turn next.

Sullivan

According to the psychiatrist Harry Stack Sullivan,[2] what is biologically determined plays a vastly smaller role for human beings than it does for lower animals. Our inborn potentialities are so labile and so much affected by experience that talking in such terms as "human instincts" is likely to be extremely misleading. We do have certain desires that are closely related to our bodily organization, like desires for food, water, and sex. But such "satisfactions" are only one of two broad classes of goals that we seek. The second, a function of our interpersonal relations rather than our biological equipment, is "security." Security has to do with being esteemed and valued, being thought of as good, important, or worthy; insecurity involves being considered in a manner that is unfavorable, derogatory, or depreciating. In one way or another, insecurity—or the anxiety that is associated with insecurity—is responsible for most of the kinds of ills psychiatrists are called upon to treat.

The role of interpersonal relations begins in life almost immediately. As all theorists recognize, the infant is born with certain physicochemical needs—for food, for oxygen, for adequate temperature, and so on. Deficiencies in what is needed produce tensions—potentialities or tendencies to action. To bring about the satisfaction of most of these needs, however, the infant requires the cooperation of someone else—a "mothering one," in Sullivan's terms. She must minister to his needs by providing food, covering, and the like; the infant cannot take care of these matters on his own. The infant can only engage in some form of behavior, such as crying, to induce what is needed. In the absence of such care from someone else, a human infant could not long survive. The very young child thus possesses not only the basic physicochemical needs but also what Sullivan calls a "need for tenderness"—for a disposition on someone else's part to care for the child and to provide what it requires.

The mother or other adult does not always know right away just what to do to relieve the infant immediately from the pressure of a need. But the infant's crying usually will lead to tenderness and efforts to provide such relief. And as the infant gradually gains more experience, he or she comes to differentiate the tensions associated with different physicochemical needs and the activities suited to the relief of these different needs. In any case, from the beginning the tensions of the infant that come from physicochemical needs tend to "integrate," or lead to and support, various interpersonal situations, such as feeding, which are necessary to the infant's survival.

The infant is also subject to another kind of tension, not based on physicochemical needs at all but brought about by interpersonal situations themselves. This tension is anxiety. Sullivan believed that when the mothering one is anxious, this induces anxiety in the infant as well. (The process by which this induction takes place Sullivan called "empathy," but he basically admitted ignorance about its nature.) Anxiety from the beginning is the cause of a great deal of disturbance. It tends to lead to the breaking up of interpersonal situations. The nursing activity of an infant who becomes anxious will be disrupted, and the cooperation of mother and child will disintegrate. Thus, when an infant becomes anxious, there is not only the tension of the anxiety itself but then also the increasing tension of the infant's other unsatisfied needs.

And what makes it all the worse, there is nothing the infant can do that is likely to result in relief from anxiety. Not only in infancy, but throughout life as well, the sources of anxiety can neither be removed, nor destroyed, nor escaped. The infant's crying won't help and will often exacerbate the situation by increasing the anxiety of the mother and thereby that of the child. Further, severe anxiety itself is like a blow on the head—the impact of such anxiety makes it extremely difficult to be clear about anything and thus to profit from experience.

Anxiety is therefore something to be avoided, if at all possible. Early on, the infant becomes extremely sensitive to signs of impending trouble, such as forbidding gestures on the part of the supervising adult. For example, if the mother becomes somewhat anxious at the infant's sucking his thumb or playing with his genitals or feces, the infant may learn to refrain from such activity or to change it in some way so that it will not upset her. As the infant becomes older, the mother tries to provide more and more training of various kinds, and she will give signs of disapproval for various actions. The overall effect is that the infant builds up a "self-system"—an organization of the experiences of oneself, or one's body, into three separate "personifications" or conceptions: the "good-me," the "bad-me," and the "not-me." The good-me is the self associated with the mothering one's being pleased with how things are going and therefore is the self associated with her tenderness. The bad-me is the self associated with the mothering one's tenseness and prohibitions and with increasing degrees of anxiety. Very intense anxiety, in turn, brings about the not-me, a kind of dissociated part of the self about which one does not feel that it belongs to oneself at all. Awareness of components of this not-me is likely to be accompanied by extremely unpleasant "uncanny" emotions like dread, loathing, and horror.

The self-system is purely a product of interpersonal experiences. Although it has some resemblance to Freud's superego, it comes into existence not by a process of incorporation or introjection but as a means of satisfying needs and avoiding anxiety. Further, Sullivan tells us, its negative aspects could be greatly modified if we lived in a more ideal society. Sullivan believed that although becoming a human being would probably always involve the development of some kind of self-system, in societies better adapted to human life there would be nothing at all like the punitive, critical superego of which Freud conceived.

The self-system, then, functions to keep anxiety down to a tolerable level. Very serious distortions may come to exist, however, in the infant's growing conceptions of what comprises the bad-me and the not-me, with severe consequences for later development as a result. The parents may have various unrealistic expectations of the infant stemming from the culture and from their own personal history in that culture; they may become anxious and transmit anxiety to their infant in quite inappropriate situations. Further, the infant's potential understanding is limited both because of his youth and poor ability to organize his experiences and because the self-system develops in just such situations that provoke anxiety, and the anxiety in turn keeps one from clarity. That the self-system is a protection against anxiety also means that it will be highly resistant to change.

As the infant grows older, his needs develop and become elaborated. A need for physical contact with others, as reflected in, for example, lying against them, manifests itself very early. Also very early there are "zonal" needs for activity of parts of the body. Zones such as the mouth area are energized in relation to the physicochemical needs such as the needs for food and water, which they are involved in satisfying. The amount of this energy may be greater than the energy required for the satisfaction of the physicochemical need itself. Thus, for example, the oral zone's energy may not be entirely used up in the acquisition of nutriment, with the result that there comes to exist a need for sucking per se. In the same way such energy surpluses eventuate in needs of the hands to feel, to manipulate, and so on. And with the maturation of further capabilities, there develop needs to manifest these capabilities too. All of these kinds of needs may readily lead to trouble since the parents may become anxious upon their manifestation. Disapproval of thumb or finger sucking or of manipulation of the genitals or feces is likely to lead to the incorporation of such activities into the bad-me or the not-me.

During childhood the need for tenderness, manifested in infancy as the need for physical contact, becomes elaborated as a need for attention and approval. If there are too many demands on the mother, if she doesn't understand what is going on, or if the mother has various "crazy ideas" about the child's spirit or will, she may consistently rebuff the child. Sometimes modifications of the child's behavior will lead to modifications in what the mother does, and everything will adjust itself and be all right. But many children are not that lucky. If their mothers continue to respond to their expressed need for tenderness in a manner provoking anxiety or pain, the children will learn not to express this need. Instead, they will come to act as if the bad-me had become central—to substitute "malevolent" behavior for manifestations of the need for tenderness. And once a start is made in this direction, it tends to snowball. The child's attitude, in which others are seen as enemies, makes it almost impossible for other people to treat the child kindly. This in turn only serves to confirm the child in the attitude.

This view of, as Sullivan called it, the "malevolent transformation," was important to him. Sullivan thought of it as "a theory which is calculated to get around the idea that man is essentially evil." He continued:

> One of the great social theories is, you know, that society is the only thing that prevents everybody from tearing everybody to bits; or that man is possessed of something wonderful called sadism. I have not found much support for these theories—that man is essentially a devil, that he has an actual need for being cruel and hurtful to his fellows, and so on. . . . And so as the years passed, my interest in understanding why there is so much deviltry in human living culminated in the observation that if the child had certain kinds of very early experience, this malevolent attitude toward his fellows seemed to be conspicuous. And when the child did not have these particular types of experience, then this malevolent attitude was not a major component.[3]

The extremely troublesome development of malevolence, then, comes about when there is too great a rebuff from crucial people during childhood. Moreover, certain aspects of interpersonal relations in this period generate problematic developments to some degree in virtually all of us. It is almost inevitable that, as a part of the training the child receives, he or she will be taught concepts of duties and responsibilities and will be expected to learn to behave in terms of the prescriptions of the culture in which the child lives. But Sullivan points out that "nowhere on earth" is there a "coherent and rationally understandable social system."[4] The societal prescriptions for different occasions tend to be contradictory; in addition, what reasonableness these prescriptions may possess is likely to be beyond the capacity of the child to comprehend.

The near impossibility of actually behaving according to the principles laid down by the adults in authority often leads to the early development of the child's abilities to deceive others and to conceal transgressions. Further, the acculturating adults in certain ways directly encourage such learning. Children are directly taught, for one thing, to use "verbalisms" to remove what would otherwise be the consequences of disapproved behavior. Thus, they are told to say "I'm sorry" when they have done something they have been warned against doing, and the utterance of these magical words is supposed to make everything all right again, or at least a great deal better. Sullivan felt that this sort of practice amounts to encouraging the taking of verbal statements to have "a superior quality of reality" compared to other actions, promoting the development of rationalization and keeping oneself from the recognition of experience that does not fit one's preconceptions.

Besides the use of verbalisms, another way that children often learn deception is by the use of "as-if performances."

Sometimes these performances amount to the acting out, in certain interpersonal situations, of roles that are quite discrepant from one another or from other aspects of the self. Another kind of as-if performance is the "preoccupation"—an activity indulged in not because it is currently interesting or profitable in its own right but simply as a way of avoiding punishment or anxiety. Sullivan gave as an example of this the behavior of one of his cocker spaniels, which when young had often been treated very roughly by her bigger siblings. If she took to digging, however, they would leave her alone. Later, older and larger, she was no longer bothered by her brother and sister. But when the garbage collecter came around, with his frightening noisy truck, she would run and bark at him, stopping briefly and digging frantically after every third bark or so. Sullivan thought that parental authority often teaches a child that, as in the case of the spaniel's digging, preoccupying oneself with some particular kind of activity will save one from unpleasantness—a forerunner of later obsessions.

Some of the kinds of learning of dubious merit that may have been promoted in the child's home become open to remedy as the child moves increasingly into contact with people outside the home. One big change comes as children go to school with their peers. If circumstances at school are favorable, children can come to correct many of their misconceptions, such as a belief in the godlike nature of their parents, and learn a great deal about getting on with their fellows. On the other hand, school children are hardly noted for their sensitivity to the feelings of others, and a child's sense of personal worth can plummet under the onslaught of ridicule from peers.[5] A child who enters the company of other children handicapped in various ways by earlier experiences at home can have a very difficult time. It may become almost impossible for such a child to maintain good self-esteem, and the child's anxiety to be approved and liked may come to overrule almost everything else.

These sorts of difficulties and others may, with luck, be overcome by experiences with a "chum" (Sullivan's term) in preadolescence. Sullivan believed that in this period there develops an extremely strong need—strong enough even to overrule severe anxiety—for interpersonal intimacy. The preadolescent is able, for the first time, sensitively to appreciate what matters to somebody else. When there is a real chum, the chum's satisfaction, status, and self-esteem take on practically equal importance to one's own. The close relationship and intimate communication that can result make possible the confirmation of one's own worth and the correction of all sorts of misconceptions through consensual validation. One comes to see oneself through another's eyes, and the erroneous ideas one may have developed about oneself—the distortions of the self-system—become open to correction. Sullivan put an enormous emphasis on the possibilities for a chum relationship to bring about the correction of earlier difficulties and "warps" of the personality.

The chum relationship is also highly significant as a kind of forerunner of the relationships with sexual partners that will be developing in adolescence and adult life. The growth of sexual motivation in adolescence ushers in a whole new range of problems. The need for intimacy now tends to become a need for a loving relationship with a member of the opposite sex. Sullivan thought that our culture gives very little preparation for these developments, and that a considerable amount of interpersonal learning is required to find satisfactory ways of dealing with sexual desire, with the need for a loving relationship, and with the ever-present need for security—all of which are motivational systems apt to collide with one another. He agreed with Freud that there were often problems in the sexual arena, and that a person's sexual interactions were important to consider. But Sullivan believed very strongly, quite differently from Freud, that problems here would typically be *reflections*, rather than *causes*, of more general difficulties in living. They would derive from inadequate or inappropriate interpersonal learning more generally.

Sullivan maintained throughout his career a firm conviction about the importance of learning and particularly interpersonal learning. People who go to a psychotherapist are people, he thought, who for one reason or another have missed out on the opportunity to undergo some highly significant educational experiences with others. Usually they have come to possess some very inadequate and inappropriate conceptions of themselves—conceptions that keep getting them into trouble but that, because of their role in maintaining security, are extremely resistant to change. Some important parts of the personalities of these individuals are seen by them as the not-me, are dissociated, closed off from experience and not integrated with the rest of the personality. Sullivan viewed a great deal of mental illness as representing either efforts to keep the sorts of things classed as the not-me out of awareness (typical of obsessive processes), or breakthroughs of this material (typical of early schizophrenia).

Such processes—to lesser degrees—are common to all of us. Sullivan felt strongly the essential similarity of all human beings—that we are all, as he put it, "much more simply human than otherwise."[6] In the case of the more fortunate ones among us, however, there have been fewer warps inculcated by previous experiences or more opportunities to correct such warps. These more fortunate individuals are not as closed to their experiences and have been better able to benefit from them. Thus, they have a greater possibility of understanding what is going on with themselves and others, of correctly foreseeing what will be the results of their actions, and of acting appropriately. Almost all people would be all right if they did not have severe blocks to understanding their experiences and profiting from them. The attempt to remove such blocks and to nurture understanding and foresight is essentially what psychiatry is all about. Sullivan believed that "personality tends towards the state that we call mental health or interpersonal adjustive success, handicaps by way of acculturation notwithstanding. The basic direction of the organism is forward."[7]

Horney

Much like Sullivan, Karen Horney[8] believed that neurosis is essentially a consequence of specific unfortunate interpersonal experiences in childhood. A person who becomes neurotic, she maintained, has almost always suffered an early lack of genuine warmth and affection. The parents may have tried hard to put on a display of love, to look after the child's best interests, and to treat the child well, but children are difficult to deceive and inevitably feel keenly the absence of genuine love. Another common denominator in the childhood history of most neurotics is behavior on the part of the parents that arouses hostility, such as lack of fairness and interference with the child's legitimate wishes. Typically, by intimidation or babying the parents have also made the child feel particularly helpless and afraid.

The child is thus in a situation that, on the one hand, keeps provoking hostile impulses and, on the other hand, makes the expression or even the awareness of these impulses extremely dangerous. As a result, the child will tend to repress them. Horney thought repressed hostility generally leads to a feeling of anxiety, as anxiety essentially is the feeling of being helpless in the face of overpowering danger. The child thus becomes anxious, and, because anxiety itself is also likely to provoke the child's hostility, matters will tend to get worse and worse.

It is no wonder, then, that—unless there are other important figures in the child's life who provide different experiences—a child growing up in this way will be particularly subject to neurotic difficulties. The child will have a broadly generalized "basic anxiety"—which Horney describes as "a feeling of being small, insignificant, helpless, deserted, endangered, in a world that is out to abuse, cheat, attack, humiliate, betray, envy."[9]

To be safe, to protect themselves from this anxiety, neurotics have developed certain general and enduring attitudes—"neurotic trends." Although Horney described these trends somewhat differently at different times, there are essentially three: moving toward people (seeking affection, approval, and support), moving against people (striving aggressively for power and success), and moving away from people (trying to shut oneself off from others, to isolate oneself).[10] Each of these occurs in all of us to some degree, without representing anything at all neurotic; each of them may also be particularly emphasized in different cultures, without this having any implications about the mental health of typical members of these cultures. But in a neurotic, one of these trends to the exclusion of the others becomes the means by which the person desperately attempts to secure safety and protection. Since this is the only bulwark for such a person against the basic anxiety that keeps threatening to engulf and overwhelm him or her, the neurotic trend becomes an insatiable and indiscriminate need that inevitably leads to conflict and difficulty. Let us consider each of these neurotic trends in turn.

1. Those who follow the trend of moving toward people in attempting to gain reassurance against their basic anxiety accept the idea that they are helpless. The only possible safety for such an individual lies in finding affection and belongingness and being "taken care of" by someone else. This kind of person thus develops the tendency to be compliant and overconsiderate. Such people subordinate themselves to others, are never assertive, critical, or demanding. They never strive for any ambitious goals. They undervalue all their qualities, talents, and abilities; other people are always much better and more worthy than they themselves. Any criticism or rejection is construed as a terrible danger or catastrophe. They are always ready to belittle themselves and to shoulder blame.

Most of these tendencies are readily conceived of by the neurotic person as virtues. Such individuals will tend to view themselves as unselfish and undemanding, as giving and kind. But these are not really genuine characteristics of theirs; they are ways in which such people try to protect themselves from the ever-threatening danger of overwhelming anxiety. The danger is never removed, and thus the neurotic strivings are never satisfied. No matter how much affection and approval the person receives, this will never guarantee safety, and thus it is never enough. The person will continue compulsively to seek more and more, indiscriminately from all possible sources.

This way of behaving is bound to lead people into difficulties. With such extreme dependence on others' reactions to themselves, people will be subject to continual feelings of rejection and humiliation. The posture of self-effacement will encourage others to take advantage of them, and they will not be able to provide a defense or even respond assertively. Further, such people must manage to talk themselves into believing that they really don't want anything for themselves, don't have any aggressive impulses or any desires to behave differently, or else this whole way of life becomes threatened. Any hostility that is felt must be repressed, contributing to even greater anxiety and an even greater need for protection against anxiety.

2. The neurotic who moves against people is almost the direct opposite of the type we have been discussing, but will have comparable difficulties. Helplessness is one of the last things to which this person would ever admit. Such an individual views the world as just as dangerous a place as the neurotic who moves toward people, but reacts with fighting instead of appeasement. This kind of neurotic believes that everyone in reality callously pursues his own self-interest; all else is hypocrisy and pretense. A neurotic of this type attempts ruthlessly to achieve power and success. All softer tendencies, all feelings of sympathy or obligation, are repressed. Clearly, such people too will be likely to have troubles in their interpersonal relationships—troubles that will only reinforce their cynical views and lead to even more hostility toward others. Once again there tends to be a vicious circle in which the effects of the neurotic trend only make it stronger still.

3. The third type of neurotic attempts to attain security by avoiding any emotional involvement with others. Neurotics of this third type neither appease nor fight; they withdraw. They attempt to be utterly independent and self-sufficient. While the first type represses feelings of hostility and the second type represses feelings of love, the neurotic who moves away from people represses both. But, as in all neuroses, the repressed tendencies are still there underneath: the detached neurotic continues to have cravings

for closeness, for aggression, and for success—cravings that harass if not paralyze such a person.

In her early writing, Horney concentrated on the conflicts among moving toward, against, and away from people. She was especially concerned with the consequences for interpersonal relationships of one of these trends becoming compulsive and indiscriminate and the others being silenced and repressed. As time went on, however, Horney became increasingly convinced of the role of *intra*personal factors in neurosis—in particular, of the significance of an idealized image of the self.[11] Neurosis no longer seemed primarily a disturbance in one's relation to others, but in one's relation to oneself.

The neurotic, Horney came to believe, is "alienated from his real self."[12] His spontaneous wishes, feelings, and thoughts have become sacrificed to the compulsive strivings of his neurotic trends. Such a person no longer develops in accordance with the spontaneous forces of the person's true self.

Thus, the neurotic—who in any case has had little opportunity to build self-confidence and a feeling of identity—functions as a house divided against itself. The neurosis only exacerbates the person's feelings of being lost, anxious, and inferior. The neurotic's conflicts are not resolved; the repressed forces push on underneath the surface. There is a means, however, that offers the promise of solving all of the neurotic's problems at a single stroke: perfecting oneself in imagination. By developing an idealized image of themselves—for example, a being of perfect unselfishness and love, simultaneously an individual of great power and wisdom, or a figure of enormous strength with no potential vulnerabilities, possessing a detached concern for all—neurotics can assure themselves of safety, appear to render compatible their conflicting strivings, and simultaneously glorify themselves. Instead of a miserable wretch suffering continual humiliation and defeat, they can see themselves as an exalted saint or hero.

But the idealized self must then be proved in action. The individual is all the more compulsively driven, therefore, to act in accordance with it. One must continually be hemmed in by taboos and rigid dictates, without any regard for what may be one's own actual best interests. Horney cites as one example of such a compulsive drive a 10-year-old girl who believed that she would prefer being blind to not being the first in her class.

And the drive to glorify oneself is again not only compulsive but also insatiable. No matter what the person accomplishes, it can never be enough. As Robert Pirsig put it:

> Any effort that has self-glorification as its final endpoint is bound to end in disaster. . . . When you try to climb a mountain to prove how big you are, you almost never make it. And even if you do it's a hollow victory. In order to sustain the victory you have to prove yourself again and again in some other way, and again and again and again, driven forever to fill a false image, haunted by the fear that the image is not true and someone will find out.[13]

Because the idealized self is so crucial to the neurotic, because this self represents to neurotics what it becomes so desperately important that they *should* be, the neurotic becomes subject to a kind of "tyranny of the should." One should always be the epitome of lovingness, generosity, consideration, and kindness; one should always be the perfect parent, spouse, worker, and so on. Or one should never permit oneself to get upset over anything, one should always be serene and in full control of oneself—but one should also always be completely spontaneous. One should never become angry, but one should never let anyone take advantage of one, and so on. The particular "shoulds" will vary with the individual, but they come to take over most of the person's life, and they universally operate with an almost total disregard for feasibility.

Neurotics expect to be able to solve their problems, to fulfill the shoulds that preempt their lives and to attain perfection, by sheer force of willpower. When this doesn't work and instead the troubles keep reappearing, when circumstances force neurotics to recognize their imperfection, neurotics then have all the more reason to despise themselves. And they hate themselves all the more still because by so doing they can at least affirm the saintliness of their standards. But all this only means an even greater drive to glory—once again, a vicious circle operates that makes matters worse and worse.

What is probably most harmful about the shoulds to the neurotic is the way that they "further *impair the spontaneity of feelings, wishes, thoughts, and beliefs*—i.e., the ability to feel his own feelings, etc., and to express them. The person, then, can at best be 'spontaneously compulsive' (to quote a patient) and express 'freely' what he *should* feel, wish, think or believe." Thus, Horney points out, if a command comes from the shoulds about what to feel, "imagination waves its magic wand and the border line between what we *should* feel and what we *do* feel evaporates. We consciously believe or feel then as we should believe or feel."[14]

Horney recognized a close similarity between her shoulds and Freud's superego. She felt that one of Freud's most serious mistakes was in identifying such inner dictates with morality. Many of the rigid requirements we set upon ourselves have nothing to do with morality, as, for example, the dictate that "I should come out first in every competition" or "I should be able to write without laborious work and effort." And even demands for moral perfection are permeated with arrogance and have as their aim the neurotic's greater glory. Indeed, when all the unconscious dishonesty involved is taken into account, Horney felt that the shoulds can be seen to be immoral rather than moral.

The shoulds also differ from genuine ideals in their coerciveness. We are obligated by ideals as well, but in the case of ideals it is we ourselves who really want, or think it right, to fulfill them. We are at one with ourselves when we try to carry out our ideals—we do it freely. On the other hand, efforts to meet the demands of our shoulds are coerced by the terrible consequences of not meeting them— condemning and despising ourselves, generating anxiety and despair.

To Horney the essence of neurosis is that neurotics are tyrannically ruled by their idealized selves and their shoulds. Their real selves are suppressed, and they need to be helped to find them again—which is the role of psychotherapy. Neurotics must give up their illusions about themselves and find and develop their real potentialities instead. Their shoulds must lose their coercive power, and they will then be able to discover their real feelings, thoughts, and wishes.

Like Sullivan, Horney had a strong faith in everyone's natural constructive forces, of which she felt the patients she had in psychotherapy gave much evidence. If neurotics in general were helped to see their illusions for what they were and to recognize the possibility of being their real selves, they would, she thought, make powerful efforts in positive directions. They would strive toward clearly and deeply experiencing their authentic wishes and feelings, toward making use of their resources for constructive ends, toward assuming responsibility for themselves. They would put considerable efforts into relating genuinely to others with a spirit of respect and mutuality and into working productively not to achieve self-glorification but for the sake of the work itself. Their concerns would no longer be so narrowly focused on their own personal interests; they would come to see themselves as part of a larger whole to which they would contribute in the most constructive way made possible by their talents.

Horney thought that Freud was wrong in believing that we are motivated only by our instinctual drives, that "nothing really new is created in the process of development"[15]—in short, that all our wishes and feelings can be analyzed into basic instinctual components. She recognized and strongly objected to the implication of his theory that "there is no liking or disliking of people, no sympathy, no generosity, no feeling of justice, no devotion to a cause, which is not in the last analysis essentially determined by libidinal or destructive drives."[16] This view she regarded as not only greatly in error but also seriously harmful, because it fosters distrust of judgments and feelings and encourages a constant effort at detection of ulterior motives. She maintained that "it is merely dogmatic to assert, for instance, that a judgment cannot be simply the expression of what one holds to be right or wrong, that one cannot be devoted to a cause because one is convinced of its value, that friendliness cannot be a direct expression of good human relationships."[17]

Much of the way Freud viewed human beings in general Horney felt was true specifically of neurotics but not of healthy people. A neurotic is indeed driven by irresistible and blind urges—albeit urges ultimately not for sex or destructiveness but for safety. A healthy human being, on the other hand, is spontaneous and genuine. Similarly, there is no inevitable conflict between the individual and the environment; in neuroses there is such a collision, although not because of the individual's instincts but because of the environment's provoking of fear and hostility. People who are free of neurosis, however, feel themselves to be an integral part of the larger world and willingly assume responsibility within it.

With her abiding faith in the human being's natural constructive forces, Horney felt there was no need for shoulds and taboos, for anything like a superego. In her view, these are all merely counterfeits of genuine morality and conscience, consequences of neurotic self-idealization. Both she and Freud saw serious problems in the restrictiveness of inner dictates, but, in her words, "Freud can aim merely at reducing the severity of the superego while I aim at the individual's being able to dispense with his inner dictates altogether and to assume the direction of his life in accordance with his true wishes and beliefs."[18]

In Horney's view, people, unless obstructed by the environment, strive autonomously for self-realization, for the full development of their human potentialities. They cannot do this without being truthful to themselves, being productively active in the world, and relating to others in ways based on trust and mutuality.[19] They will thus—if the environment permits—of their own accord develop in positive and constructive directions; there is no need for inner shackles or commands. Destructive forces will be outgrown as we become increasingly aware of ourselves and understand ourselves better. The appropriate goal for us, then, "is the liberation and cultivation of the forces which lead to self-realization."[20]

Fromm

Erich Fromm was a far-ranging thinker concerned with understanding historical and political developments and with bringing psychology to bear on efforts to improve society. One of his goals was to facilitate the construction of social arrangements that would better meet our fundamental human needs. A great many of the troubles of our current period, according to Fromm,[21] are related to changes in the nature of society since the time of the Middle Ages. While human beings have become progressively more free, they have also become progressively more separated from one another and from their communities. And people have a deep need for relatedness and belonging. They cannot bear to feel alone and apart from the rest of the world, segregated from other human beings. To become fully isolated is to become insane.

In medieval society, each person had a clearly defined role that was unchanging and unquestioned. One's position in the social order was essentially determined by birth. There was no possibility of choice among different ways of living, but neither was there doubt about one's situation or the meaning of one's life. People hardly thought of themselves as separate individuals, but rather considered themselves in terms of the roles they played in the social groups of which they formed a part. They had little freedom, but they were secure.

When feudal society started to disintegrate in the late Middle Ages, all this began to change. With the rise of capitalism, traditional social groups declined in significance. One no longer had a fixed place into which one was more or less born. People came to discover themselves as individuals.

This trend continued apace with the further development of industrial society. People became increasingly free from traditional bonds and sources of authority, but at the same time became increasingly isolated and separate. Further, while in one sense the individual became more and more important, in another sense the individual became subordinated to the workings of the economic system itself. Our society does not serve the full, concrete person with all of that person's human potentialities; rather, the individual is now largely a cog in the vast economic machine. The individual has become an instrument for this machine's purposes, and all of one's relationships are imbued with its spirit of manipulation and instrumentality. Another person is one's "employee," whom one "employs" or uses—or, inversely, is one's "employer"; another person is one's customer, whom one manipulates rather than whose aims one is concerned to satisfy, and so on.

The modern person, according to Fromm, has won freedom from traditional authorities and bonds; such a person has become an independent individual. But at the same time, that person has become separated, alienated, anxious, and powerless. People in modern society have attained "negative freedom," freedom from bondage, but have not achieved "positive freedom," freedom to live actively and spontaneously—to realize themselves, their individual potentialities. We must now develop our freedom to be ourselves, to live productively, and to be productively related to the world. Much of Fromm's later writing is directed toward clarifying the objective of self-realization and the possibilities of its attainment, which we shall discuss further.

For the moment, however, let us consider what happens when positive freedom in this sense does not exist; let us consider what happens when—as has been typical of our era—there is freedom from but not freedom to. According to Fromm, relatedness is a fundamental need of human beings; it is crucial to our very sanity. But negative freedom without positive freedom means isolation and alienation. It is therefore an intolerable state—a condition not to be

borne. Thus, when people cannot progress to positive freedom, they try to escape from freedom altogether.

One can try to escape from freedom by giving up one's
independence and submerging oneself in some larger whole.
This was the basis of the appeal of the Nazis, Fromm believed, to large groups of the German people. Political and
economic developments after World War I had exacerbated
their feelings of isolation, insignificance, and powerless-
ness. The Nazis offered them the possibility of overcoming
their separateness and uniting in what was to be a glorious
higher power. In Goebbels' words, they were to "submit
the I to the thou"; they were to sacrifice "the individual to
the whole."[22] They had to give up their rights of asserting
their own opinions and interests, their rights of pursuing
their own happiness. But in return, they were to participate in "the uplifting of mankind itself."[23]

Fromm believed that not only the Germans who followed Hitler but also the majority of "normal" people in
our own society have "escaped from freedom." We have
not been thinking for ourselves; we have been conforming.
The authority we have submitted to is that of public opinion instead of that of a dictator, but we have submitted to
authority nonetheless. Like subjects influenced by hyp-
notic suggestion, we have been under the illusion that our
feelings and thoughts are our own while they have really
been imposed on us from the outside. What we have been
aware of feeling or wanting is mostly not anything we
really felt or wanted at all, but just what we thought—on
the basis of those around us—we were supposed to feel
or want. Similarly, "our" opinions have typically not been
the result of our own deliberations, but mostly just a function of what has been suggested to us by others. We have
become a society of largely identical automatons. Being
like everyone else, we no longer feel alone and anxious,

but the price is very high: we have given up our individual selves.

In Fromm's view, psychiatrists, instead of recognizing these problems, have mostly gone along with the general cultural pattern. They have stressed as characteristics of mental health such qualities as adjustment, not being "too emotional," and security (here Fromm takes Sullivan, among others, to task). But how can a person who is sensitive to the actual conditions of our existence ever feel really secure or adjusted? Fromm asks.[24] In Fromm's view, "Country of the Blind," a story by H.G. Wells about doctors in an isolated tribe, provides an apt illustration of the situation of many of our psychiatrists. The members of this tribe are all congenitally blind, and a young man named Bogota, from outside the tribe, has come to live with them. This sighted man is examined by the tribe's doctors, who are much disturbed by his peculiarities and differences. Finally, they come to the conclusion that the trouble with Bogota is his abnormal eyes—they are diseased, and all that is necessary to restore him to health is for his eyes to be removed.[25]

There is no need, however, for people to give up their own individuality in order to avoid being powerless and alone. When we have only negative freedom, says Fromm, we are bound to attempt escape. But there is another alternative. There is the possibility of positive freedom, which human beings can attain by the realization of their selves, by active expression of their emotional, intellectual, and sensuous potentialities. We have positive freedom when we act spontaneously, when our feeling, thinking, and behavior are the expression of our selves. Small children, Fromm tells us, offer a good example of such spontaneity—what they feel and think and do really comes from them. Certain artists offer another example.

With activity that is spontaneous, one realizes oneself while at the same time uniting oneself with the world. Genuine love, productive work, and productive thinking are all important kinds of such activity. They are not functions that are imposed on us from the outside—they are freely undertaken activities in which we realize our individual potentialities. And they relate us—productively, creatively—with others and with the world. Real love, for example, is a free action in which we unite with another. It involves care and responsibility: *"Love is the active concern for the life and the growth of that which we love."*[26] It also involves knowledge and respect, seeing the other person as he or she really is, and wanting that person to grow and develop for that person's sake and not for our own purposes. When one truly loves another, one realizes one's own self by actively striving for the other's growth and happiness.

What Fromm means by self-realization is clearly something different from what is ordinarily meant by selfishness. But Fromm is also worried by the extensive promulgation of the idea that one should not be selfish. This tends to mean, he says, not only that one should have concern for others, but also " 'don't love yourself,' 'don't be yourself,' but submit yourself to something more important than yourself, to an outside power or its internalization, 'duty.' 'Don't be selfish' becomes one of the most powerful ideological tools in suppressing spontaneity and the free development of personality."[27]

According to Fromm, the traditional doctrine of the sinfulness of loving oneself and seeking one's own self-interest rests on a confusion about the meaning of love and self-interest. People who are really selfish—who are interested only in having, never in giving, who look at things only in terms of what they can get out of them—do not love themselves too much, but rather too little. They are not serving their own objective interests, which have to do not with grasping what they can for themselves but with realizing their inherent potentialities.

We *should* love ourselves, Fromm tells us. But this does not mean that we should strive for pleasure, material gains, power, or success. It means rather that we should be concerned for ourselves as individuals, with all of the intellectual, emotional, and sensuous potential that we possess. We cannot genuinely love another person unless we also, in this sense, love ourselves. Love that is rooted in weakness, in lack of love for oneself, is not really love at all. Similarly, the "unselfishness" that derives from insufficient care for oneself is not conducive to the welfare of others either. The child of an oversolicitous, self-sacrificing mother is not a happy, joyful child.

Loving oneself and loving others are not, according to Fromm, alternatives. Rather, they go together. Fromm puts it this way: "Respect for one's own integrity and uniqueness, love for and understanding of one's own self, can not be separated from respect for and love and understanding of another individual. The love for my own self is inseparably connected with the love for any other self."[28] We are all human beings, and the proper love of any other member of the human species implies love of humankind in general, including oneself. Thus, "my own self, in principle, must be as much an object of my love as another person."[29]

In Fromm's view, then, we should love ourselves and attempt to realize our potentialities. When we move toward the realization of our capacities, we are united with the world while maintaining the integrity of our selves. In a word, we are happy. Happiness and joy accompany all productive activity in thought, feeling, and action. Morality and happiness are intertwined. "Happiness is the criterion of excellence in the art of living, of virtue in the meaning it has in humanistic ethics."[30] Indeed, Fromm also said, "Happiness is man's greatest achievement."[31] He has stressed, however, that the happiness at which we are to aim is not to be understood in the sense of satisfaction of felt desires or subjective wishes.[32] What we are aware of wanting is by no means necessarily the same as what we objectively need. It is this latter that should receive our attention. Fromm thought there were a number of such objective needs, apart from physiological ones, that arise out of the conditions of human existence. In the beginning of his work, he stressed mainly relatedness. He then added others, such as the need for a frame of orientation and devotion, for a sense of identity, and for effectiveness.[33] It is these needs on which our happiness depends and which we can fulfill by productive realization of our potentialities.

If conditions permit, we will naturally strive toward such realization. This is part of our nature as human beings. Individuals who grow under proper conditions, who can productively use their capacities, will try to do so. They will want to further their own life and that of others. They will love themselves and those around them; they will be productive and they will be virtuous. But this kind of fulfillment may be blocked; obstacles may prevent the productive realization of our potentialities. It is here, according to Fromm, that we have the conditions for evil. A person blocked in this way can become psychically crippled. Such a person can become passionately attracted to death instead of life, to destruction for the sake of destruction.

What we need, then, if we are to attack the evil that exists in the world and to nurture the good, is not a system of rewards and punishments, not relentless suppression of evil strivings. Rather, what we need is the removal of obstacles in the environment that prevent people from following their natural inclinations. If these environmental obstacles are not too great, people will spontaneously attempt to realize their potentialities and relate themselves creatively with the world.

A person for whom the obstacles are too great, who cannot make use of his or her inherent powers, is inevitably in trouble. This person may succumb to a dictator or become a conforming automaton. Or the person may develop a neurosis. Neuroses need not be the consequence of particularly strong pathogenic forces; on the contrary, in a society such as ours in which the majority of individuals do not live spontaneous and productive lives, neuroses may be the result of particularly strong, healthy forces that are refusing to go along with the cultural pattern. A neurosis is the result of conflict between a person's powers and the interferences that are blocking the development of those powers. The healthy part of the person fights against the blocking; neurotic symptoms are the expression of that fight.

Fromm gives an example of a successful teacher, in psychoanalysis because of dizzy spells for which there is no organic cause, to illustrate this kind of conflict. The teacher mentions casually that in his job he has to express views with which he does not agree. He believes—and has "proved" to himself by means of various complex rationalizations—that he is managing to maintain his integrity while doing what his job requires of him. However, it becomes clear that this is not the case, and that his spells of dizziness are a reaction to the violation of his basically moral personality, to his going against his own conscience.[34]

Conscience—when it is our own voice, as opposed to the internalized voice of an authority—is very important to Fromm. Such conscience, again, sends us in the direction Fromm is continually urging—that of our real self: "It is the voice of our true selves which summons us back to ourselves, to live productively, to develop fully and harmoniously—that is, *to become what we potentially are.*"[35]

The full development of our own powers is always what Fromm sees as our main task in life. It is a mistake to think that our ideals and purposes lie outside of us—to search for answers by looking to history, to what the world might become, or to the order of the universe. The person who makes this mistake "will go outside himself and seek fulfillment where it can not be found. He will look for solutions and answers at every point except the one where they can be found—in himself."[36]

Notes

1. Fairbairn, 1952.
2. Sullivan, 1947, 1953.
3. Sullivan, 1953, pp. 213–214.
4. Sullivan, 1953, p. 207.
5. Sullivan, 1953, p. 230.
6. Sullivan, 1953, p. 32.
7. Sullivan, 1947, p. 48.
8. Horney, 1937.
9. Horney, 1937, p. 92.
10. Horney, 1945.
11. Horney, 1950.
12. Horney, 1950, p. 13.
13. Pirsig, 1974, pp. 210–211.
14. Horney, 1950, pp. 81–82, italics hers.
15. Horney, 1939, p. 42.
16. Horney, 1939, p. 187.
17. Horney, 1939, p. 188.
18. Horney, 1950, p. 375.
19. Horney, 1950, p. 15.
20. Horney, 1950, p. 16.
21. Fromm, 1941/1965.
22. Quoted by Fromm, 1941/1965, p. 258.
23. Hitler, as quoted by Fromm, 1941/1965, p. 259.
24. Fromm, 1955, p. 174.
25. Fromm, 1955, p. 171.
26. Fromm, 1956, p. 26, italics his.
27. Fromm, 1947, pp. 131–132.
28. Fromm, 1947, pp. 133–134.
29. Fromm, 1947, p. 135.
30. Fromm, 1947, p. 192.
31. Fromm, 1947, p. 194.
32. Fromm, 1976, pp. 3–4.
33. Fromm, 1955, 1973.
34. Fromm, 1947, p. 226.
35. Fromm, 1947, p. 163, italics his.
36. Fromm, 1947, pp. 249–250.

6

Sullivan, Horney, and Fromm: Opposing Prescriptions and Restraints, Promoting Self-Realization

The neo-Freudians, as we have seen, reject Freud's instincts as the sole basis of all motivation. They regard human beings as possessing important needs besides the ones Freud recognized—in particular, needs having to do with other people. They stress our lack of self-sufficiency and the interdependencies that exist among us.

But, notwithstanding their emphasis on the role of human beings in relation to one another, the push toward selfishness that is implicit in Freud's theory turns out to be accelerated, we submit, by the neo-Freudians. Freud still believed—along with the vast majority of humankind over the ages—that it was important for people to be guided by prescriptions and restraints. While he thought that too much constraint could be very harmful to an individual, indeed could be responsible for neuroses, considerations of the common good made it absolutely essential to limit the extent of the direct gratification of wishes by any one of us.

This idea the neo-Freudians no longer accept. They view prescriptions and restraints as still more harmful than did Freud. And while Freud thought that the unchecked release of the instinctual forces of human nature inevitably leads to evil, Sullivan, Horney, and Fromm believe that such an outlook rests on far too negative a view of what constitutes human nature. Rules, regulations, and taboos are not necessary to keep us from evil. They are far more likely to contribute to evil by alienating us from our true selves. Freud—consistently or not—urges that we sublimate, that we direct our energies away from what would be most inherently gratifying, deflecting these energies toward ends of greater social value. What the neo-Freudians urge, rather, is that we direct ourselves toward our real interests and not deceive ourselves in regard to what these are. The emphasis, increasingly present from Sullivan to Horney and from Horney to Fromm, is on spontaneous expression of our selves, self-realization, and maximum development of our potentialities.

These ideas were strongly contributed to by Rousseau and Nietzsche, and within psychology and psychiatry by Jung, Adler, and Rank. In the growing liberal sentiment that was mobilizing against totalitarianism, these ideas seem to have gained strength in part from their relationship to the political ideals of freedom and democracy. Indeed, Fromm made the connection explicit. Such a linkup is not without irony, of course, since a connection could also be drawn to the totalitarianism that the neo-Freudians abhorred—witness Hitler's invoking of Nietzsche for the self-development of the German people under National Socialism.

In any case, clearly there is much that is important in what the neo-Freudians advise. But we believe that too much opposition to prescriptions and restraints, along with the view that people should act only spontaneously and toward their own maximum expression or development, can be extremely harmful and is not warranted. Next we turn again to the writings of Sullivan, Horney, and Fromm, this time focusing on the specific ways in which they opposed constraints and favored self-realization. We will then consider problems in the arguments they advance.

Self-Realization and the Attack on Restraints

We begin once more with Sullivan. It is true that Sullivan did not explicitly urge self-realization as such, and he recognized that some prescribed ways of doing things—when appropriately understood and not distorted by the mind of a child—might facilitate human relationships. Nevertheless, Sullivan too, along with Horney and Fromm, held that evil was not a natural consequence of what human nature is like when unconstrained, but rather a result of unfortunate early experiences. In further general agreement, Sullivan also held that the main need was not for prescriptions and restraints, which had mostly negative effects, but rather for the removal of blocks to understanding one's experience and profiting from it.

Sullivan believed that societal prescriptions tend to be unreasonable, contradictory, and impossible to carry out. And the insistence of authorities upon them leads to anxiety and all its negative consequences, as well as promoting misconceptions and the development of techniques for deceiving others and also oneself. Frequently there is, Sullivan said, "a great deal of training—that is, experience which is presumed, erroneously I think in a great many cases, to be educational—in which the idea of *ought* is very conspicuous."[1] The reactions of the mother or other authorities to the transgressions that inevitably occur cause more anxiety in the child. There is no way anxiety can be gotten rid of, and when one is anxious, everything tends to go awry.

Sullivan, then, was much concerned with how prescriptions and restraints get people into trouble. We would all generally be able to stay out of trouble were it not for anxiety, erroneous ideas about ourselves, and blocks to understanding. What Sullivan primarily urges is the avoidance or correction of misconceptions and the removal of obstacles to clarity and to profiting from experience. Prescriptions and restraints are not a help in this task, but a hindrance.

In Horney, there is explicit urging to self-realization. She believes that, if we but permit them to do so, people will of their own accord strive to be constructive, responsible, and productive and to develop in positive directions. Prescriptions, restraints, constraints, requirements are all unnecessary and as much as possible to be done away with. This goes not only for the external constraints on which Sullivan principally focused, but particularly, also, for our inner dictates or shoulds. These serve no useful function, but only cause misery and distress for the person—most of all, tending to alienate us from our genuine selves and to keep us from spontaneity and self-realization.

Although we tend to think of our shoulds as essentially moral, Horney believed this was a serious mistake. Their real source, she held, lies in compulsive drives for safety and self-glorification. Unlike genuine ideals, which we try to carry out because we really want to do so, our shoulds rule us by coercion—by the self-condemnation and anxiety that ensue if we fail to obey their dictates. Many of the shoulds, such as that one should win in any competition, are not related to morality at all. And shoulds whose content is integrally related to what we think of as morality are also in a similar fashion not really directed toward ethical aims, but at the satisfaction of neurotic drives. Feeling that one should always be unselfish, for example, may be part of one's neurotic moving toward people—a way of attempting to assure that they will like one, look after one, take care of one. It may represent a refusal to assume responsibility for oneself and a claim upon others to do so instead.[2] And unselfishness may be a crucial aspect of one's idealized self, the image of which one is desperately attempting to shore up and maintain. Given the unconscious dishonesty involved, Horney believes that the shoulds are positively immoral.

What Horney finds most damaging about the shoulds is the way in which they serve to separate us from our real feelings, thoughts, and wishes. Neurotics, tyrannically ruled by their shoulds, can no longer sense their own true feelings and wishes. They are conscious only of what they think they should feel, or believe, or want, not what is actually the case. A neurotic's real self has been pushed into hiding, and the major task of psychotherapy is to help bring it back to light.

While Horney is mostly concerned with self-realization as a counter to neurosis, Fromm is concerned with its general and fundamental value. Everything that he views as good and to be striven for—the fulfillment of our objective needs, the development of our potentialities, productive thought and work, love, happiness—depends on the spontaneous, genuine realization of our selves.

Again and again, Fromm tells us that what should really be our fundamental aim in life is to be spontaneously ourselves, develop our powers, realize our potentialities as fully as possible. It is a mistake, he believes, to look for values and purposes outside oneself. In recurring statements with which Horney and Sullivan both expressed their explicit agreement, Fromm maintains that the traditional condemnation of loving oneself and pursuing one's self-interest rests on erroneous conceptions of love and self-interest. Indeed, because genuine love for another human being implies love of human beings as such, real love of self is inseparable from love of others. The dictum against self-love, rather than furthering the person's own well-being, is seen by Fromm largely as an ideological tool sanctimoniously used by authorities whose real purpose is to compel obedience to what the authorities want people to do.

Like Horney (who was strongly influenced by him), Fromm believed that human beings—if they are permitted to do so—will spontaneously try to make productive use of their powers, to further inherent tendencies toward growth, to be constructive. It is only when the obstacles become too great that people may turn to evil. If the obstacles standing in the way of our natural tendencies toward self-realization can be removed, we will spontaneously strive toward productive work and love.

All three of our neo-Freudians—Sullivan, Horney, and Fromm—thus in various ways keep opposing restraints on people, rules, regulations, prescriptions, taboos. Horney and Fromm explicitly urge spontaneity, the maximal development of one's powers, self-realization. On the face of it, we have here a striking contrast to Freud, who believed that constraints and sublimation were indispensable to civilization.

But recall that there is a kind of tension, if not contradiction, in Freud's position. On the one hand, he wanted to urge that we restrain ourselves from too direct an expression of our impulses, sublimating our energies instead toward the attainment of higher values. But on the other hand, his theory implies that direct gratification is always what would be preferred if it were possible and is also what would be most conducive to our health. Freud urges us to restrain ourselves and to sublimate, while at the same time admitting that we would be better off if we didn't have to do so.

The neo-Freudians in effect solve this problem by arguing that we don't have to restrain ourselves and sublimate. We are not by nature evil, and the spontaneous expression of our impulses will not lead to harm; on the contrary, maximal spontaneous self-realization would be best for all concerned. The neo-Freudians are, in a sense, rejecting one of Freud's conflicting principles—that we must restrain ourselves and divert our energies toward socially useful ends—while carrying the other one—that direct gratification is what is really best for people—to its logical conclusion.

Can the General Good Be Served Without Restraints?

The neo-Freudians argue—validly, it seems to us—that the provision of regulations and taboos does not necessarily make people better moral beings, and it may even make them less moral. Some regulations, like the one requiring a teacher to express views with which he disagreed, may lead the individual to suppress not what is evil, but what is good. And we may require many things of ourselves ostensibly because we think they are right or good, but really for reasons that are not commendable. One may try always to be considerate, for example, less because of a belief in the value of behaving this way than because one is afraid of how others will respond if one behaves otherwise.

Further, rules and regulations can have unfortunate side effects, whether or not they lead to good. They can contribute to anxiety and promote deception and concealment, both in relation to others and to oneself. They thus raise the likelihood of misconceptions and failures in understanding and learning. Prescriptions and taboos, particularly when one requires of oneself that they be followed, can lead to problems in the awareness of one's own feelings and wishes, as well as misconceptions regarding what these really are. Anxiety, concealment, and such misconceptions certainly do seem to cause serious troubles for people.

However, none of these points can be taken to imply that prescriptions and restraints are really unnecessary for the general good. That prescriptions can be evil and that even what would seem to be good prescriptions can lead to harmful consequences does not mean that it would be better for all concerned if there were no prescriptions, and people simply acted spontaneously instead. At the most, these points might imply that it would be better, for any given individual, if that person could act spontaneously and not be constrained. (Whether this is true we will consider later.) But this is very different from claiming that the greatest general good for all would be served by getting rid of prescriptions and maximizing spontaneity.

It seems extremely unlikely that this could be so. What is to happen when there are conflicting interests among us? Could it really be better to have no rules and no guidelines? To have no common expectations as to what we could count on each other to do and not to do? This is what the neo-Freudians seem to be saying. But such a state of affairs could actually be better for all concerned only if we all spontaneously looked out for everyone else's interests as for our own, a situation that clearly is not the case.

That it would be better for everyone if people simply acted spontaneously toward their own self-realization without norms, regulations, or taboos seems so implausible on its face that one may wonder how the neo-Freudians could ever have been able to accept such a proposition. Their work as therapists with clients who came to them for help with psychological problems may have had a great deal to do with this, not only by causing them to be continually aware of the roles of prescriptions and restraints in clients' problems but in other ways as well. The very arrangement of therapists working with individual clients is unlike all the rest of what transpires in the world; the clients have practically no responsibilities to anyone but themselves, and the therapists have practically no responsibilities except to help their clients. This situation would seem highly conducive to the view that self-realization is the ultimate good. This view would be likely to be strengthened by the concern that the therapist is not to impose the therapist's own values upon the client. Further, the clients who came to the neo-Freudians for therapeutic help seem to have been, for the most part, people with strongly developed values and ideals, deep commitments to ethical behavior, and serious concern for others. With such people as one's frame of reference, it would be a great deal easier to believe that spontaneous self-realization would serve the general good.

Particularly important is the fact that therapists inevitably tend to focus on psychological problems as their highest priority, seeking all possible ways to minimize them. In the prevailing atmosphere of increasing skepticism and doubt concerning traditional values, the neo-Freudians apparently let *psychological* values preempt all others. They began to identify evil essentially with neuroses and good with mental health.

Freud had been subject to some of the same influences. But his belief that the best interests of any particular individual are served by the satisfaction of that individual's own bodily needs, coupled with his concern for civilized values and people's attitudes toward one another, meant that he saw what was good for the individual as inevitably in conflict with what was required for the good of society. Having broadened the scope of what is viewed as the individual's needs, the neo-Freudians no longer believe this conflict to be necessary. The general good as well as the good of the individual will be furthered, in their view, by maximally freeing the individual from all prescriptions and restraints. But, as we have argued, this would only be true if we all spontaneously cared as much about everyone else as about ourselves.

Do Restraints Necessarily Oppose the Interests of the Individual?

The neo-Freudians disagreed—unwarrantedly, we have argued—with Freud's principle that prescriptions and restraints are needed if the general good is to be served. It was Freud's belief in this principle that kept him from carrying to its logical conclusion another principle in which he also believed: that prescriptions and restraints go against the interests of the individual. On this principle the neo-Freudians agreed with Freud, and, disbelieving the first one, they were free to extend the second principle further, indeed to carry it to the point of general opposition to prescriptions and restraints.

Let us now consider whether this second principle is correct: whether prescriptions and restraints are necessarily opposed to the interests of the individual. Given Freud's conception of motivation, this has to be the case, with the exception of constraints required by the nature of reality. According to Freud, what is good for the individual is satisfaction of the individual's bodily needs; what motivates the individual is the stimulation brought about by these needs, stimulation that the activity in turn is designed to reduce. The natural and spontaneous actions of the individual thus always tend to be in the individual's own best interests, except insofar as his or her actions fail to take sufficiently into account the nature of reality. Any prescriptions or restraints that prevent individuals from doing what they would spontaneously undertake to do must then be opposed to their interests, except for those that help in achieving greater need satisfaction by taking better account of reality (the reality principle).

It is striking that most interpretations of motivation after Freud, despite all sorts of other modifications, continue to assume that, with the qualification concerning reality, what the individual spontaneously tends to do is always what is in the individual's best interests to do. But if our interests are not all fundamentally a matter of reduction of stimulation that leads us to act, our interests may not always be furthered by spontaneous action, modified only by the reality principle. Indeed, once individuals are conceived of as possessing the kinds of concerns that the neo-Freudians attribute to them, there is compelling reason to believe that submission to some prescriptions and restraints is often required by the concerns that we have.

Sullivan, Horney, and Fromm recognize the individual as possessing interests such as the development of the individual's powers, the maintenance of justice, and the good of other people to whom the individual is devoted. They deny that these interests are related to the kinds of needs Freud held to be at the root of all motivation. They do not think of behavior supporting these interests as resulting from any kind of stimulation that the behavior is designed to reduce. Why, then, should we still assume that the individual will naturally and spontaneously always take these various interests appropriately into account? It would seem far more likely that we will tend to pay particular attention to those of our interests for which immediate reminders are available.

If one is hungry, one does not have to try to keep it in mind, because exactly the kind of stimulation that Freud thought was at the root of all motivation does tend to occur in the presence of a physiological need like the need for food. Under normal conditions and when reality permits, this stimulation will lead the individual more or less spontaneously to seek out food and eat when it is in the individual's interest to do so. But, unless we somehow build them in by prescriptions or restraints, similar automatic reminders do not exist for, say, our concern for other people or for justice. Someone who is hungry may forget all about others' needs for food unless specific efforts are made to avoid this. Such interests as we may possess that are not represented by immediate stimuli may thus be furthered, rather than opposed, by prescriptions and restraints.

If there can be undertakings we wish to carry out that are not fundamentally a matter of reducing bodily stimulation, these undertakings may require some kinds of regulation for their very possibility. Without submitting oneself to rules, one cannot, for example, perform music or play a game, even by oneself, let alone with anyone else. The distinction between a musical composition and noise, between a game and random activity, between a dance form and flailing about, implies some kind of sensitivity and adherence to rule systems.[3] The development of one's capacities, which the neo-Freudians were so concerned to encourage, is hardly possible without some discipline. And most kinds of relationships with others—teacher, teammate, spouse, friend—require that one make some commitments and not keep oneself free from all constraints.

Thus, much of what the neo-Freudians believe we most want (and much of what we indeed seem most to want) often apparently can be attained only if we are willing to subject ourselves to some prescriptions or restraints. These regulations then are not opposed to our interests, but are necessary for their furtherance.

But while they recognize motivations that would seem to require prescriptions and restraints, the neo-Freudians assume that all constraints must derive from something other than a person's genuine desires. They seem to believe that any restrictions must have sources that are external to the individual ("authority" or simply the group or society, to which one blindly conforms) or sources that are internal but in some way not real but inauthentic or neurotic. They do not seem to realize that people might submit to certain rules and prohibitions precisely in order to further their genuine interests and desires. Constraint seems automatically to imply to the neo-Freudians not only a restriction against spontaneity but also what seems to be taken as almost the same thing, a restriction against fulfillment of the person's true desires and interests.

Thus, for Horney, the kind of prescription that a person feels as a should is inevitably the result not of a genuine desire but of something neurotic. It is coerced by the self-condemnation that would follow upon its violation, while a genuine desire is carried out spontaneously and freely. But desires of the kind Horney takes to be genuine are not, as we have argued, always carried out spontaneously and freely. They may instead sometimes depend for their furtherance on aid from prescriptions and restraints, indeed, at times on just the kind of coercion that Horney views as characteristic of neurotic trends. Will we not also condemn ourselves if we go against something that we genuinely want or believe in—if, for example, we teach what we think are falsehoods or if we harm our children? That we do something because we think we should and would condemn ourselves for doing otherwise cannot be taken to mean that it is necessarily neurotic and opposed to our real interests. We might condemn ourselves precisely because of our genuine desires.

For Fromm, it often seems as if going along with the norms or prescriptions of a group were inevitably a kind of blind conformity, opposed to the real interests of the individual. He does not seem to consider the possibility that such compliance may be motivated by genuine desires to do one's part in the group or to support and maintain trust and other aspects of social life. But the upholding of certain norms or regulations—for example, telling the truth, carrying out promises—would seem essential to the maintenance of the kind of community of which most people want to be members. These norms and regulations are then required not only for the general good but also for the good of each of these individuals. Far from being counter to the genuine interests of the individual, they are vital to these interests.

It thus seems a grievous error to think of submission to prescriptions and restraints apart from external sanctions as necessarily a matter of a neurosis or blind conformity. Rather, such submission would frequently seem to be a matter of serving genuine desires of the individual, desires that may be as simple and as unrelated to other people as playing a game of solitaire or as complex and concerned with others as the furthering of justice. Prescriptions and restraints may often further our real interests instead of opposing them.

This is not to say, of course, that most prescriptions and restraints are in our true interests. A society's rules and regulations frequently do fail to serve the interests of all its members; some of its conventions are misguided, some represent only the efforts of those in power to further narrow interests of their own. We personally share Horney's and Fromm's strong value for self-determination: having individuals themselves, as much as possible, determine what they do instead of leaving this up to some presumed authority or anything else external to the individual. But this does not mean that the individual's own issuance of prescriptions and restraints should be minimized.

Prescriptions and restraints for which the sources are internal to the individual are, of course, not necessarily good ones either. Certainly some of the shoulds that people hold for themselves derive from sources that are in some way inauthentic. But this seems far from true for all of them. Some of the constraints that individuals place upon themselves seem crucial to the furtherance of what they most value and care about. What seems called for, rather than trying to minimize prescriptions altogether, is a careful distinction between prescriptions that do further the person's genuine interests and those that do not.

We have been arguing that our genuine desires are not necessarily spontaneously carried out and that a person may submit to prescriptions or restraints not only because of external sanctions or neurotic or conformist tendencies but also precisely to further the person's real interests and desires. But are we not forgetting about the role that prescriptions and restraints play in people's troubles and difficulties? The neo-Freudians have pointed out how they may foster anxiety, conceal what goes on in us, and promote misconceptions about ourselves and others. Constraints not only keep us from acting on our spontaneous feelings and wishes but also often keep us from even knowing what we feel and what we wish. And anxiety and such a lack of contact with one's own experiences seem to play a significant role in the troubles of people who come to psychotherapists for help.

But the very prescriptions and restraints that cause difficulties for a person may still derive from the person's most genuine desires. Just as it is not only neurotic shoulds whose violation can lead to self-condemnation, so it is also not only neurotic or conformist or otherwise inauthentic constraints that can result in anxiety or self-deception. If one genuinely wishes to be fair, for example, one may become anxious when acting unfairly, or fail to perceive what one is doing, or give such behavior a false interpretation. If speaking the truth is held by one as a genuine ideal, one may become anxious when one is not honest or be taken in by one's own lies.

As soon as we have any ideals for ourselves, there is no escaping that these will imply constraints, which may function as sources of discomfiture. The neo-Freudians certainly do not want to discourage us from affirming ideals. Indeed, to do so might lead to further trouble in its own right, particularly, the exacerbation of the feelings of meaninglessness that are already so common a complaint. But then perhaps the possibility of anxiety and self-deception simply has to be accepted as part of the human condition, and all that one can do is try to be honest with oneself, while recognizing that one may not always be successful at it.

Opposition to prescriptions and restraints that people impose on themselves, then, may not be at all in these people's interests but rather against them, and this holds true even when these prescriptions and restraints are causing a person anxiety or other kinds of trouble. It is, of course, a particular temptation when one is disturbed about having violated some prescription or when a therapist is confronted with a client who is so disturbed to try to minimize that prescription's force or validity. To succumb to this temptation may, however, be harmful rather than helpful; the prescription may be related to a strongly felt concern or ideal. Not to take seriously requirements one has for oneself or to encourage others not to take their self-imposed requirements seriously may be to engage in or to foster a harmful kind of self-deception.

Thus, while prescriptions and restraints may indeed foster anxiety and self-deception, this too does not mean that they are simply to be opposed. Some constraints seem essential in the furtherance of what we ourselves really want. Even when they are involved in a person's difficulties, trying to counter such constraints may do the person much more harm than good.

Recapitulating the Argument

Let us now sum up where we have been going. Freud, we said, believed that prescriptions and restraints are opposed to the interests of the individual, but are necessary for the general welfare. The neo-Freudians agreed with Freud that prescriptions and restraints go against the individual's good, but disagreed on their necessity for the general good. They then ended up arguing against prescriptions and restraints altogether, urging instead spontaneous self-realization and the maximum development of the individual. Ironically enough, in view of their conviction about the existence of human interdependence and mutual concern, it turns out that the neo-Freudians thus encourage the cultivation of selfishness to a far greater extent than did Freud.

We have argued the diametric opposite to the neo-Freudians on both these points. Human beings hardly seem always so ready spontaneously to consider the good of others as their own good that prescriptions and restraints are not required for the general welfare. On this point Freud seems to us clearly correct. But we believe Freud and the neo-Freudians and the vast majority of psychologists since to be wrong in their view that prescriptions and restraints are in principle opposed to the interests of the individual.

Quite apart from the problem of its potential blindness to reality, spontaneous action does not always maximally further what the individual most wants. Prescriptions and restraints can help the individual keep sight of interests that are not represented by immediate stimuli and can be necessary for the possibility of carrying out some of the undertakings that a person considers most important. At times it will thus be more in people's interests to subject themselves to constraints than to act spontaneously. Both on the grounds of the general welfare and of the good of the individual, then, a general opposition to prescriptions and restraints seems unjustified and misguided.

Notes

1. Sullivan, 1953, p. 206, italics his.
2. Horney, 1950, p. 50.
3. Wallach, 1967.

7

Maslow and Rogers: Further Calls to Actualize and Be Oneself

We have seen how Horney and Fromm put much emphasis on the development of one's potentialities and being one's true self. They held, as did Sullivan and indeed Freud as well, that we cause ourselves a great deal of distress by suppressing our real desires, feelings, and thoughts and permitting awareness only of what we think we should or are supposed to feel or want. We need to give up our illusions and self-deceptions and to allow ourselves to strive spontaneously toward self-realization. Within the past twenty-five or thirty years, these ideas have been developed further in various directions.

New forms of therapy have become widespread that stress (in varying degrees) awareness, here-and-now experience, spontaneous self-expression, and the rejection of prescribed behaviors and false exteriors. For all of them, authenticity is a central concern. They accept the basic existentialist stance[1] that we tend to take the mode of our existence as given, as if we were required to play out the roles that we are assigned in life, although this is to live inauthentically. In actuality, we are free to choose and are responsible for ourselves. (This view, together with Marx's conception of our alienation, or estrangement, from our own humanity, clearly was important for Fromm as well.) The European existentialist therapists, who became influential in this country particularly through the work of Rollo May,[2] attempt to help their patients become aware of their potentialities and become capable of acting upon them by entering as fully as possible into their experiences. The therapist who has probably argued the most vehemently against letting others define us to ourselves, R. D. Laing, has described schizophrenia itself as "a natural way of healing our own appalling state of alienation called normality."[3]

Authenticity is also a focal goal for various therapies otherwise less related to existentialism. Berne seeks to help the patient to advance "beyond games and scripts"[4] through analysis in terms of "child, parent, and adult" aspects within the patient as modeled on Freud's id, superego, and ego. Client-centered therapy[5] stresses, like the existentialist therapies, empathic understanding by the therapist of the experience of the client and attempts to help the client achieve awareness of his or her own feelings and desires through the therapist's communicating this understanding with genuine acceptance. Once there is awareness, there will be constructive self-actualization. In Gestalt therapy,[6] a number of different games and exercises are carried out involving considerable role playing, sometimes of different parts of the self. The activities are intended to induce the patient's here-and-now awareness and to bring about the reowning and integration of excluded parts of the self with, again, self-actualization and growth the expected result.

As this brief characterization of these therapies already makes evident, they tend to view the person coming for therapy less as someone with an illness or explicit problem needing "correction" and more as someone who is being obstructed in growth, in the development of his or her potentialities. One of the major extensions of the ideas of self-actualization and being oneself in the past thirty years has been that of placing increased emphasis, quite generally, on the positive potentialities of human beings. Sullivan, like Freud, was mostly concerned with alleviating his patients' suffering; Horney began somewhat and Fromm much more to think about the heights that human beings might, at their best, attain. In recent years, a large number of psychologists came to feel—as Maslow[7] expressed with particular clarity—that far too much attention had continually been paid to disturbances, to abnormalities, and to ways in which functioning could be impaired. They urged consideration of what it is possible for us to become under good conditions, what we can be like when we do actualize ourselves, and what the conditions are that would permit such an occurrence.

This concern with positive human potentialities has meant that it was no longer only people in particular psychological distress who were expected to benefit from greater awareness and self-actualization, but all of us. There has been a tremendous rise in the offering of psychological services not just to those with special difficulties but also to people who simply want to grow, to develop their potentialities, to live more satisfying, rewarding lives. In particular there has been the extensive spread of encounter groups, in which usual constraints operating in social interaction are abolished and one is urged to be spontaneous and to express what one really feels.[8]

These various directions in which the ideas of actualizing and being oneself have been taken in recent years seem to us to contain much that is significant and useful. But they also seem to have contributed still further to the trend toward selfishness. The most systematic and influential presentations of the newer directions are those of Maslow and of Rogers, whose work we will now consider more closely.

Maslow

Abraham H. Maslow was one of the psychologists who felt most strongly that psychology had focused altogether too much on problems, on the less than optimal, and had failed to take our positive potentialities adequately into account. He, perhaps more than anyone else, was concerned with attempting to articulate a point of view that would not only be able to account for our lower levels of functioning (as he felt extant theories did) but also could recognize and do justice to what we are capable of at our best.[9] His concept of a hierarchy of needs with self-actualization at the apex plays a central role in this endeavor.

Most psychological views of human motivation, Maslow pointed out, put a great deal of emphasis on physiological needs such as the needs for food and rest. These needs, he agreed, are "prepotent," in the sense that if they are unsatisfied, they tend to overwhelm everything else. If one has been deprived of food for an extended period of time, one is likely to be interested mostly in food, to think mostly about food, and to bend most of one's efforts in the direction of attaining food. Food is likely to seem more important than anything else in the world. But for most of us, luckily enough, such deprivation actually is extremely rare. Our physiological needs in general are usually relatively well gratified. And when a need is gratified, Maslow said, it does not play any active role in our lives; it is not a motivator. Physiological needs, then, are not actually motivating us much of the time.

Maslow believed that when lower needs are taken care of, other higher needs immediately tend to emerge, which are just as much a part of human nature, just as biologically given, as the lower ones. When our physiological needs are gratified, unfulfilled safety needs may surface— needs for security, stability, freedom from fear and anxiety, and so on. Safety needs are particularly evident in young children, who of course are relatively defenseless and do not inhibit the expression of these needs, unlike adults in our society. There are also neurotic adults whose motivational lives seem largely dominated by fear and desires for safety. Such people seem to live as if they were continually located at the edge of catastrophe, in a hostile, threatening world. They are well described, Maslow thought, in Karen Horney's writings about "basic anxiety."

In situations of real and serious danger, strong safety needs will also manifest themselves among normal, healthy adults. When there are actual threats to law and order, when the authority of society threatens to break down, safety needs will become predominant in practically everyone. At such times people may be ready to give up almost everything else for safety and will far more readily accept military rulers and dictatorships than at other times.

But again, as with the physiological needs, for most people safety needs tend to be fairly well taken care of under normal circumstances. Like the physiological ones, safety needs actually motivate us only rarely.

When both physiological needs and safety needs are gratified, then needs for love and belonging emerge. Now people will, if they do not have them, strive mightily for friends, for a wife or husband, for a group to join. Maslow, like many others who have thought about psychopathology, held that the thwarting of these needs was the most frequent core of mental disturbance. Like Fromm, he recognized that in technologically advanced, industrialized societies the gratification of needs to belong was particularly difficult. He believed that the great and rapid proliferation we have been experiencing recently of training groups (T-groups), along with other kinds of personal growth groups and communal living arrangements, is due largely to widespread alienation and loneliness, exacerbated by the breakdown of traditional groupings, by urbanization, and by mobility.

With the need for love gratified, Maslow felt there was yet another need that would seek satisfaction—the need for esteem, both from the self and from others. Lack of gratification of this need can again give rise to psychological illness. Thus, like Adler, Sullivan, and increasing numbers since, Maslow thought basic self-confidence was also extremely important for our well-being.

We have, then, as part of our biological nature, these four basic kinds of needs: physiological needs, and needs for safety, love, and esteem. It was of the greatest significance to Maslow that these needs are all based on deficiencies of one kind or another. When lower needs are satisfied, they are set off by deprivations. We are motivated by hunger when we lack food, by safety when we are in danger, by needs for love and esteem when we are lonely and lacking in self-confidence. The majority of psychologists viewed all motivation as based in this way upon deficiencies.

But this viewpoint appeared to Maslow to be a crucial fallacy. He was convinced that human beings were not motivated only by lacks that they tried to fill, that striving was not always a matter of deficiency motivation. Some other kind of motivation also had to be recognized, a tendency toward growth and fulfillment of one's potentialities, or self-actualization. Maslow thought of what he was doing here as articulating and giving voice to something sensed by an increasing number of psychologists and psychiatrists, something for which more and more evidence was becoming available.

He agreed with Sullivan, Horney, and Fromm in their conviction that what went on in therapy could not be accounted for without postulating some such positive tendency toward growth. Maslow was much impressed by Goldstein's findings of patients' adaptive reactions to brain injuries, reactions that would allow them to make the best use of whatever capacities they still possessed.[10] He thought that children's interest in and enjoyment of the development of new skills and abilities were indicative of a basic trend toward the fulfillment of potentialities. And further, he thought that there was much evidence of such a trend in his own studies of what he called "self-actualizers"— people whose basic needs were gratified and whose activities he felt could be understood only in terms of their attempting to make full use of their capacities. These studies will be described later; for the moment what is crucial is Maslow's strong conviction that above and beyond the deficiency-based needs for physiological necessities, safety, love, and esteem there could be a quite different kind of need for actualization of the self.

Maslow conceived of this need for self-actualization as also being biologically given. It was the highest-level need, a need that could motivate us when all of our more basic needs had been relatively gratified. Maslow had, thus, the conception of a hierarchy of innate needs, extending from the physiological needs through safety needs and needs for love and esteem (all deficiency needs) to the positive need for self-actualization. In general, the lowest need in which there was a deficiency would dominate, and the needs above it in the hierarchy would not appear. When a need was met, there would usually be transient happiness, and then higher needs would tend to emerge.

There were certain exceptions noted to the general rule. Long deprivations can lead to needs dropping out altogether. Thus, a person who has had too little to eat for many years may never aspire to much more than providing for the satisfaction of physiological needs. People who have, from the beginning of their lives, experienced very little love may lose any desire for it and become psychopathic personalities. On the other hand, people whose basic needs have been well gratified, particularly in their early lives, can become capable of withstanding a great deal of frustration of these needs later on. The gratification strengthens their characters and can enable them to remain on higher levels even under conditions of severe lower-level deprivations.

Maslow thought that as a person went up in the hierarchy from the lower to the higher levels of needs, this meant, typically, that he or she was not only increasingly gratified in basic needs, but also increasingly psychologically healthy. For example, apprehensiveness, anxiety, tension, and nervousness all resulted from frustration of the safety need. They would disappear when this need was satisfied; the person would then be relaxed and secure. Gratification of the needs for love and belonging and for respect would allow a person to become affectionate and self-confident, and so on. The more the basic needs were gratified, the higher the level of needs that would motivate the person, and the healthier the person would be. The most healthy individuals were those whose deficiency needs were satisfied and who were engaged in the process of self-actualization.

Most of the existing psychology of human personality and motivation, it seemed to Maslow, had concentrated on the unhealthy, lower levels of human functioning. It was concerned with the thwarting of deficiency needs and with threats to basic necessities. He believed we needed to study healthy people, to see what human beings were like at their best. As he put it, "To oversimplify the matter somewhat, it is as if Freud supplied to us the sick half of psychology and we must now fill it out with the healthy half."[11]

Maslow's investigations of self-actualizers—the people who seemed to him the healthiest and functioning at the highest level of the hierarchy—began, as he described it, "as the effort of a young intellectual to try to understand two of his teachers [Ruth Benedict and Max Wertheimer] whom he loved, adored, and admired and who were very, very wonderful people. . . . My training in psychology equipped me not at all for understanding them."[12] Maslow did not at first think of what he was doing as actual research but rather as a private venture. But he soon came to feel that trying to characterize and understand what self-actualizing people were really like was so significant that he had to proceed and do his best, despite the methodological problems involved.

From among personal friends and acquaintances, as well as contemporaneous and historical public figures, Maslow tried to select individuals who, in his estimation, made full use of their potentialities, doing the best of which they were capable, whose basic needs were gratified, and who showed no neurotic, psychopathic, or psychotic tendencies. He modified his criteria somewhat as he went along, in an effort at a spirallike process of self-correction. For example, it soon became clear that foibles and imperfections should not disqualify a person from being considered a self-actualizer, or else no one would be able to pass the test. Maslow tried to study in any way he could the people he regarded as self-actualizers: with interviews, observation, and examination of available documents. Maslow was often not certain whether a given individual should really be classed as a self-actualizer; it was usually impossible to get as much information on the candidate as he wanted. He ended up with a relatively small number of subjects: only 18 who he considered highly probable actual cases.[13] Nonetheless, he felt that it was possible tentatively to describe some significant characteristics of people who seemed to actualize themselves.

For one thing—as is consistent with the theories of Horney and of Fromm—such people are relatively spontaneous, natural, and simple. They are not particularly unconventional superficially in their usual behavior since they do not wish to make issues of trivial matters. But they are unconventional and spontaneous in their impulses and their thinking. They are much more aware than most people of their own subjective reactions—their thoughts, opinions, feelings, and desires. And in matters that they consider important, they will not allow convention to stand in their way.

Self-actualizers are not much concerned about themselves. They usually have some kind of task or vocation to which they are dedicated. They tend to live and view things in the widest possible frame of reference, *sub specie aeternitatis.*

Their perception of reality is much sharper than that of other people, and they continue to perceive and appreciate the world freshly, preserving a childlike sense of wonder. They are more accepting of themselves and others.

They are highly autonomous individuals, very independent of their environments. What opinion others hold of them or how others feel about them is not a significant determinant of what they do. They are active agents in the world.

They have a certain reserve and detachment and are more likely to enjoy being alone than most of us do. They need other people less than is the case for most and may actually be hampered by them. But they have deep feelings of sympathy and affection for human beings in general and profound relationships with a limited number of particular individuals.

Self-actualizers are highly ethical, although their standards are frequently quite different from those typical of the society in which they live. Many issues and differences that their culture may take seriously—for example, what kinds of clothing or eating patterns are permitted or customary—they care little about one way or the other. They distinguish clearly between ends and means, and in general they are focused strongly on whatever they consider to be worth treating as ends in themselves. Being far more likely to enjoy activities for their own sakes, they may, however, often regard as ends what other people tend to treat as no more than means.

Self-actualizers often fuse into unities what in less healthy people appear as opposites or dichotomies. Their desires tend to be in accord with reason, and so their hearts and their heads are not in conflict. Finding pleasure in being altruistic, they fuse selfishness and unselfishness. Work and play are not opposed, because for them work *is* play.

Maslow wrote in a number of different ways about self-actualizers' motivation. He was convinced that the usual ways of thinking about motivation would not do for them:

> The motivation of ordinary men is a striving for the basic need gratifications that they lack. But self-actualizing people in fact lack none of these gratifications; and yet they have impulses. They work, they try, and they are ambitious, even though in an unusual sense. For them motivation is just character growth, character expression, maturation, and development; in a word self-actualization.[14]

Maslow emphasized that the self-actualizer is motivated from within, by inner rather than outer determinants. Such a person is free, self-determined, autonomous—his or her authentic self. The environment is viewed essentially as something to be transcended; one paper by Maslow was titled "Health as Transcendence of Environment."[15] Self-actualizers, he said, "are not dependent for their main satisfactions on the real world, or other people or culture or means to ends or, in general, on extrinsic satisfactions. . . . The determinants of satisfaction and of the good life are for them now inner-individual."[16] There is, of course, contact between the self-actualizing person and the environment, but the intrinsic nature of the person is the primary determinant, and "The environment is primarily a means to the person's self-actualizing ends."[17]

Sometimes Maslow spoke of self-actualizers as *unmotivated* and *nonstriving;* in his later writing he often used the term *metamotivated,* which he said meant "beyond striving."[18] To be metamotivated was to be in the "B-realm" (*B* for being) as opposed to the "D-realm" (*D* for deficiency). One was not striving for anything at all, but just being. For example, love in the B-realm—unlike love in the D-realm, which is based on something we need from the one we love—is an entirely disinterested, unselfish kind of love, in which one simply rejoices in the nature of the loved person and in freely giving to that person. It is spontaneous, not something one does in order to achieve or attain anything or because one had a prior need for it. (Maslow rather charmingly suspected that such love may occur in its purest form in what some grandparents feel for their grandchildren.[19]) One can be similarly just admiring and appreciative, without having any further purposes therein, when gazing at a painting, listening to music, observing a baby, or watching a sunset. These would all then be experiences belonging to the B-realm. Maslow thought that what was so important here was akin to something found in certain Eastern philosophies, particularly, the kind of yielding fostered and celebrated in Lao-tzu's Taoism.[20]

Of particular interest to Maslow were B-realm experiences that were especially intense and ecstatic, which he called "peak experiences." In peak experiences one is wholly engrossed in something outside of oneself, transcending one's own ego. One is open to and perceiving aspects of reality of which one typically is not aware; one's consciousness is expanded. The world looks different, and one is now able to perceive its intrinsic values. Most of the time, Maslow thought, we are much too means oriented. We tend to perceive things and think about them in terms of their usefulness to us, their instrumental significance; we are preoccupied with means and too little concerned with ends, with what really matters. In peak experiences, we are aware of the values of the B-realm—the ultimate values—truth, beauty, goodness, justice, life, and so on. At times Maslow spoke of self-actualizing people as being metamotivated by these values.

Ultimate values were of the greatest concern to Maslow. Although in his earlier writing[21] he thought pathology could only be caused by thwarting or threatening of basic needs, he later came to believe that what he called "metapathology" could result from deprivation of intrinsic values, for which we have "metaneeds." Much of the current anomie and emptiness found among affluent people seemed to him due to a kind of value starvation. People who are not affluent have something to strive for, and such striving itself tends to give life a meaning. But when there are no lacks to focus on, our spiritual hunger surfaces and makes itself strongly felt.[22]

It was a major aim of Maslow to contribute to working toward "a validated, usable system of human values, values that we can believe in and devote ourselves to because they are true rather than because we are *exhorted* to 'believe and have faith.' "[23] Human beings have a higher nature, he said, that is part of their essence. Science has ignored this realm, declaring it unreal. But, he countered, one can make progress toward objective knowledge here. The self-actualizers show us what is possible, and their experiences and choices can help us to understand what is really important in life, what really matters.

Rogers

The other psychologist who, besides Maslow, has probably been most influential in the more recent currents of thought about self-actualization and being oneself is Carl R. Rogers. Rogers began his work, like most of the writers we have discussed (though unlike Maslow), with efforts to aid people who were in distress. It was only after many observations of such people in counseling or psychotherapy and much thinking about what seemed to be successful ways of helping them that he came to formulate his views on what was best for human beings generally. We shall, therefore, begin with the observations and ideas emerging from Rogers' activities as a therapist.

One of the significant things Rogers felt he learned early in his work with clients was the importance to them of their concepts of themselves. These concepts would keep coming up as he tried to get them to describe their difficulties and feelings. They would say things like: " 'I feel I'm not being my real self.' 'I wonder who I am, really.' . . . 'I never had a chance to be myself.' "[24] In the beginning of therapy, clients usually made a great many negative statements about themselves and often expressed feelings of worthlessness. During the course of therapy, their concepts of and attitudes to the self would frequently undergo large changes, sometimes fluctuating widely between positive and negative extremes. And when therapy was successful, clients seemed to see themselves at the end as much more adequate and worthwhile persons than they had at the beginning.

Clients at the end of successful therapy seemed not only to feel more positive about themselves but also at the same time to be more realistic, more objective about themselves and their life situations. They seemed to perceive their own feelings and other experiences more fully and more accurately, with much less distortion than before. And they seemed much more ready to rely on themselves for their standards and evaluations, rather than on what others desired or expected. Such changes with therapy were not only documented by Rogers' subjective impressions but were also supported by research that Rogers, together with his students and associates, carried out on recordings of therapeutic interviews and clients' ratings and answers to questions.

There were essentially three aspects of therapy, Rogers came to believe, that were crucial in bringing about these changes. His own "client-centered therapy" focused on these points, but he thought they were the critical part of all forms of successful psychotherapy. The three points are as follows:

1. Therapists should themselves be open to their own experiences and genuine in their relationship with the client. They should not be "putting on" anything, such as appearing to like or understand the client better than is the case.

2. The therapist should have "unconditional positive regard" for the client. He or she should feel warm and accepting toward the client, without reservation. This positive attitude should be consistently maintained, rather than depending on the client's behaving or feeling certain ways.
3. The therapist should have empathic understanding of the client's world as it appears to the client.

Rogers believed that these three conditions—given that a client, who was in a troubled state, was in contact with the therapist and perceived that the conditions were being met—were necessary and sufficient for constructive personality change to take place.[25] They did not have to be met perfectly, but the more openness and genuineness on the part of the therapist, the greater the degree of noncontingent warmth and acceptance, and the more empathic understanding that was present, the better the outlook for constructive personality change occurring. The early results of Rogers' research largely support this contention, although later evidence is more problematic.[26]

The central process in psychotherapy that Rogers thought was responsible for its power to produce constructive changes in the client—one to which all of the thinkers we have discussed-would have assigned a primary role—is the increasing of the person's undistorted awareness of his or her own experience. There is less self-deception, less filtering of what one permits oneself to have in awareness, less thinking of oughts and what others wish or expect of one. "During the process of therapy the individual comes to ask himself, in regard to ever-widening areas of his life-space, 'How do *I* experience this?' 'What does it mean to *me*?' . . . He comes to act on a basis of what may be termed realism—a realistic balancing of the satisfactions and dissatisfactions which any action will bring to himself."[27]

Rogers felt that the goal of psychotherapy was well expressed by Kierkegaard's phrase, "to be that self which one truly is."[28] The client comes to realize that it is not necessary to present a facade, that one doesn't have to try to be any different from the way one feels like being. As with the neo-Freudians, Rogers believed that it was a mistake to fear that such "being what one truly is" would lead to evil. We are not evil, unsocialized, uncivilized creatures. Free and undistorted awareness means rather "an organism which is as aware of the demands of the culture as it is of its own physiological demands for food or sex—which is just as aware of its desire for friendly relationships as it is of its desire to aggrandize itself—which is just as aware of its delicate and sensitive tenderness toward others, as it is of its hostilities toward others."[29]

Such an organism will act constructively upon the basis of what Rogers took to be the one fundamental motivational force in human beings: the tendency toward growth or actualization, which he conceived of as similar to Maslow's self-actualization need. Like Sullivan and Horney, Rogers was tremendously impressed by the way in which his clients again and again would move forward, taking positive, constructive steps with their lives, when it became possible for them to see their situations clearly. The difficulties came from misperceptions and a lack of awareness of actual experiences.

Rogers believed, much like Sullivan, that such distortions and unawareness were the result of significant people in his clients' pasts having given them love and approval only when they behaved in certain ways and not others. We start out in life, as infants, with a certain amount of clarity about what feels good and bad to us, what we like and do not like. Hunger is negatively valued; when one is hungry, food is positively valued. Pain is negatively valued; relief from pain is positive; and so on. There is an "organismic valuing process," according to which experiences that "maintain, enhance, or actualize the organism" are valued positively, and those that do not, negatively. But the infant is also much in need of love and strongly affected by the disapproval of the mother and other significant figures. When the infant engages in an activity such as pulling a baby sister's hair, which the infant finds satisfying but which leads to scolding and rejection, the infant himself comes to adopt this negative attitude as well. Hair pulling, which is actually experienced as positive, comes to be seen by the infant as something bad. What the important adults in his life approve of comes to be regarded by the infant as good, even if it provides no actual satisfaction; what they disapprove of comes to be regarded as bad and is rejected, although the experience may really be a satisfying one by which the infant is maintained and enhanced.[30]

The same process continues as we get older. One may feel that one's parents behave in unloving ways when one thinks of entering a certain occupation, for example, becoming an artist. Then one may oneself come to believe that the occupation is not worthwhile and fail to recognize one's positive experiences in drawing and painting. Or one may find oneself rejected upon any expression of hostility, come to believe that hostility is always bad, and deny awareness to hostile feelings when one experiences them. In these and many other ways, we come to take over the attitudes of others and lose touch with our own experiences. We do this because the love and approval of these other people is so important to us, and they give it contingently; we can obtain their love and approval only when we behave in line with their values and expectations and not otherwise.

It is this counterproductive process that is rectified by the unconditional positive regard of a psychotherapist who is being genuine and understanding. Approval, caring, and acceptance are then consistently provided instead of being contingent upon particular behaviors or expressions on the part of the client. Rogers stresses the significance of the therapist fully accepting the client as he or she is. The therapist must be willing to give the client complete freedom, including the freedom "to choose goals that are social or antisocial, moral or immoral."[31] The therapist in client-centered therapy essentially tries to enter into the world of the client as the client perceives it and to reflect back in a warm, nonjudgmental manner the client's feelings about this world by communicating understanding and acceptance. The client then becomes able to accept his or her own feelings as well. The necessity of denying or distorting these feelings is removed, and the individual is once again in touch with his or her actual experiences. He or she then gains the freedom to be guided by the organismic valuing process instead of by the wishes or expectations of others and to behave in accordance with the basic tendency toward actualization.

In Rogers' words: "Less and less does he look to others for approval or disapproval; for standards to live by; for decisions and choices. He recognizes that it rests within himself to choose; that the only question which matters is, 'Am I living in a way which is deeply satisfying to me, and which truly expresses me?' "[32] Rogers is quite explicit that "the criterion of the valuing process is the degree to which the object of the experience actualizes the individual himself. Does it make him a richer, more complete, more fully developed person?" He goes on to say, "This may sound as though it were a selfish or unsocial criterion, but it does not prove to be so, since deep and helpful relationships with others are experienced as actualizing."[33]

As his thinking proceeded, Rogers became less focused on psychotherapy and what it specifically could bring about and increasingly interested in what he saw as wider implications. The kind of person he had described as emerging from successful psychotherapy was closely related to the kind of person he now regarded as a general ideal. And the way in which he had described a good therapist as acting toward a client was also essentially the way in which he now recommended that all people should behave toward one another.

What Rogers viewed as a general kind of ideal for personality was spelled out in "A Therapist's View of the Good Life: The Fully Functioning Person."[34] In this article, the good life was a process in the direction of becoming a more and more fully functioning person. A critical aspect of what this meant was an increasing openness to experience. One became less and less defensive and also less and less inclined to impose structure on oneself and one's experiences by means of preconceptions. Every moment was a new one, and the person tended increasingly to live wholeheartedly in each moment. There was also increasing self-trust—faith in one's own reactions, in what felt right to one. Because the person was open to his or her experience, the information would be available on the basis of which the best possible decision could be made about how his or her needs might be satisfied. Here as elsewhere, Rogers stressed that the person who was functioning freely and openly would naturally be constructive and trustworthy. He believed that his experiences as a therapist had clearly demonstrated that when the individual was freed from defensiveness, "his reactions may be trusted to be positive, forward-moving, constructive."[35]

Rogers also believed that what he had found to be helpful for a therapist to do in psychotherapy could be applied to human relationships in general. Genuineness, empathic understanding, and unconditional positive regard would tend to foster the growth of any person being treated in this way, to encourage him or her to become a more aware, more fully functioning individual.

Such an individual would then not only be better off himself but would also have better relationships with others. It was an important point to Rogers that understanding and acceptance of the self led to better understanding and acceptance of other people as well. A defensive person views others as threats to the self. But when one is not defensive, one can see others as they really are, and interact with them appropriately. For example, a woman who sees herself as a good and loving mother is threatened by a son who sometimes makes her feel aggressive toward him. The only way she can justify these feelings to herself is in terms of claiming he is bad and deserves to be punished. It is only when the mother becomes able to accept her sometimes having negative feelings toward the boy that she can relax and see the child as he really is, with both good and bad features. Only then can a spontaneous and genuine relationship develop between mother and son—not positive at all times, but frequently so, and satisfying to both of them.[36] As the example suggests, Rogers felt that nondefensive openness and genuineness should take precedence over unconditional positive regard when the two conflicted, but that nondefensiveness would make for greater acceptance of the other.

Rogers thought there were enormous potentialities for a facilitative kind of chain reaction as people came to accept themselves more thoroughly. Their self-acceptance would lead to their being more understanding and accepting of others, which would in turn lead these others to increased self-acceptance. Then these people would in turn be more understanding and accepting of still others, and so on.[37]

With the passing years, Rogers' writing came more and more to focus on urging people to behave toward one another in such a way that would facilitate each other's personal growth. This was always to be accomplished essentially through the key elements of genuineness, understanding, and acceptance. Such attitudes would be helpful in the family,[38] in education,[39] and in all kinds of organizations and groups.[40] He became very much involved in the encounter-group movement,[41] seeing in the better kinds of encounter groups an embodiment of the attitudes he propounded. He believed that people came to a greater knowledge and acceptance of themselves as they expressed their true feelings to one another in such groups and found these feelings accepted by the others. They developed more closeness and intimacy than they had known even with members of their own families, and better relationships thereafter outside the group as well.[42]

It was only late in Rogers' career that he undertook explicitly to address political issues of power and control. But he then came to see himself and his writings as part of a broader force that was attempting to diminish the power of institutions and authorities and place it in the hands of the individual. Rogers believed he could see a new kind of human being emerging, a kind that might lead to a fundamental change in the nature of society. These persons are first and foremost authentic individuals, straightforward, open and honest, wholly without phoniness or hypocrisy. They refuse to conform to the bureaucratic requirements of structured institutions, believing that it is only human purposes that matter. They are unconcerned about material goods or about personal ascendancy or achievement. They are caring people, with a deep desire to help others directly, person to person. They recognize the temporariness of contemporary life and are trying in response to develop new forms of intimacy and community, forms that can be quickly established and without too great regret left behind. They distrust science and technology. They want to explore "inner space"—feelings, dreams, altered states of consciousness, and all kinds of occult and psychic phenomena. They are aware that they are always in process, always changing. They trust their own experience and profoundly distrust all external authority.[43]

As Rogers acknowledges,[44] despite the lateness of his explicit concern, he has in a sense been teaching and practicing politics all along. He has always been strongly antiauthoritarian; he has again and again stressed respect for the individual and urged the individual's freedom and autonomy. Already as an undergraduate, he admired Luther's rejection of external authority.[45] As a young theological student, Rogers was a member of a group that "wanted to explore our own questions and doubts and find out where they led,"[46] after which he decided to leave the field of religion to guarantee his freedom of thought.

It is a critical feature of client-centered therapists, as opposed to both Freudian and behaviorist therapists, that they do not stand in the position of authorities but rather place control and responsibility in the hands of the client. It is a crucial part of what Rogers urges in the classroom, that teachers share their power and encourage self-direction. It is central to what he recommends for every aspect of life, that one individual is not to be set above others and put in a position of taking control. Distrust of external authority and trust in a person's own experience and natural tendency to strive constructively toward growth have

always formed a central tenet—perhaps the central tenet—
in Rogers' thinking.

Notes

1. See, for example, Warnock, 1970, for a clear introduction.
2. May, 1958a, 1958b.
3. Laing, 1967, p. 167.
4. Berne, 1976.
5. Rogers, 1951.
6. Perls, Hefferline, and Goodman, 1951.
7. Maslow, 1970.
8. Rogers, 1970.
9. See, for example, Maslow, 1954, 1970.
10. Goldstein, 1939.
11. Maslow, 1968, p. 5.
12. Maslow, 1976, p. 40.
13. Maslow, 1970, p. 152.
14. Maslow, 1970, p. 159.
15. Maslow, 1968.
16. Maslow, 1970, p. 162.
17. Maslow, 1970, p. 68.
18. Maslow, 1968, p. 72.
19. Maslow, 1970, p. 183.
20. Lin, 1948.
21. See, for example, Maslow, 1954.
22. Maslow, 1964, p. 38.
23. Maslow, 1959, p. viii.
24. Rogers, 1959, p. 201.
25. Rogers, 1957.
26. See Parloff, Waskow, and Wolfe, 1978, for a recent overview.
27. Rogers, 1961, pp. 103–104.
28. Quoted by Rogers, 1961, p. 166.
29. Rogers, 1961, p. 105.
30. Rogers, 1971.
31. Rogers, 1951, p. 48.
32. Rogers, 1961, p. 118.
33. Rogers, 1971, p. 15.
34. Rogers, 1961.
35. Rogers, 1961, p. 194.
36. Rogers, 1951, pp. 511–512, and p. 521.
37. Rogers, 1951, p. 522.
38. Rogers, 1961, 1972, 1977.
39. Rogers, 1961, 1969, 1977.
40. Rogers, 1970, 1977.
41. Rogers, 1970.
42. Rogers, 1970, p. 9.
43. Rogers, 1977.
44. Rogers, 1977, p. 4.
45. Kirschenbaum, 1979.
46. Rogers, 1967, p. 354.

8

Maslow and Rogers:
Determination from Within Ourselves,
Not from Outside

When we compare Freud to the neo-Freudians and the neo-Freudians to Maslow, Rogers, and other recent thinkers with related ideas, there seems to be increasing concern about the way the individual is restricted and limited by society and by other individuals. Freud recognized and, for their role in neuroses, lamented the existence of prescriptions and restraints. But he believed in their necessity. Were the instinctual drives allowed direct expression and satisfaction, people would find it impossible to live with one another. There must be inhibition and sublimation in order for any kind of civilized life to take place.

The neo-Freudians, rejecting the idea that constraints and shoulds were necessary, were all the more disturbed by their ubiquity. They elaborated upon the ways in which constraints were harmful above and beyond preventing the expression of impulses and the satisfaction of needs. Sullivan detailed how the disapproval of authorities causes anxiety and misconceptions. Fromm and Horney stressed how attempting to follow prescriptions and restraints separates us from our real feelings and desires, keeping us from becoming that of which we are capable. For Sullivan and Horney, the onus still was more on constraints themselves than on the social world as a source of constraints. Horney, in fact, seems at least as concerned—if not more so—about prescriptions and restraints that issue from the individual as she is about those issuing from others. With Fromm, in turn, the way we let others impose their thoughts and feelings on ourselves becomes a major issue.

When we reach Maslow and Rogers, much of society and of our relations with other people is seen as obstructing our growth and the development of our potentialities. Self-determination becomes a matter of overriding significance. We start, then, with the push toward selfishness that seems inherent in Freud's basic ideas on motivation and find it increased by the neo-Freudian rejection of what Freud saw as the need for restraint and sublimation. This push is exacerbated still further, we submit, when Maslow and Rogers urge us to determine our own lives and not let society or others do it for us. In the next section we review what Maslow and Rogers say on these issues. After that, we consider some problems in their position.

No Determination from Outside the Self

Much as Horney and Fromm urged what they called "self-realization," Maslow and Rogers urge "self-actualization." The meanings are very similar. All four psychologists intend minimal prescriptions and restraints and maximal spontaneity, awareness of one's own true feelings together with the freedom to act upon them, and the development of one's potentialities. With Maslow and Rogers there is now also an added emphasis on being determined from within and not by what is outside: I am responsible to myself alone.

An essential feature of those whom Maslow thought of as self-actualizers was that they were free and self-determined, their own authentic selves. They did not allow themselves to be much affected by what others thought of them or the standards others held. While not going out of their way to be unconventional, they did not hesitate to go against the patterns of their society when something mattered to them. They had a kind of detachment and less need for others than most people do.

The environment could serve as a means to the self-actualizer's ends, but other than this it was to be transcended. The self-actualizer's satisfactions did not come from the external world or other people, but rather were inside the individual. Self-actualizers had much greater awareness than others of their subjective reactions, and their own states of consciousness were of particular significance to them.

These characteristics might suggest that self-actualizers were basically wrapped up in themselves and relatively unconcerned with other people or with anything else outside of themselves, but this was not the case. Those studied by Maslow showed little self-concern and were usually dedicated to a task or vocation. Although they could find other people hampering, they had a great deal of sympathy and feeling for the human race and deep relationships with certain individuals. Again, while their standards often differed from those of others in their society, the self-actualizers were extremely ethical. They were also more likely to love others in an unselfish way and were more aware and appreciative in general of what is of value in the world. In fact, it was through them that Maslow thought more could be learned about what the ultimate values really are.

Self-actualization was, for Maslow, a very different matter from being selfish. (He even became concerned that the term "self-actualization" suggested selfishness and a neglect of ties to others and began to hesitate about using it so much.[1]) The dichotomy of selfishness–unselfishness was itself, he thought, characteristic of a level of development that self-actualizers transcend. Much the same way as Fromm had felt that love for oneself was involved in real love for another, and hence the two were not alternatives but of a piece, so Maslow thought that for the self-actualizer, altruism itself was pleasurable; thus, hedonism and altruism were not opposed but unified.[2]

Maslow went, if anything, still further than Fromm in the extent to which he believed that concern for others required, first of all, concern for self. Gratification of one's own needs was prerequisite, in Maslow's view, to concern for anyone or anything outside the self. The higher levels of his need hierarchy are attainable only when lower-level needs have been satisfied. Physiological and safety needs must be taken care of before love can play much of a role. And all one's basic needs must be gratified before one can become a self-actualizer, no longer focused on what one may lack but on such matters as ultimate values.

Turn now to Rogers. For the individual to be aware of and to act upon his or her own feelings, thoughts, and inclinations is always what Rogers is trying to encourage and foster. The major obstacle he sees consists of other people and the institutions of society, and he is repeatedly attempting to counter their interference. He is opposed to the exercise of all authority—in therapy, in education, in the family, in all organizations and relationships. It is always the individual's own reactions that are to be trusted and relied upon. The newly emerging human type that he saw on the horizon and so admired accepts no impositions and permits neither institutions nor other individuals to tell one what to do. The encounter groups he has expounded on and fostered call upon people to drop typical social forms and restraints on interaction and instead to express themselves freely and genuinely.

At the core of all psychological difficulties, according to Rogers, is lack of understanding and acceptance of the self, which results from other people who do not permit one to be oneself. We are born with a natural disposition to value as positive what we experience as satisfying—what maintains and enhances us—and to evaluate the opposite as negative. But this valuing process is interfered with by others approving only of some of the things we do and disapproving of other things, giving us acceptance and regarding us positively only when we do what they approve of. If their love and approval are sufficiently important to us, we come to evaluate positively what they approve, even when it does not really lead to our own satisfaction; we also evaluate negatively what results in their disapproval, even though it may be exactly what is satisfying to us. This damaging effect of others is what the Rogerian psychotherapist's unconditional acceptance and positive regard are intended to undo, thereby freeing the client to become his or her real self.

When psychotherapy is successful, Rogers says, clients come less and less to rely on others for standards, evaluations, and decisions, and increasingly to rely on themselves. Instead of allowing the approval and disapproval given by others to guide them, they ask themselves how they feel. What matters to them is no longer what someone else believes or thinks, but rather that they actualize and express themselves.

Like Maslow, Rogers did not think of self-actualization as implying selfishness. He said that although actualization of the self might sound like a selfish criterion, in fact it was not, since we will feel actualized by relationships that are truly helpful to others. And also like Maslow, Rogers stressed still more than Fromm the extent to which the ability to benefit others depends first of all on being good to oneself. We cannot, he says, understand and accept others—or have good relations with them or aid their growth— if we do not understand and accept ourselves first. Without this we will be defensive, viewing other people as threats rather than as they really are, and will be unable to develop genuine and spontaneous relationships. "Each person is an island unto himself, in a very real sense; and he can only build bridges to other islands if he is first of all willing to be himself and permitted to be himself."[3] Rogers had high hopes for an ever-expanding ripple effect in people's acceptance of themselves and consequent greater acceptance of others, this in turn leading to these others also accepting themselves more and therefore accepting still others more, and so on. In this manner we would all increasingly facilitate one another's growth.

Let us now consider what Maslow and Rogers are asserting in the context of our preceding discussions of Freud and the neo-Freudians. The neo-Freudians, we said, rejected Freud's principle that civilization and the general good require that we restrain ourselves and sublimate, while accepting and carrying further his principle that direct gratification is the best course for the individual. They believed that Freud greatly overestimated our natural inclinations toward evil and greatly underestimated those toward good. If human beings could follow their genuine feelings and wishes, spontaneously express their impulses and gratify their real desires, this would not be harmful but, rather, for the good of all concerned.

Maslow and Rogers follow the neo-Freudians here and go still further. They oppose not only prescriptions and restraints, but all determination from outside the self. Freud had seen the direct expression of inner impulses as leading to evil; good—the fruits of sublimation, for example—results from constraints that originate outside, some of which then become internalized. Maslow and Rogers, by contrast, see all external determination as a source of evil and what comes genuinely from within as leading to good.

Self-expression and the gratification of one's own needs are urged even more strongly by Maslow and Rogers than by the neo-Freudians. According to Rogers, it is self-acceptance and following one's own inclinations that essentially define psychological health. And for Maslow, health is defined in terms of the height of one's ascension up the hierarchy of needs, with the higher levels emerging as the lower needs are satisfied. Furthermore, not only will individuals be more healthy to the extent that they look to the satisfaction of their own needs, but this policy will be best for everyone else too. Greater self-acceptance, according to Rogers, leads to greater acceptance of others as well. And Maslow's notion of the hierarchy of needs turns Freud's concept of sublimation completely upside down. Instead of saying that we contribute to the higher things of life only insofar as we are denied direct instinctual satisfaction, Maslow says we only become concerned with these higher aspects when our basic needs are satisfied.

In Chapter 6, we considered the problems stemming from blanket opposition to prescriptions and restraints. Freud seems correct that some constraints are required for the general welfare. And we argued that the interests also of the individual—contrary to Freud and the neo-Freudians and now Maslow and Rogers as well—are not necessarily hindered by constraints but can be promoted by them. These arguments will not be repeated here. What seems to call for further consideration at this point is the rejection in Maslow and Rogers of all determination from outside the self.

Can Freedom from External Determination Serve the General Welfare?

To advocate that one should seek self-actualization and not be determined by society or other individuals seems inevitably to urge the individual to look to his or her own needs, desires, and fulfillments, in preference to those of others. It seems inevitably to suggest that what one should do in any situation is to maximize one's own benefits rather than aiming at benefits for others, or justice, or anything else outside of oneself.

Maslow and Rogers do not appear to believe that this is the outcome. Together with Sullivan, Horney, and Fromm, they expect that in the absence of obstruction to our natural inclinations, we will tend toward constructive caring for others and being helpful to them. What is needed, therefore, in their view, is simply the freedom to realize or actualize ourselves. We can then, as Maslow says, find pleasure in altruism and transcend the dichotomy between selfishness and unselfishness. Or, in Rogers' terms, we will then be helpful to others, because helpful relations are themselves actualizing.

But this outlook seems simply to ignore the possibility that what will most further one's own actualization may conflict with what is best for other individuals or for one's group. If one is to evaluate all available alternatives according to whether they advance one's actualization or help to more fully develop one's potentialities, it is not enough that helpfulness and caring are among one's potentials and are themselves actualizing. There may always be alternative possibilities to pursue that would develop one's potentialities even more. What is most actualizing for one person cannot simply be assumed to coincide with what is going to be best for others as well.

Consider the current example of an artistic mother with several small children, who finds herself left with little time or energy to carry on her artistic work. She may find it fulfilling to care for the children, but she may find this less fulfilling and actualizing than painting. If that is the case, Maslow and Rogers clearly imply that what she ought to do is to paint, whether or not she could make arrangements for the children that would be equally good for their development. Sometimes, perhaps, this is what such a mother ought to do. But in cases of conflict between our own development and that of others, is it really always true that we should choose what is most beneficial to ourselves? Suppose the woman felt that although it would be more conducive to her own development to make some other arrangements for the children and to spend her time painting, it was more important to her to help the children develop their potentialities.

Marriage, on which Rogers wrote extensively,[4] provides further examples. The development of one of the two partners cannot be assumed always to be maximized by the same actions that will maximize the development of the other or of the couple or family as a whole. A move to another city might be excellent for the husband's work and difficult for the wife or vice versa. The move might be good or bad for the children's development and might interfere with or facilitate joint pursuits of the family. All sorts of possible household arrangements may obviously be good for one spouse and bad for the other. Once again, it is clear what Maslow and Rogers recommend: our own fulfillment, actualization, or development always should be the paramount consideration. Indeed, according to Rogers, the marriage itself is to be continued only if it is actualizing for both of its members. He describes with approval the outlook that "a relationship between a man and a woman is significant, and worth trying to preserve, only when it is an enhancing, growing experience for each person."[5]

What is to happen when one partner, say, becomes ill and needs help, and is able to contribute little to the fulfillment of the other? Rogers said the data on marriage breakdowns clearly demonstrate that all vows of commitment notwithstanding, a couple "cannot hold to them unless the marriage is satisfying. . . . The value of such outward commitment appears to me to be just about nil."[6] But what meaning can commitment have if it is always one's own growth and actualization that one is to care most about? May the prevalence of this belief itself be contributing to these marriage data?

While Maslow and Rogers do not wish to encourage self-concern as opposed to concern for anything outside ourselves, their urging of self-actualization and opposition to external determinants seems to have precisely that consequence. A different illustration of this point can be seen in Maslow's writings on values—an ironic example, given his concern for values.[7] His conviction that primary significance attaches to what is within ourselves and not what is without seems to lead Maslow to exalt our experiences of values, which are within, and to offer no encouragement for our actively trying to advance what we value in the world. What we are to do about values is simply to yield to them and appreciate them, to savor them; as he says, our attitude should be one of "being" instead of striving. Maslow may well be right that we are overly utilitarian. But when there is something that we value quite apart from any usefulness, we need not only passively appreciate it. Should we not also promote what we value?

The idea that what matters is within oneself fails to encourage any efforts to further that which is valued, but
instead encourages focusing on one's own subjective experiences. Maslow himself was concerned about this possibly leading to an ever-escalating search for triggers to
wonderful experiences, with the rest of the world all but
forgotten.[8] However, although he clearly did not intend to
encourage such an attitude, his doctrine seems inevitably
to do so.

What Maslow and Rogers urge seems, if anything, still
more problematic when we consider its implications for
groups larger than families and for the society as a whole.
If we are always to be governed by our own dictates and
never from the outside, this hardly encourages us to subject ourselves to the external constraints that inevitably
accompany commitment to any group or institution. If we
always should be trying to actualize ourselves, this hardly
encourages our seeking to further community or societal
goals. Maslow and Rogers each say little about the broader
social structures in which human beings are embedded
except for lamenting the ways in which these structures
interfere with self-determination and self-actualization.
Maslow's self-actualizers show detachment from their cultures. Rogers' newly emerging human type feels the deep-
est antipathy to institutions. And Rogers surveys with evident satisfaction the current decline in the power of
institutions of all kinds, including governmental, religious,
and educational organizations.[9]

Again we find what is hard not to see as the romantic
illusion that all will be well if only we are free to actualize
ourselves. Maslow and Rogers seem merely to assume that
no one will try to take anything away from us or attack
us, that justice will prevail, that we will all be in a position
to develop our potentialities amicably. No formal arrange-

ments are required for such ends; no one needs to take specific responsibilities for achieving them. They will all come about automatically if only obstructions are removed. This scenario, however, is difficult to credit with much likelihood.

Maslow and Rogers certainly want people to be caring and helpful to one another, to pursue common goals, to try to deal with the problems of their communities and broader groups. But what they advocate seems designed rather to prevent this than to bring it about. Maddi has strikingly pointed out the problematic nature of Rogers' writing on these issues.[10] For example, Rogers argues that the increasing violence in our cities is virtually unknown in the People's Republic of China because there, unlike here, people feel a part of an ongoing, purposeful, larger process. But the nature of current Chinese social institutions hardly seems to fit the principles Rogers—and Maslow—advocate. These principles are surely better exemplified in our own society, one where little or no sense of common purpose is fostered.

If we are always to be determined by what is within rather than outside ourselves, if we are always first and foremost to seek our own growth and actualization, this inevitably seems to push toward concern for the self at the expense of others. But what about the argument that we must look first of all to our own concerns if we are to be able to look usefully to any that lie beyond? According to Rogers, it is only when we understand and accept ourselves that we can understand and accept other people and thus be of benefit to them. According to Maslow, it is only when our lower needs are satisfied that our higher needs can emerge. Both of them see satisfaction of one's own needs as a necessary prerequisite to good relationships with and helpfulness to others.

It certainly seems true that our own unsatisfied needs can get in the way in our relations with other people; we are then a hindrance rather than a help. Fromm and Rogers each described mothers who made life difficult for their children precisely because they had too little concern for and acceptance of themselves; Fromm wrote of the over-solicitous, self-sacrificing mother; Rogers discussed the mother unable to accept any hostile feelings in herself. Horney described neurotics who were overconsiderate, always subordinating themselves to others in an indiscriminate striving for affection and approval. Such people may indeed be more helpful to others if they look first to what their own needs and interests require and try to provide for them.

That sometimes it will be most beneficial for all concerned if individuals take better care of their own needs cannot be taken to imply, however, that this is true in general. One might argue that Maslow and Rogers themselves are guilty here of just what Maslow wanted to avoid: taking the "sick half of psychology" as if it applied to everyone. It hardly seems likely that, for example, it would be good for children generally if their parents always thought in terms of what would be best for themselves, rather than how they can help their children to grow and to flourish. Nor does it seem likely that we can solve our nation's problems, such as unemployment, the depletion of energy resources, and the dangers of nuclear destruction, if each of us concentrates on our own self-actualization.

Even if helpfulness to other individuals or to groups requires a certain degree of self-acceptance or satisfaction of one's own needs, that it should in general be best for all concerned if we focus on personal needs, self-acceptance, or actualization seems exceedingly unlikely. Maslow and Rogers could probably never have believed anything like this if it were not for their strong faith in people's natural goodness, which meant that they thought of people as actualizing themselves by helping others and deriving pleasure from being altruistic. But as we have illustrated, no matter how naturally inclined we are to care for and about other human beings, what will most actualize ourselves may well conflict with what is best for others.

Maslow and Rogers would likely also never have held that the general good is best served by individuals' focusing on their own needs and actualization if psychological values had not come to be so significant to them that they outweighed or preempted all other considerations. They ignore what may matter apart from feelings themselves, such as fair distribution of scarce resources, caring for society's children, or the availability of socially constructive roles rather than useless or frivolous or dysfunctional occupations. What seems to have happened is that the process, already begun with the neo-Freudians, of identifying evil with neuroses and good with mental health, has become very near complete.

In sum: It is unlikely that the general good is promoted by urging us to actualize ourselves and not be determined by anything outside. Maslow's and Rogers' presumption of natural concern for others does not keep such urging from discouraging helpfulness and the pursuit of broader goals, because what is good for the self often will differ from what is good for other individuals or for the general welfare—our possible natural concern for others notwithstanding. Nor can advocating top priority for self-actualization be seen as furthering the general good on the grounds that it is prerequisite to being beneficial to others. There are sharp limits to when consideration of self over others is actually better for all concerned.

Is Freedom from External Determination
Best for the Individual?

It was not, of course, the general welfare that was foremost in the minds of Maslow and Rogers when they urged self-actualization and opposed determination from outside the individual, but the welfare of the individual. They believed it was crucial for the individual that he or she "grow from within," be aware of his or her own feelings and beliefs, and act in accordance with them. We are not to let external pressures lead us to become what we are not and to do what does not feel right to us.

This concern for freedom and autonomy is what seems to have made it possible for Maslow to come to think that ideally people are "not dependent for their main satisfactions on the real world, or other people or culture" or anything else "extrinsic"[11]—and that the environment should be "primarily a means to the person's self-actualizing ends."[12] Should we not gain satisfaction from seeing our children thrive? Should we not try to improve our environment (or at least keep it from devastation)? The same concern for autonomy enabled Rogers to come to feel that the only real criterion for an individual to consider is whether something makes him or her "a richer, more complete, more fully developed person"[13]—and that "the only question which matters is, 'Am I living in a way which is deeply satisfying to me, and which truly expresses me?' "[14] Should we not consider whether we are furthering what we value in the world?

These statements by Maslow and Rogers are difficult to reconcile with their own views that people have direct concerns for other human beings and the world outside. Rogers says the organism has a desire for friendly relationships and is sensitively tender toward others. Maslow says his self-actualizers are dedicated to a task or vocation and are

particularly likely to love others unselfishly and to appreciate what is of value in the world. It is hard to see how
we could have direct concerns outside ourselves without
also having external ends and satisfactions, as well as criteria that matter to us other than our own development.
If there is someone whom you really care for, you will be
affected by what affects that person; what is good for him
or her will tend to be a satisfaction for you as well and will
be able to serve as a criterion that guides a part of your
conduct.

Their interests in the individual's being free and determined by his or her own feelings and desires do not require Maslow and Rogers to have gone as far as they did
in urging absence of all determination from without. If
people do care about other people and about other matters
external to themselves, then they can be responsive to events
outside themselves because of their own feelings and
wishes. If you really want to make a child happy, to reduce
the incidence of cancer, or to improve conditions for migrant workers, then you will—because of your own, genuine desires—tend to be affected by what will further these
goals. To have ends outside ourselves does not mean that
we are not being determined by our own thoughts and
values. Rogers and Maslow may have been so concerned
about freedom and autonomy that they lost sight of the
different kinds of ways in which outside events can have
effects on us. But we can freely aim at something in the
world outside; our choices can be our own, internal, while
our ends are external.

Whether or not an individual is acting freely or according to his or her real feelings seems an altogether separate
and independent question from that of whether the actions
are aimed at something internal or outside. Not only may
one be led by one's own feelings to try to further some-

thing outside of oneself, but also others may influence one precisely in the opposite direction—to look toward one's own welfare. It is, for example, not uncommon to find college students with high ideals and aspirations being urged by their parents to go into a more prestigious and secure occupation, rather than one that has a greater possibility of benefiting humanity.

Concern for freedom and autonomy thus does not warrant the Maslow and Rogers position, which opposes what they themselves say in other places, that it is better for the individual to aim always at his or her own actualization or development and not at external ends. What can be harmful—and here we agree with them—is being pressured to go against our own feelings and judgments, to be or do otherwise than what seems right to us. Parents and spouses may insist on our earning a living through types of work we find alien or do not respect; schools and other institutions may demand our performance of tasks that seem meaningless or worse; governments may require that we fight in wars we deem unjust. When such demands are made that one go against one's own values, we too feel that one should attempt to oppose those demands and, if that does not succeed and what is at issue is of sufficient significance, refuse to comply.

But that others may try to make us go against our own beliefs does not mean that we should have no aims external to ourselves. Of course, one might attempt to ground the Maslow and Rogers position instead on a different argument: that it will be best from the point of view of the individual's welfare to aim directly at whatever defines it, and this of necessity has to be something like personal happiness or well-being and not something external. That argument, however, ignores the ancient wisdom, which will be further pursued in Chapter 11, that such matters as our own well-being and happiness may be more readily attained when not aimed at directly.

In any case, it seems clear that Maslow and Rogers' explicit argument that the individual should act according to his or her own feelings and desires does not justify opposition to our having external aims. It does not even seem to justify broadside opposition to letting ourselves be influenced by others' evaluations or constraints. Influence of this kind does not necessarily go against our own feelings and desires either. It may support them. Like internal prescriptions and restraints, external ones also can help us keep sight of matters that we ourselves care about and can facilitate our accomplishing things that we ourselves wish to carry out. Following the instructions of a baseball coach can make possible better playing and a greater contribution to one's team. Are such instructions just to be viewed as impositions? Following the conductor of an orchestra can enable the musicians to perform a symphony. Is it simply a loss of freedom to subject oneself to the conductor's direction? (Fellini's film, *Orchestra Rehearsal*, portrays the chaos that results when an orchestra's musicians refuse determination from anywhere else but within and, by extrapolation, when the members of a society make a similar refusal.)

As we see it, Maslow and Rogers and many other psychologists at the present time are so concerned about potential threats to freedom and autonomy that they attempt to shield us from external influence to a degree far beyond what is in fact good for us. Although it is true that misuses of authority are legion, it does not follow that all authority is illegitimate and to be avoided—such as that of all team coaches and orchestra conductors, or that of all parents, teachers, and judges.[15] Nor does it follow from the existence of demands to go against our own values and beliefs that all long-term commitments are to be viewed as chains and all kinds of human institutions as so many forms of imprisonment. Do we really become more free if, like Rogers' favored new emerging type, we reject long-term commitments, or do we lose much more in positive possibilities than we gain? And how far could we get in the development of our potentialities without any societal structures or institutions?

In summary, it seems misguided to think that total independence and freedom from all external determination actually is best for the individual. Determination that results from our having external aims, so that we are affected by what bears on those aims, seems in no wise against the individual's interests. These aims can reflect our real wishes and desires. And even external prescriptions and restraints are not necessarily opposed to, but may support, what individuals really feel and want.

Freud's Opposing Principles Revisited

Let us now look again at the ideas of Freud with which we started our inquiry and consider what has become of them. Recall Freud's antinomy between what is best for the individual and for the common good. From the point of view of the individual, Freud said, what would be best was the greatest and most direct possible gratification of internal needs. Ideally, each of us could freely and spontaneously express our inner impulses. Consideration of the common good, however, makes it essential that there should be restraints and sublimation.

This second principle—the necessity for restraints, for redirecting of energy—has been much questioned. The neo-Freudians and later also many others, particularly Maslow and Rogers, rejected it, believing that it followed from what they viewed as Freud's overly pessimistic interpretation of human nature. This in turn made it possible for them to carry ever further the implications of Freud's principle about what is best for the individual's welfare, opposing all prescriptions and restraints and all forms of external determination. The actualization of what is within the self became essentially the only thing that mattered.

We have argued that this position is inevitably opposed to the common good. It simply fails to take into account the facts of conflicting interests; indeed, it seems to ignore altogether the existence of any considerations outside the individual, such as a world in danger of destroying itself, and to let presumed psychological values preempt all others. The conception that all would be well if only we were each free to actualize ourselves seems ultimately difficult to see as anything other than a form of romantic illusion. On the issue of the general welfare, then, the neo-Freudians and Maslow and Rogers disagreed with Freud. We are maintaining that Freud was correct. On the other hand, when it comes to the issue of what is best for the individual, Freud's views have received very little critical consideration and have largely been taken for granted, but here we believe that Freud was wrong.

Within the Freudian conception of motivation, it has to be best for the individual to be essentially free of prescriptions and restraints, and free of determination from outside. The individual's good is ultimately defined in terms of the satisfaction of bodily needs; these needs are what lead to activity; the activity is designed to reduce the needs. The spontaneous and unrestrained actions of the individual will thus always be in his or her best interests, except when they may be unrealistic. Prescriptions and restraints and any form of external determination will serve the individual's interests only when they make possible a more accurate weighing of the implications of reality for how internal needs may be satisfied. Apart from this, they are inevitably opposed to the good of the individual.

In Chapters 3 and 4, we argued that Freud's reasons for believing that all behavior is aimed at the satisfaction of bodily needs turn out not to support this belief after all; the belief is actually untrue. It was rejected by the neo-Freudians and by Maslow and Rogers, all of whom believe, as we do, that human beings can have direct concerns with what is outside of themselves. Once Freud's conception of motivation is relinquished, however, it is no longer evident that the individual's spontaneous activity is necessarily in his or her best interests (given that reality is taken into account) and that whatever interferes with this activity or affects it from outside will likely be contrary to those interests. Without prescriptions or restraints, we may lose sight of concerns that are not represented by immediate bodily stimulation but are nevertheless ours. And much that we may want to do that is not a matter of satisfying bodily needs seems in principle possible only if we subject ourselves to certain constraints and forms of discipline, including at times ones necessarily external to ourselves. Further, to have direct concerns outside ourselves, to be in part determined by external aims (so that events bearing on those aims affect us) does not oppose, but is required by, our own feelings and desires.

Not only from the point of view of the larger group, but also from that of the individual, it thus seems quite unwarranted to oppose all determination from outside the self, to urge concern only with what is within, and to advocate self-realization or self-actualization as all that matters. We shall soon argue that, rather than its being helpful to a person to focus on actualization and development of the self, it is often quite detrimental and that, for the sake of the individual as well as the group, a different kind of focus would be preferable. We have, however, mostly been looking at influential trends bearing on these issues only in the area of clinical psychology and personality. Before we continue with this argument, let us look at some other kinds of work in psychology in which we might expect the push toward selfishness to be less in evidence.

Notes

1. Maslow, 1968, p. vi.
2. Maslow, 1968, pp. 139–140.
3. Rogers, 1961, p. 21.
4. Rogers, 1972, 1977.
5. Rogers, 1972, p. 10.
6. Rogers, 1972, p. 200.
7. Maslow, 1964, 1968, 1976.
8. Maslow, 1976, pp. 332–333.
9. Rogers, 1977, pp. 266–267.
10. Maddi, 1978, p. 300.
11. Maslow, 1970, p. 162.
12. Maslow, 1970, p. 68.
13. Rogers, 1971, p. 15.
14. Rogers, 1961, p. 118.
15. See Sennett, 1980.

9

Current Academic Psychology on Human Conduct

To what extent is psychology in its more academic and less clinical aspects implicated in giving support to selfishness? The formulations that we have been considering are not unconnected with academic study and research, but they have arisen largely in the context of therapy and counseling. There are other areas of psychology that have addressed themselves to questions regarding human conduct, and we must ask how they fit in. We will examine some recent, influential trends bearing on the issues that concern us. In particular, two academic specializations have gained attention in recent years that seem highly relevant, but arose at some remove from the clinical sphere—"social psychology" and "developmental psychology," centering on studies of social interaction and of changes with age, respectively. If we take some examples of major current ways of thinking in the research of these academic specialties, what will we find?

Some who decry our culture's drift toward selfishness may hold certain aspects of clinical psychology responsible, but do not see academic psychology as blameworthy. An example would be Robert Coles, who is ready to fault the concentration on the self, on "one's thoughts, feelings, wishes, worries," that comes through in forms of "pop" psychology that advocate personal liberation, or in encounter or training (T) groups.[1] But Coles carefully exonerates "the kind [of psychology] fairly often taught in college and university courses (a scholarly discipline conveyed as such)"[2] and even exonerates Freudian psychoanalysis as well. Already in Chapter 1, the nature of what is taught in college courses gave us pause. Now we will explore that academic work further.

The kinds of "pop" psychological advice that Coles criticizes would include the writings of someone like Theodore Roszak, an historian strongly impressed by the very ideas that Coles deplores.[3] Roszak celebrates therapies that focus on self-awareness and self-expression. He says we should carry out "a redisposition of attention toward the inner self"[4] and embark upon an "adventure of self-discovery."[5] We should trust our innocence and speak our minds, which means that what looks like incivility and lack of respect for others—the "collective egoism" that Coles views as problematical—is rather a healthy refusal to put oneself down.

But even in the "scholarly discipline" of psychology one can find encouragement to ventilate those personal "thoughts, feelings, wishes, worries" on which Coles says we concentrate too much. For example, the widely used text by Aronson that aims "to spell out the relevance that sociopsychological research might have for some of the problems besetting contemporary society,"[6] praises T-groups and advocates that close friends and marriage partners should freely voice their complaints and negative views about one another. Further, there are certain other ways in which academic psychology seems much more strongly to lend support to selfishness.

The most outstanding of these ways is simply the assumption that selfishness is inevitable. As this chapter will indicate, academic work seems repeatedly to take for granted as a motivational premise that what ultimately matters to each of us is just ourselves—our own affective states, satisfaction of our own needs. The past fifteen years or so have seen increasing interest in the area of helping behavior and altruism.[7] But, as noted by Wispé,[8] with relatively few exceptions even the psychologists working in this realm have not put aside this theoretical preconception. They still assume that we cannot really have direct concern for others. The many kinds of altruistic behavior that have now been documented and studied are almost always still explained (explained away?) in terms of positive outcomes for the helping individual. Doing things for others is continually traced to the expectation that one will get something back in return, or at least will make oneself feel good.

Let us now take a closer look at current scholarly work. In this regard, a broad distinction can be drawn between more "conservative" and more "liberal" approaches in developmental and social psychology. Some researchers, for example, may believe that, however complex the behavior, the relevant paradigm for understanding it should come from certain simple assumptions of associationistic learning or of decision making in games, or that one must demand the rigor of putting theory in tight propositional form and conducting experiments; they may be viewed as "conservative." Others, for instance, may wish to document creativity as it occurs in human society, even if its explanation must be ambiguous, or may be more open to drawing upon diverse kinds of data and making rough approximations; they may be viewed as lenient or "liberal." We will sample from both trends.

A Sampling of "Conservative" Academic Trends

Among those subscribing to rigorous theory and experimentation in social psychology, a tilt toward cynicism about the bases for social concern is frequently encountered, as we glimpsed in Chapter 1. Scientific parsimony has led many in the direction of a "debunking" attitude toward what humans mean for one another. Thus, White studies the progress of human courtship by focusing on physical attractiveness of partners, and compares two theories, both of which assume that partners are consumers trying to extract advantageous deals from each other.[9] And after a review of experimental gaming studies that are expected to indicate how people react to social dilemmas, Dawes finds nothing to deter him from the general belief that "most people in the world will compromise his or her altruistic or ethical values for money or survival."[10]

Research on interpersonal relations by Kelley and Thibaut[11] offers a programmatic outlook with a significant academic following. For this reason, we may find it useful to consider at some length. In accordance with their approach, how people act toward one another, and how they should act, depends on the personal benefits that accrue to each. What ultimately guides your social acts, however concerned for another they may seem, are the outcomes to yourself. To be sure, you may set aside your own outcomes and act out of purely moral considerations, such as commitment to honesty or justice as an ideal, or out of concern for the welfare of others. At some level, however, you keep an accounting of the consequences that these actions produce in benefits to yourself. If not sufficiently favorable, you will and should arrange to improve your balance of returns.[12] Rather than always maintaining a particular commitment, such as, for instance, to justice, you are expected to do so "conditionally, depending on the situation and the partner."[13]

As indicated, Kelley and Thibaut mean their discussion to be prescriptive as well as descriptive. The most reasonable thing for you to do psychologically, in terms of what is presumed to be your nature, is to accept the pivotal significance to you of your own outcomes. Of course, your way of doing so should be enlightened rather than the blatant pursuit of personal advantage, since the latter is not an effective strategy. Thus, "being considerate of other persons' needs and helping them attain their goals will often be found necessary in order to obtain the cooperation from them that the individual desires."[14] But if the tactic doesn't work, consideration and helpfulness may have to give way before a reassessment of where your personal advantages lie. Of course, you might still end up deciding to show consideration or concern for others, since your society could impose sanctions that lead you in that direction. Once again, however, personal advantage would determine whether or not you do. When people act on behalf of others, then, personal benefit is at the bottom of it.

Perhaps most crucially, what Kelley and Thibaut urge is flexibility in how one relates to others. The wisest course is to keep one's relations conditional: "the functionally optimal rules are highly contingent."[15] Reciprocity is what one hopes to establish. Life with others is viewed as a negotiation process, using the carrots and sticks at one's disposal in pursuit of reciprocity. Cooperate if the other person does, too, but don't let anyone take advantage of you. Commitment to another person, faith or trust in another, with its implication of steadfastness, of *uncondition-*

ality, becomes a gambit or move that is tendered to induce reciprocation. It is a risk that, in the favorable instances, pays off by inducing the other to act in ways rewarding to one.

Since it is ultimately premised on trying to improve one's own outcomes rather than on one's feelings about the other, commitment needs to be kept within limits. The rational approach becomes the kind of partial or tentative commitment that leads one to be looking for evidence of reciprocation and to consider ending involvement. This makes it in one's interest to have alternative options of other possible relationships available, to avoid getting caught in a situation in which one can be exploited because of having nowhere else to turn. To the extent that one's available alternatives are better than one's partner's, one's bargaining power in the relationship is greater; one is in a better position to ensure reciprocity. Commitment, with its implication of insensitivity to personal advantage, carries the danger of entrapment, and we ought to be wary of it.

Commitment as a danger, conditionality as the key to keeping one's relationships healthy and happy, is a theme sounded by many researchers. Thus, Staub warns against opening ourselves to exploitation in his asserting that "when we give unconditionally without any returns, what we give loses value; hence the protective character of insisting on reciprocity."[16] Consciousness raising about seeking reciprocity as one's just due, keeping one's commitments limited and contingent on the returns that come in, is viewed as only sound since then each party will be alert to the other's sense of what parity requires.[17] Each will be sensitized to the importance of increasing the other's outcomes, upon threat of tit-for-tat forms of reprisal that will decrease one's own. Note, however, the built-in element of instability when having attractive alternatives available is a means of giving teeth to demands for reciprocity. A certain precariousness would seem to attend relationships that are based in this way on flexibility, conditionality, and insistence on reciprocity, rather than on commitment. To opt nevertheless for contingency as what is rational reflects again the root assumption that only one's own outcomes ultimately matter. For that means if reciprocity is not maintained, one in fact is better off elsewhere and can only be made unhappy in the present situation.

The possibility of another's outcomes having direct reward value to one, apart from the connections that hold between these outcomes and one's own, has no place in this approach. One must be careful, therefore, to make sure enough benefits are accruing to one in the relationship to justify what one is "paying" for it. It is only realistic to weigh what one's best returns would be elsewhere, to establish comparisons, since this lets one know the limits on what the present relationship is worth. Not to be careful in these ways is to court the disaster of letting investments outrun what is warranted by returns, warns Rusbult: "High investments and/or poor alternatives may sometimes serve to 'trap' the individual in an unhappy, unsatisfying relationship."[18]

Even when, as with Levinger, preoccupation with "fairness" is acknowledged as a danger signal in marital or other close relationships, this is understood as meaning that one or both of the partners may no longer be receiving sufficient reward to justify the investment.[19] The implication is that, to make the relationship work better, each partner has to be assured of deriving sufficiently favorable net benefits from maintaining it. Neglected is the possibility that instead the very terms of the analysis—as applied both by the couple and by the psychologist—are at fault. What may be wanting is not more attention to balances of returns but an approach to relationships that views another's welfare and commitment to furthering it as primary considerations.

Is it the case then that, as Kelley and Thibaut assert, "the functionally optimal rules are highly contingent"? Is conditionality so important to maintain, and is unconditional giving such a danger? Perhaps not, at least according to work that has carefully tried to separate the contributions of—on the one hand—level or rate of positivity and negativity in exchanges between marriage partners and—on the other hand—sequential dependency or conditionality in these exchanges. Research by Gottman, Markman, and Notarius[20] compared distressed and nondistressed married couples in the discussion of a personally salient marital issue, such as budgeting money. The two kinds of couples were clearly differentiated in terms of the ratios of agreement to disagreement in their verbal behavior and even more so in terms of the degrees of negative affect conveyed in their nonverbal behavior such as facial cues of frowning, sneering, or disgust, or vocal cues of impatience or sarcasm. There were higher rates of agreement and less negative affect in nondistressed couples.

But is conditionality a good thing? When Gottman, Markman, and Notarius controlled for base-rate differences and looked for sequential dependencies in the affects expressed, some dependencies were found, but they were complex. It was certainly not the case that the nondistressed couples showed overall greater reciprocity. On the contrary, where conditionality seemed most pronounced was in the reciprocation of negative affect by the distressed couples. As Gottman, Markman, and Notarius indicate: "This finding would be consistent with clinical folklore which suggests that clinic couples are more likely to be involved in negative cycles than nonclinic couples."[21] What seems to happen, then, is that in unhappy marriages, expressions of negative affect tend to be responded to in kind, while in happy marriages there is a much lower degree of expression of negative affect altogether—an *unconditional* eschewing of the negative, rather than conditionality. In other words, the happy marriages seem to involve more of something like commitment or trust. Perhaps this kind of goodwill has the pivotal role to play in marriage, friendship, parent–child relations, and interpersonal relations generally, in contrast to giving what you get.

As another example from the conservative end of the research spectrum, consider "social learning theory"—an outlook of wide influence that is viewed as accounting for complex human phenomena in scientifically parsimonious ways. Closely linked to the name of Albert Bandura,[22] social learning theory again makes the root assumption that all an individual can fundamentally care about are personal outcomes. For example, why are you likely to become disturbed by the suffering of a friend? The social learning answer is automatically cynical: You are moved by adversities befalling a friend because they mean that you are likely to be adversely affected also. When others are distressed, your experience has been that they are less likely to treat you amiably; further, what has happened to your friend may happen to you as well.

In line with this example, social learning theory asserts quite generally that what is outside ourselves has little direct significance for us. Only physical experiences involving such things as food and comfort are intrinsically rewarding. We come to care about social approval and disapproval because, through their association with the physical consequences we experience in the course of development, approval and disapproval from others become predictive of physical effects. The same is true of regard for ourselves, which we acquire in turn primarily through the intermediary of evaluations of ourselves by others. But whatever matters to us does so only because of its implications for our own personal gains and losses. As with our concern for a friend, so for our interest in playing a musical instrument or solving an intellectual problem.

For instance, Bandura argues, without apologies to tuba players, that "there is nothing inherently rewarding about a tuba solo. To an aspiring tuba instrumentalist, however, an accomplished performance is a source of considerable self-satisfaction that can sustain much tuba blowing."[23] It is only because it has been hooked to self-evaluation that tuba playing is now a meaningful activity. Similarly, inducing people to care more about their fellows, to be of greater benefit to others, or to devote themselves to ideals of beauty or truth as represented in music, in art, or in the pursuit of knowledge, depends on making any of these a means for improving one's balance sheet of personal outcomes. What matters to the individual is never really such activities in their own right, but the approval or disapproval from others and from self to which they may give rise.

The way in which personal benefits and losses are viewed as the ultimate controllers can be illustrated further by considering how Bandura answers the question of why people would ever be self-critical or punish themselves, which would increase one's negative outcomes. If self-punishment were taken at its face value, it would violate the assumption that we act to minimize personal losses and maximize personal gains. Bandura sees self-punishment, therefore, as a way we have learned of mitigating still worse punishment. When we are self-critical or self-punitive, it is because this alleviates the distress our thoughts generate and reduces the extent to which external agencies would otherwise punish us.[24] Thus, any anguish over what we did has an ulterior motive; the self-punishment serves to bring us less punishment than we would otherwise experience. Rather than accepting the reality of remorse, the social learning analysis turns remorse into a minimizing of our pain; we are responding in the way that will make us suffer as little as the circumstances permit.

Whatever our modes of behavior and our goals happen to be, they are to be understood as the particular instrumentalities we have learned for favorable personal returns. Again, then, as with Kelley and Thibaut, the best that can be hoped for in relations with others is bargaining based on those personal returns to "foster reciprocity through balancing of interests."[25] Promises of gain and threats of loss must be used to fashion people's conduct into mutually beneficial patterns. In fact, legalistic negotiating of quid pro quo contracts is acknowledged by Bandura as a form of reciprocal influence that has enlarged its dominion over human affairs in recent times, and he views this trend with approval. He, like Kelley and Thibaut, merely sees it as psychological realism about our natures.

When the ideas of social learning theory are directly applied with an eye to enhancing the likelihood of socially constructive action and reducing selfish behavior, the result is work like that of Rushton.[26] According to the social learning formulation, we imitate what others do in expectations of social approval and avoidance of social disapproval. We observe, take over, and internalize others' standards, making these standards the basis for self-regulation when others are no longer present, in the expectation that this will lead us to rewards and the avoidance of punishment. Thus, imitation and internalization of an altruistic model will be based, Rushton tells us, on some kind of expected personal gain. Similarly, when the agents of approval and disapproval urge us by preaching, exhortation, or reason toward virtuous courses of action, our compliance will be a function of expected rewards. A model or a "preacher" of altruism will be followed to the extent that our own positive outcomes are linked with doing so.

Modeling of or exhortations to altruism coming from, say, a more powerful individual, one with a high degree of control over us, will thus be likely to lead to greater unselfishness on our part than similar behavior from a weaker person. And if we see beneficial outcomes accruing to a model for altruistic behavior, such "vicarious reinforcement" will be a message not lost on us, and we will be more likely to imitate the model as a result. In the first case, the prediction in social learning studies is that, for example, a prestigious person urging donations to a worthy cause is more likely to induce children to donate money given to them than a person lacking prestige. In the second, it is predicted that if a model receives praise for generosity in making donations to a worthy cause, children are more likely to imitate the model than if the model receives no praise.

Indeed, some support for predictions of this kind can be found. Children sometimes do make more donations when urged to do so by someone whom they regard as important or powerful or when they observe someone being praised for such behavior. But this is far from indicating that the children are not really affected by the anticipated consequences of their donations for the recipients per se. As a matter of fact, one of the studies that Rushton cites for showing the role of power[27] also contains evidence that describing the implications of donations for the recipients is more effective than normative exhortations. Experimental demonstrations that prestige or power or praise is capable of increasing altruistic behavior by no means show that expected rewards are always the explanation of why we behave altruistically when we do. The crucial role that social learning theory ascribes to personal gain seems to be present more as an article of faith than as a conclusion compelled by the evidence.

Nonetheless, a social learning theorist such as Rushton seems to take for granted that the only way in which people could be brought to less selfishness is to arrange for unselfish behavior to become in their self-interest to carry out, to attach it to personal advantage. The cynicism that this fosters may well have the ironic effect of undermining the calls to altruism that Rushton seeks to implement. Real altruism is not even regarded as a possibility; benefiting others is always ultimately a function of one's own rewards. And though we may have internal standards to behave unselfishly, even such standards are maintained only because their maintenance is linked with positive outcomes for ourselves. But if this is the case, doesn't it make sense always to seek one's own advantage, fine-tuning our internal standards so they get in our way as little as possible?

It is hard to avoid the implication from social learning theory of right being conferred by might. If all that ultimately matters to you are outcomes to yourself, all that can ultimately commend one course of action as against another is the greater satisfaction to you that will result. What you can manage to get away with, then, would seem to be what you deserve. There is nothing to keep this from extending as well to the control of others for the purpose of furthering your own interests. You can even do so by the manipulation of rewards and punishments to sanction cooperation and compliance so highly recommended by Rushton. This method has been invoked time and again, of course, by oppressive authorities wishing to suppress dissent and keep people subservient.

A Sampling of "Liberal" Academic Trends

Other academic trends may be more tolerant in their demands for theoretical parsimony or the rigor of tight experiments. They may even have evolved in opposition to, or in response to uneasiness about, an outlook like social learning theory. What are their assumptions like? Do they avoid the push toward self-centeredness that seems implicit in the preceding illustrations? Already their language may raise our concern. Consider a recent psychological analysis of originality in musical composition, seeming to move beyond a social learning type of formulation; it refers to "the developmental transition from mere imitation of role models to full-fledged self-actualization."[28]

An emphasis on being true to oneself can be gleaned in some of the work of academic liberals. A major rallying point, for example, has been Lawrence Kohlberg's formulations about moral development,[29] which are widely viewed as an antidote to what is taken to be the narrowness or astringency of academic conservatives. In Kohlberg's theory, the individual's development of morality ideally proceeds from Level I, the "preconventional," where rules and social expectations are simply imposed from without, to Level II, the "conventional," where the person identifies with or internalizes these rules and expectations, to Level III, the "postconventional," where the person shakes loose from external authority altogether. At this highest of Kohlberg's levels, we have a person "who has differentiated his self from the rules and expectations of others and defines his values in terms of self-chosen principles."[30] The self has moved above social rules and expectations and is responsible now only to its own dictates.

Kohlberg seems to have little doubt that those self-chosen principles will be good ones, for, not unlike Horney or Fromm, or Maslow or Rogers, he considers the aspirations of the self to be essentially wholesome. But it is difficult to see how the general good will be furthered by one's always giving one's own principles precedence over the laws and agreements of one's group, in line with Kohlberg's ideal of the highest level of functioning.[31] Although this is clearly not what Kohlberg intends, his view of the basic motivation for morality almost seems to imply that one's principles really ought to be self-serving. This motivation has nothing to do with feelings for others or appreciation of the role of morality in promoting the general good; it is, rather, "a generalized motivation for acceptance, competence, self-esteem, or self-realization."[32]

Until recently, Kohlberg took the position, in sharp contradiction to social learning theorists, of being against the teaching of any value content, or what he called "indoctrination." Kohlberg held such teaching to be in violation of the rights of those being taught. However, as Oldenquist has pointed out,[33] Kohlberg always has pushed for, or "indoctrinated", certain values such as, for example, the desirability of freedom to make one's own choices, independent of shoulds imposed by anyone else. (In tune with the times, rights have seemed to weigh more heavily than obligations in Kohlberg's view.) In fact, Kohlberg now admits[34] that indoctrination of particular value content is necessary, which would seem to imply more explicit (albeit somewhat paradoxical) fostering of the personal autonomy focus that Oldenquist argues has been there all along.

The connection between Kohlberg's ideas and those of a personality theorist such as Maslow is made explicitly by Simpson, for whom such a link is seen as a virtue.[35] Noting that Kohlberg's preconventional and conventional levels of moral development are grounded in external authority, while his postconventional level is based on internal principles expressive of the self, Simpson suggests that Kohlberg's highest level of morality corresponds to Maslow's need for self-actualization. Both men are arguing that with greater maturity comes greater reliance on autonomously fashioned internal standards, and less reliance on the outer society or the group. All of this is understood in terms of needs of the self for something like competence, mastery, or fulfillment. Kohlberg's ideal, like Maslow's, places the self in the driver's seat and expects it to do the right thing if we but respect its needs as legitimate.

Some liberals particularly decry the individualism that gains support from conservative theoretical assumptions. They may question the premise that our basic state of being is unsocial or that personal acquisitiveness and concern for personal advancement are necessary aspects of human nature. They may want to replace such assumptions with premises that take individualism less for granted and that offer a stronger basis for human community. Even for these psychologists, however, the fundamental role of self-interest in all motivation can remain unquestioned. Take Hogan, Johnson, and Emler[36] and Baumrind[37] as examples.

Hogan, Johnson, and Emler do not believe that children start out with a natural antagonism to adult society that socialization must overcome. Hogan, Johnson, and Emler consider sociability to be more basic than this view would imply. What then do they offer to account for social life in a manner that, presumably, will deemphasize individualism? They postulate three needs: for positive attention or approval from others, for predictability, and for aggressive status seeking or dominance. The first of these needs is presumed to underlie affiliative behavior and thus social cohesiveness; the other two form bases for the hierarchically organized and orderly nature of life in social groups. Ironically, then, in light of Hogan, Johnson, and Emler's antiindividualistic outlook, all that affiliation can come from is one's desire for positive attention—to get something, not to give something. If you show concern for others, you are really motivated by your need for social approval. Your interest in others depends on what they, or someone else, will do for you in return. Once more we find Kelley and Thibaut's assumption that only your own outcomes can ultimately matter to you.

For Baumrind, in turn, opposition to individualism goes so far as to make her a self-proclaimed Marxist. As such, she presumably sees individualism, with its emphasis on personal success at the expense of others, as an outgrowth of a particular economic system—free-enterprise capitalism. The profit motive would be, in this view, a result of the conditions of production. These conditions should be changed to encourage people to conduct themselves for the good of the community and the collective. Yet, for all the Marxist tracing of individualism to capitalist economics, Baumrind still considers self-interest to be psychologically fundamental. What presumably motivates us is "the drive to survive and flourish. Wisdom refines and educates narrow self-interest; self-interest becomes enlightened as the individual is socialized."[38] Enlightened self-interest once again is the best we can hope for, and cynicism is a necessary, although unacknowledged, implication.

Perhaps a particularly good illustration for the liberal side of the academic spectrum is provided by the work of Eleanor Maccoby,[39] a psychologist highly regarded for the breadth of her orientation toward human development in its social context. Her disinclination to be limited by theoretical dogma makes especially interesting what she takes for granted. This seems to include an instrumental outlook concerning the relation of other human beings to oneself. From the infant's earliest manifestations of attachment onward, others appear to exist in order to be used for one's own ends.

In the case of attachment, for example, Maccoby criticizes a view that would interpret the infant's attachment to caretakers as grounded exclusively in their ability to relieve the infant's distress. Rather, she sees attachment as also coming about because adults function as "agents" to help the infant in its emerging push to master the environment. By responding predictably to the infant's actions, adults permit the infant to accomplish what it couldn't do alone. This addition to earlier ideas, then, notes that caretakers serve as tools to amplify the infant's competence for achieving what it wants from the environment, not just as providers of comfort. Maccoby's extension is reminiscent of White's[40] earlier positing of competence motivation and in the same way leaves the organism still focused on itself, pursuing its own competence.

The reason for emotional bonds to a caretaker thus becomes no less instrumental than it was before. Maccoby's way of treating the cynical implication that attachment should decay when it no longer serves the child's interests is simply to reassure us that we will always remain of use. Parents needn't worry about losing the love of their offspring, because children "do not stop needing to know that their attachment figures are available in situations that are frightening or beyond their capacity to handle."[41] Since the reason for cynicism is still there, however, the reassurance rings a bit hollow.

Maccoby recognizes the early existence of sympathy, which, one might suppose, could suggest that children at least sometimes do care directly about others and how they feel. But without even considering direct concern for others as a possible alternative, she accepts Aronfreed's[42] interpretation that becoming distressed at the distress of another results from associations between the signs of the other's distress (such as crying) and one's own misery. The idea is that the child has, for example, frequently heard the sounds of his or her own crying while experiencing unhappiness. Now the crying of another will evoke the associated feelings of the child's own unhappiness. It is assumed without question that there is no intrinsic connection between the distress of the other and the distress of the child. Instead, according to this formulation, the child is upset because his feelings have been arbitrarily linked to signs of the distress in the other.

Rather like Bandura or Kelley and Thibaut, for Maccoby acquisition of social ability as the child grows up involves coming to use bargaining ploys to manage others in ways that induce their cooperation toward one's goals. It is understood that this means children need to learn to speak out of both sides of their mouths, and this is accepted as the necessary developmental reality. With enough maturity, children gain the skill "to tailor their actions for different audiences, depending on the nature of the social self that they wish to project."[43] And what they wish to project depends on the contingencies, as when a young man wants to project a macho image in discussions with his male friends but appear tender when with his girl friend.[44] Most of the time, Maccoby seems to accept, as Rushton does, the idea that people act altruistically when, and only when, it is in their self-interest to do so—when altruistic actions, rather than aggression, say, are the ways to get what they want. It is the familiar assumption that we can do no better than bring people to moral conduct or unselfishness through enlightened self-interest, but now made perhaps even worse by seeing this basis for morality as not just "social learning" but also as some kind of inexorable given of development.

A good example is Maccoby's discussion of work by Damon.[45] Damon found that children may, in a hypothetical situation, advise equal division of candy with peers, but when actual candy is present want more for themselves, at the expense of the other children in their group. Maccoby analyzes this finding as an illustration that the children haven't learned to postpone gratification, since the child's long-term interests would be better served by seeking less candy now and promoting mutual trust in the group. Justice seems to be understood here as based on the children's coming to calculate that their greater gain really consists in promoting an atmosphere of trust with the other children rather than in how much candy one can have right now. Again, in Maccoby's words, unselfish behavior depends on "weighing future gains against present ones" to determine where one's greater advantages really lie.[46] Yet Maccoby does not seem put off by the cynicism of this formulation.

When all is said and done, Maccoby seems well aware of what it means for children and their parents, say, to have a truly constructive relationship with one another. The irony is that little from the psychology she has presented seems to account for the difference between families that have such a relationship and those that do not. She characterizes life in the kinds of families she admires as follows:

> It was as if parents and children agreed that the table needed to be set, clothes hung up, consideration shown by all family members to one another. . . . The children seemed to carry out their part in family enterprises spontaneously as if they were doing it of their own accord instead of because their parents demanded it. . . . When this sense of mutual sharing exists, bargaining or dominance of one member's objectives over another's becomes less important.[47]

She then goes on to admit that psychology knows little about how to foster what she admires here.

Maccoby understands that what matters is for the family members to be committed to values that are shared, to have a sense of working together toward the same ends. She seems unable, however, to offer much from psychology that will help move families in that direction. And she seems unaware as well of the extent to which the ideas she has elaborated, which keep self-interest as the premise of our conduct toward one another, actually foster the issues of bargaining, dominance, and control, about whose effects on families she seems to have her doubts. The best she seems able to do is point to an extrapsychological factor—religion—as a possible source of shared values for some of the families who behave in this harmonious way that she admires.

How can someone like Maccoby, who is clear about what she believes good family life is like, reach this kind of impasse? The answer may have to do with the fact that even she, who criticizes social learning theory for leaving out developmental forces, tends to accept without questioning the idea that all we can ultimately care about is the satisfaction of our own needs.

This assumption, a fundamental cornerstone for Freud, has continued to be taken for granted not only by Freudian psychoanalytic thinkers but by the vast majority of academic psychologists as well. We have seen how it plays a crucial role in Kelley and Thibaut's understanding of interpersonal relationships being based on balances of individual returns, in Bandura's interpretations of interest in things outside ourselves being caused by their implications for personal rewards or punishments, and in Rushton's conception that "altruistic" behavior is carried out in the self-interests of the performer. Even thinkers like the Hogan group and Baumrind, who are attempting to counter individualism, presume that what ultimately motivates us are needs—whether for positive attention, predictability, and dominance or just to survive and flourish—for ourselves.

A few academic psychologists, analogously to the more clinically oriented thinkers who disagreed with Freud, believe that there can be matters of direct concern to us other than those connected to gratifying our own needs. In Kohlberg's view, for example, a person at the higher stages of moral development is regarded as fully committed to principles. But what is apparently most important for Kohlberg is that the principles be the person's own, be expressive of the self. What seems to happen in academic psychology when (occasionally) people are not viewed as completely egoistic is that, just as with the neo-Freudians and with Maslow and Rogers, self-realization becomes the highest good. It is not only the more clinical parts of psychology that lend support to selfishness.

Notes

1. Coles, 1980, p. 137.
2. Coles, 1980, pp. 135–136.
3. See, for example, Roszak, 1978.
4. Roszak, 1978, p. 316.
5. Roszak, 1978, p. 317.
6. Aronson, 1980, p. xiv.
7. See Bar-Tal, 1976; Hornstein, 1976; Mussen and Eisenberg-Berg, 1977; Wispé, 1978; Staub, 1978, 1979; Rushton, 1980; and Rushton and Sorrentino, 1981, for recent reviews.
8. Wispé, 1978, p. 318.
9. White, 1980.
10. Dawes, 1980, p. 191.
11. See, for example, Kelley and Thibaut, 1978.
12. Kelley and Thibaut, 1978, pp. 22–23, and p. 324.
13. Kelley and Thibaut, 1978, p. 22.
14. Kelley and Thibaut, 1978, p. 179.
15. Kelley and Thibaut, 1978, p. 319.
16. Staub, 1978, p. 374.
17. Staub, 1978, p. 414.
18. Rusbult, 1980, p. 175.
19. Levinger, 1980, p. 536.

20. Gottman, Markman, and Notarius, 1977.

21. Gottman, Markman, and Notarius, 1977, p. 474.

22. See, for example, Bandura, 1977.

23. Bandura, 1977, p. 106.

24. Bandura, 1977, p. 152.

25. Bandura, 1977, p. 209.

26. Rushton, 1980.

27. Eisenberg-Berg and Geisheker, 1979.

28. Simonton, 1980, p. 982.

29. See, for example, Kohlberg, 1976.

30. Kohlberg, 1976, p. 33.

31. For example, Kohlberg, 1976, p. 35.

32. Kohlberg, 1976, p. 48.

33. Oldenquist, 1979.

34. Kohlberg, 1978.

35. Simpson, 1976.

36. Hogan, Johnson, and Emler, 1978.

37. Baumrind, 1978.

38. Baumrind, 1978, p. 64.

39. Maccoby, 1980.

40. White, 1959.

41. Maccoby, 1980, p. 74.

42. See, for example, Aronfreed, 1970.

43. Maccoby, 1980, p. 292.

44. Maccoby, 1980, p. 269.

45. Damon, 1977.

46. Maccoby, 1980, p. 360.

47. Maccoby, 1980, p. 391.

10

Must Psychology Promote Selfishness? The Assumption of Egoism

We have seen in earlier chapters how selfishness is promoted by urging realization and expression of the self. Those who have done this urging—particularly Horney, Fromm, Maslow, and Rogers—have held that if people are really actualizing themselves, they will in fact be good to one another. But, as we have discussed, this cannot keep the encouragement to focus on oneself and one's own development from supporting concern for self in contrast to concern for others. Far as it was from their intention, these psychologists inevitably promote selfishness by asking us to realize ourselves, to love ourselves, to view the environment as a means for our own self-actualizing ends, and to consider whether something will contribute to our own development as the only real criterion for what we should do.

This position of the neo-Freudians and Maslow and Rogers has been opposed by a sizable number of other psychologists. People are not, in their opinion, naturally so good that all that is needed is to remove constraints and allow individuals freely to actualize themselves. This was, of course, the point of view of Freud: we must restrain and sublimate our natural impulses. It is also the position of psychologists otherwise as different from Freud as, for example, Rushton: we must provide models and rewards to lead people to consider the needs and desires of others. A few years ago, Campbell gave voice to the misgivings of many about what was seen as psychologists' widespread opposition to restrictions and inhibition and their encouragement of impulse expression.[1] In view of human beings' natural selfish tendencies, Campbell urged psychologists to respect the wisdom of evolved social traditions and recognize the need for cultural controls.

The issue seems to be joined in terms of these two points of view, ones that cut across the boundary between academicians and clinicians. The neo-Freudians, Maslow and Rogers, and like-minded current clinicians believe human nature does not require prescriptions or restraints, or, indeed, any form of external determination: people should seek their own realization. They are supported, at least in part, by a few of the liberal academic psychologists, such as Kohlberg. On the other hand, Freud and the psychoanalysts who remained closer to his tradition, together with large numbers of other academic psychologists—liberals as well as conservatives—regard this view as unrealistic and "tender-minded." We must, they say, be "tough-minded" and recognize that people are ultimately out for their own good; society has to supply rewards and punishments to bring about appropriate consideration of the needs and desires of others.

But this second position, we submit, rather than serving as an effective counterforce to the encouragement of selfishness by the first, itself sanctions selfishness in another way. If all that we can ultimately care about is ourselves and the satisfaction of our needs, then why should we ever act in ways other than what is ultimately in our own interests? The tough-minded position seems inevitably to foster cynicism and to imply that all that it is rational for us to do is to try, in the terms of Kelley and Thibaut, to maximize our "balance of returns."

To be sure, this position calls for taking into account the reactions of others to our behavior and considering our own evaluations of ourselves. As to the first, it will benefit us in the long run to show some consideration of other people's needs and desires, since it is only then that they will show consideration of what we want. But note that if one really takes the tough-minded position seriously, it is only when it is in our self-interest—and insofar as it is in our self-interest—that consideration for others makes any sense. To the extent that we can get away with seeking our own advantage, this becomes what it is obviously appropriate for us to do.

Again, we may suffer from our consciences if we act with too flagrant a disregard of moral principles. Our consciences find little real support either, however, in the tough-minded position. If motivation is all ultimately egoistic, then conscience cannot originate within ourselves. What internal standards we have must then be imposed on us from the outside. Accordingly, Freud's superego represents an internalization of external authorities; Bandura's and Rushton's internal standards derive from the modeling and the rewards and punishments of such authorities. But if what sometimes keeps us from concentrating too much on our own self-interest is merely an external imposition, would we not be well advised to minimize it as best we can? As we said earlier with respect to Freud, the implication seems to be that we would each be better off if we could be less good.

The tough-minded point of view itself, then, pushes for selfishness. Some consideration for others is called for in that this will lead to long-term gains for ourselves, and we must somehow reckon with our consciences. But at best what the tough-minded position promotes is acting on the basis of enlightened rather than immediate self-interest. According to psychologists as disparate as Freud, Maccoby, and Kelley and Thibaut, not to act to ultimately further one's own good is simply irrational.

If the tender-minded position calls on us to put the development and realization of the self above all else, and the tough-minded one implies that looking toward our own self-interest is all that can make any sense, then is psychology inevitably doomed to the promotion of selfishness? Are we caught between the Scylla of self-love and the Charybdis of cynicism? Or are, perhaps, both views mistaken? May the tender-minded be wrong that what is always best for people is to seek self-actualization, and may the tough-minded also be wrong that all motivation is fundamentally egoistic? This chapter will be devoted to a consideration of the assumption that all motivation has an egoistic base, and Chapter 11 will consider what is actually best for people and most therapeutic.

Isn't Egoism the Only Possibility?

It is often thought that motivation must be, at bottom, egoistic. This has long been a topic of philosophical concern.[2] Would we ever do something for another person if we didn't think it would, ultimately, gratify ourselves? Would the idea that an action was right ever lead us to carry it out if we didn't expect to feel better for doing so?

To be motivated to do something without expecting to satisfy our own wish or desire in the process may indeed be a contradiction in terms. What we are motivated to do is necessarily directed at the satisfaction of our own wants. This in itself, however, does not imply that motivation must ultimately be egoistic. That would seem to depend on what it is that we do want, on what our motives are. If they are necessarily always self-directed, if our ultimate motives must (like hunger, thirst, or relief from pain) always be concerned with states of ourselves, then non-egoistic motivation is not possible. But the fact that what motivates us must be our own desires or wishes carries as yet no implications whatsoever about the content of those desires or wishes. They might well be directed outward— to other people, to furthering values like justice—and still be our own.

The argument that motivation must ultimately be egoistic goes deeper, however. When our wants or desires are satisfied, we tend toward happiness. Inevitably we expect to have positive feelings (or at least a diminution of negative ones) upon the attainment of what we wish for. It is these feelings, so the argument goes, that are really the bases for our motivated actions. Whatever our wishes, we are ultimately motivated by the happiness or pleasure we expect to derive from their satisfaction. Even if you may genuinely wish to help someone, for example, the ultimate basis for your motivation is the pleasure you expect to derive from doing so.

But the only type of egoism that this argument is capable of supporting is an egoism of a very trivial kind. That our actions tend to promote favorable hedonic outcomes does not really mean much more than that they tend to promote the satisfaction of our own wants. Critically important in either case is *what* it is that we want or that provides us with good feelings. Suppose that you are motivated to help someone, and that it makes you happy to do so. When this is the case because you expect to gain some benefits in return or because you will then be in a position of superiority, then your motivation is truly egoistic. But the situation would seem very different if the other person's relief from distress or the other person's happiness is itself what you want to achieve and what would make you happy. Only in the most trivial sense (what you are ultimately attaining in either case is your own happiness) could you be said to be just as egoistic in the second case as in the first. You would clearly be recognized as much less egoistic if your happiness were a direct result of the other person's happiness than if it derived from expected rewards for yourself.

A good part of the widespread cynicism about motivation may derive from a confusion between the trivial and the nontrivial senses of egoism. People often seem to become convinced of the necessity of egoism in what is actually the trivial sense, without noticing this triviality, and then believe that the necessity of a nontrivial egoism has been established. Thus, one may recognize that we expect to attain satisfaction or pleasure or happiness from our motivated actions, become convinced that we are always ultimately motivated toward such feelings, and go on to believe that therefore all that ultimately matters to us is our own satisfaction and that we can never have direct concern for another person or for anything external to us. Our satisfaction and happiness themselves, however, depend on what happens that we care about. We are satisfied or pleased if we attain what we (really) want; we are made happy if something that we (really) wish for comes to pass. Nothing has been shown about what it is that our happiness and satisfaction rest upon, or, thusly, what it is that actually matters to us. This unknown could still be anything at all, external as well as internal to ourselves.

Indeed, the reason for the apparent persuasiveness of the argument that we are always motivated toward our own satisfaction or happiness is that these feelings can be consequences of attaining *anything* we might wish for, including such things as the happiness of another person. It is thus paradoxical to turn around and try to use this argument to demonstrate that an event that, so far as has yet been shown, might cause our happiness—such as the happiness of someone else—cannot matter to us. It is only a very trivial kind of egoism, then, that is supported by the argument that we are always ultimately motivated toward our own satisfaction or pleasure. For any serious kind of egoism the argument collapses, because being directed toward our own satisfaction or happiness in no way precludes these feelings from depending crucially on events external to ourselves.

Let us now return to the psychological theories that assume that all motivation is fundamentally egoistic. It is important to realize that the sense in which they assume this is not just the trivial sense, not just the sense in which one might legitimately argue that all motivation ultimately must be egoistic. Freud is not simply saying that we are always seeking our own satisfaction or pleasure. According to his theory, all that can ultimately affect our satisfaction or pleasure is the fate of our own internal needs. As we saw in Chapter 2, the theory does not permit the existence of concern for anything outside ourselves except as it derives from these internal needs.

Such psychologists as Kelley and Thibaut, Bandura, and Rushton are similarly not just claiming that at the bottom of motivation will always be found states of oneself, such as pleasure or positive affect or "being reinforced." Rather, they are claiming that these states always depend on one's own outcomes. That is, one will not feel pleasure about or be reinforced by events—for example, someone else's good fortune—except insofar as these events have implications, however indirect, for what happens to oneself. Recall Bandura's interpretation of reactions to a friend's misfortune. We are sorry when our friend suffers, in Bandura's scheme of things, because it makes us realize that such adversities could also befall us and, further, that our friend is now less likely to treat us well. Such a formulation excludes the possibility that we might directly care about our friend's distress apart from any further implications for ourselves.

Some psychologists in recent years have urged recognition of the existence of empathy or sympathy.[3] But, with a few possible exceptions,[4] even psychologists who do recognize these phenomena seem to assume that there cannot be any direct connection between one's feelings and what happens to anyone other than oneself. We have seen how, in Aronfreed's and Maccoby's discussions of empathy, our sorrow also, as with Bandura, is not caused directly by seeing that a friend is distressed. When a friend's misfortune saddens us, in Aronfreed's or Maccoby's view—as in that of most who write on empathy—this is because of an arbitrary linkage between the friend's feelings and our own. Signs of distress, such as crying, have become associated with our own distress from previous occasions on which we were unhappy and made those signs ourselves. Now when they are created by a friend, they still evoke the associated feelings. Or the friend may have been together with us at times when things happened that upset each of us, thus making the friend's distress a conditioned stimulus for our own. Our feelings and the misfortunes of our friend are connected simply because of the happenstance of earlier co-occurrences. Without that happenstance, our friend's distress would not move us.

These various psychological theories, whatever their differences, thus all presume that only when there are implications for, or prior linkages with, what happens to ourselves, can we ever be affected by what happens to anyone else. This is egoism of a nontrivial kind, and it cannot be supported by the kinds of arguments that we have been considering. However, that such egoism cannot be supported by these arguments does not, of course, mean it is false. That motivation might not have to be ultimately egoistic does not yet show that it is not. The psychological theories must be evaluated on their own merits. We turn next to a consideration of how these theories developed and what basis there may be for believing them.

Psychological Theories of Motivation, Past and Present

Psychological theories of motivation are, almost without exception, fundamentally egoistic, in a nontrivial manner. We will argue that this is the case for reasons that are historical rather than substantive. The striving, seeking, purposive, goal-directed character of so much of our activity presented a difficult problem for attempts at scientific explanation of behavior. Whence came our ends, our aims? To presume them innate seemed mysterious, metaphysical. Yet they could not be ignored. The idea that our motives are a function of our needs seemed, as we will delineate, to provide a satisfactory scientific solution to the problem; once this was clear, psychologists seldom considered further possibilities.

There was little consideration of motivational concepts at all in early academic psychology—the period of the end of the nineteenth and beginning of the twentieth centuries. They did not play much of a role in analyses of consciousness as engaged in by Wundt and Titchener or in the sort of thinking about animal behavior and learning that grew out of the work of Pavlov. But this was soon felt to be a crucial lack. As William McDougall wrote, psychology without purposes or motives "was like the playing of 'Hamlet' with the Prince of Denmark left out, or like describing steam-engines while ignoring the fact of the presence and fundamental role of the fire or other source of heat."[5]

The behavior of a living organism, McDougall pointed out, is fundamentally different from the mechanical movements of, for example, a billiard ball.[6] The ball does not move unless some sort of force is applied to it; if pushed, it moves in that direction until it has no more momentum or until a new path is determined by some resistance. Living things, however, do not move just as external forces dictate; they can direct their own behavior, pursue their own ends. A guinea pig taken out of its nest does not remain stationary but runs back toward its hole; if it meets any obstacles, it tries to get around them. It seems clear that the guinea pig's behavior is purposive, that it is striving toward the goal of returning to its nest.

McDougall believed[7] that purposive action was action governed in some way by prevision—sometimes clear and sometimes cloudy—of what was yet to happen, of the goal to be attained. What accounted for such action, he thought, was instinct. Human beings, like other mammals, have innate, goal-directed tendencies to care for their young, to fight against obstruction, to seek food, to escape danger, to mate, and so on. McDougall's list of instincts also included curiosity, avoidance or repulsion, gregariousness, self-assertion, submission, acquisitiveness, construction, and appeal for aid and comfort in distress; other psychologists developed other lists.

This attempt to provide what seemed to be missing from psychology through the concept of instinct proved short lived. Anthropologists were documenting the extreme diversity of behaviors in different cultures; Watson and other psychologists were arguing for the power of the environment and learning in determining human behavior. Further, positing an instinct for one or another kind of purposive behavior didn't seem to explain it. Even worse, the notion of innate ends or goals seemed metaphysical; it seemed to imply a return to a forsaken philosophy of inborn ideas.[8]

However, while few psychologists believed for long that McDougall's solution was tenable, it was difficult to avoid the recognition that there was indeed a problem. Freud's work began to receive increased attention around this time, making it all the more impossible to ignore the question of motivation. Increasing numbers of thinkers came to feel that if psychology was going to provide an explanation of what animals and people did, it would have to recognize and take into account some sort of internal springs of action—instincts or no.

In 1918, Woodworth enunciated an influential formulation of the problem. It was not enough, he said, to consider the issue of mechanism, of how we do something. To explain an activity, an account is also needed of why we do it, what induces us to do it. What sets the activity in motion, what instigates it, what arouses us to it? That too needs explanation, Woodworth wrote; he called this the problem of *drive*. Sometimes, as in simple reflexes, when behavior is merely a result of an external stimulus, there is little difficulty in accounting for why the behavior occurs. But with more complex behaviors we are forced to recognize the existence of internal drives. Consider, for example, a hunting dog pursuing its prey. It is not simply responding to external stimuli; if so, it would stop as soon as it lost the trail, or simply go back at that point. Instead it explores, seemingly trying to find the trail again. "This seeking, not being evoked by any external stimulus (but rather by the absence of an external stimulus), must be driven by some internal force."[9]

Not long after Woodworth had drawn this distinction between a mechanism for an activity and a drive that serves as an instigator or energizer, an acceptable scientific solution to the problem of motivation seemed at hand. Drives, it was thought, could be identified with bodily conditions corresponding to biological needs of the organism. These physical conditions would be what excites the organism to motivated activity—just as had earlier been proposed by Freud. (Freud's basic motivational forces—*Triebe* in the German in which he wrote—are usually translated as "instincts," but should have been translated as "drives" had that term been in use by psychologists then as it came to be later.) As we described in Chapter 3, the conception that motivated behavior results from bodily conditions corresponding to states of need was in close accord with the thinking of biologists and physiologists under the influence of Darwin. It viewed behavior in its functional role of enabling adaptation and survival, and it followed the general scientific consensus of the period that the normally quiescent organism was goaded into activity by excitation. Further, there was already evidence that in states of strong excitement, such as fear or rage, physiological changes take place that increase the availability of energy to the organism.[10] Evidence also began to accrue that animals' activity levels were closely associated with states of biological need.[11]

The problem of motivation thus seemed soluble in terms of drives associated with biological needs of the organism. Activities that could not be accounted for in terms of external stimulation could be explained by the internal conditions represented by these drives. The appropriateness and goal-directedness of complex behaviors—that aspect of these behaviors for which McDougall was trying to account in his problematic notion of prevision—did not have to be regarded as having any innate basis whatsoever. All that had to be assumed as innate, and what seemed highly likely to have evolved on the basis of natural selection, was a tendency to increased activity with increased need, along with some simple learning mechanism that led the organism to repeat actions that resulted in satisfaction. Specific goal-directed behaviors could then be learned on the basis of experience. A young organism that was hungry, thirsty, or cold was expected to engage in increased activity of varying sorts. Such activity that would satisfy its need—for example, searching in places where food might be found and eating it—would be strengthened or reinforced and likely to occur again under similar conditions in the future. In this way, the organism, "driven" by biological needs, would learn to engage in appropriate, adjustive, goal-directed behavior.

Most academic psychologists thus came to accept the identification of internal motivating forces with biological needs of the organism. Dashiell heralded what soon became the view of the vast majority when in 1928 he wrote:

> The primary drives to persistent forms of animal and human conduct are tissue-conditions within the organism giving rise to stimulations exciting the organism to overt activity. A man's interests and desires may become ever so elaborate, refined, socialized, sublimated, idealistic; but the raw basis from which they are developed is found in the phenomena of living matter.[12]

There was for a time broad agreement that basic biological needs represented the fundamental building blocks of motivated behavior—that these needs were the "primary drives" to activity. Some researchers[13] assumed there were a number of drives corresponding to different bodily needs; others[14] thought there was a single, general drive to which all the needs could contribute. Some investigators[15] believed that drive consisted of specific forms of local stimulation such as stomach contractions and dryness of the mouth; others[16] thought it represented a more central state. But almost all academic psychologists agreed that, except for simple responses resulting directly from external stimulation, it was ultimately basic biological needs that led the organism to activity. As we noted, this was also how Freud had proposed to account for motivation.

According to the original drive theories, then, those of the academicians as well as Freud's own, all behavior that is motivated, purposive, goal directed, all but perhaps the most simple activity, is instigated by bodily states of need or something associated with such need. What is sought or liked, what is rewarding or reinforcing, is whatever reduces bodily states of need or has been associated with such reduction. This position—as we have already seen in relation to Freud—inevitably implies that motivation is necessarily egoistic. All our purposeful activity is assumed to be ultimately directed at the reduction of needs or drives of one's own. The external environment has no motivational relevance for our behavior except insofar as it provides for or interferes with the satisfaction of our own needs.

Any motivation related to other people is, in such a theory, necessarily derivative from needs for oneself. Freud viewed positive feelings toward others usually as based upon sexual desires, homosexual if not heterosexual; sometimes he also saw them as derivative from rivalrous hostility, transformed into its opposite. The early academic drive theorists similarly took it for granted that any kind of social motivation could not simply be direct, but had to be derived from something else. Thus, it was generally held that children acquire some kind of motivation to please others, to gain their approval, because of the children's dependence on their caretakers for satisfaction of their biological needs. Anything one did in relation to another person had to be ultimately directed at one's own need satisfaction. Again, for both Freud and the academicians, all moral aspirations had to be indirect attempts at fulfilling one's own needs. The usual explanation of moral behavior by those academic theorists who concerned themselves with it was much the same as Freud's: both held it generally to be fear of punishment—first from one's parents and other authorities, later also from oneself—that motivated efforts toward the good.

Few psychologists today adhere to the original drive theories. We have considered in earlier chapters some of the dissonant phenomena that led to the changes. Already Freud had been bothered by the realization that sexual excitation was itself pleasurable quite apart from ultimate gratification, but had never really solved the problems to which this gave rise. Sheffield and his co-workers showed that even organisms as lowly as the male rat found copulation without ejaculation rewarding.[17] And Fisher[18] showed that when male rats have copulated to the point of apparent loss of sexual interest, such interest could be restored simply by the availability of a new potential mate—a finding since replicated in a number of other species as well.[19]

That eating can readily be induced in the absence of actual hunger by the presentation of highly appetizing foods could, of course, not long go unrecognized either, especially in America with its plethora of sweets and over-weight people. It is also clear that eating—and the behavior leading to it of acquiring something appetizing to eat—is not dependent upon the consumption of substances providing actual nourishment. Even rats work for saccharine,[20] and do so despite having just been fed.[21]

Yet another problem for the drive theories was that the early indications[22] of relationships between activity levels and states of biological need failed to fulfill their promise. The idea that these needs instigate general activity was not substantiated after all. There were alternative explanations for a number of the original findings, and there were many later investigations in which no general increase in activity level with increased deprivation was to be found.[23]

Moreover, there seemed to be other motivations that had nothing to do with biological needs. Hartmann, Piaget, and others raised the question of accounting for all the lively motor and cognitive activities of human infants. Such activities did indeed serve to develop abilities that could be used in bodily need satisfaction, but were quite incapable of serving this function when they first began and furthermore tended to occur just when these needs were in abeyance. Butler[24] and Harlow and collaborators[25] presented evidence that looking through a window or creating stimulus changes could per se be rewarding to monkeys. Montgomery[26] and others demonstrated that even rats would repeat behaviors that simply allowed them to explore, without leading to anything that could satisfy a biological need. Bexton, Heron, and Scott[27] found that people's mental functions deteriorated and that they became restless and uncomfortable when kept for long under conditions of minimally changing, homogeneous environmental stimulation—a situation of "sensory deprivation," not of any form of deprivation that seemed to be related to biological need.

Harlow and Zimmermann showed that the attachment of infant rhesus monkeys to their mothers was not a function of their mothers' provision for their biological needs.[28] Recall that such infant monkeys clung to and seemed comforted by an artificial mother surrogate whose body was covered with terry cloth, while this was not the case for a wire-mesh surrogate, even though the latter provided food. And Suomi, Harlow and Domek went on to demonstrate that rhesus monkeys reared without any mothers but in the company of other young monkeys developed extremely strong attachments to one another despite the lack of evident basis in biological need satisfaction.[29]

In the face of data like these, a great many psychologists gave up the view that biological needs such as hunger, thirst, and sex are at the base of all motivation. But the changes that have been made consist mostly in broadening the concept of needs and adding further ones. The assumption that all motivated behavior is a function of one's own needs—together with its egoistic implications—has seldom been reconsidered. Before we consider what seems wrong with this assumption, let us first look at some of the more recent developments in psychological thinking about motivation. We will see that what is striven for or rewarding, according to these accounts, is still almost always assumed to be ultimately the satisfaction of one's own needs.

The evidence on human infant motor and cognitive activity, animal curiosity and exploration, and the effects of restricted stimulation has suggested to many psychologists that organisms need and strive to attain stimulus novelty, variation, and change, or certain levels of physiological arousal that are a function of such factors.[30] Under these conceptions it is no longer only bodily tissue conditions of immediate significance to the survival of the individual or of the species that can provide a basis for motivated behavior. But what is added are still needs of the organism, analogous to, albeit different from, such needs as hunger, thirst, and sex. To act under a need for stimulus variation or novelty or for certain levels of arousal is still to act toward the satisfaction of one's own needs.

Other psychologists have dealt with the same kinds of data in somewhat broader terms. We have already described in Chapter 4 the proposals of motivation for competence[31] and primary energies of the ego.[32] Again under these conceptions, behavior is still regarded as directed toward aspects of oneself. Needs of a psychological rather than physical sort—for competence and for development—are proposed, but the assumption continues that behavior serves the interests of one's own needs. Indeed, something very akin to competence and development needs is today widely considered to be a major source of motivation for behavior that does not appear to be in the service of biological needs. De Charms[33] sees such actions as a function of our striving to be causal agents, to be the locus of causation, or the origin, of our behavior. Deci[34] closely follows White but adds a need for self-determination to that for competence. These concepts clearly are closely related as well to Maslow's and Rogers' ideas regarding self-actualization.

It seems to us that there is a certain irony in the fact that such motives as competence, self-determination, or causing one's own behavior are so often now called upon to explain what is even explicitly called "intrinsic motivation." Use of this phrase suggests recognition of the idea that some kinds of behavior may not be directed at extrinsic goals, that what one undertakes need not always be instrumental, carried out "in order to" achieve something else.[35] But de Charms accounts for "intrinsically motivated behavior" in terms of striving for personal causation.[36] The satisfaction we obtain is that of accomplishing something by our own efforts—the knowledge of our own effectiveness. And according to Deci: "Intrinsically motivated behaviors are behaviors which a person engages in to feel competent and self-determining."[37] Such behaviors are said to be "motivated by a person's need for feeling competent and self-determining in dealing with his environment."[38] It could hardly be made more clear that the relevance of the external environment continues to be understood as depending entirely on its relation to the needs that we have for ourselves.

What other people mean to us, in current views, again quite explicitly continues to depend on our own needs. Where earlier academic psychologists saw desires such as wanting to be with others and to gain their approval as developing from children's dependence on their caretakers for satisfying physical needs, and Freud saw them as based upon sex, psychologists now include other sources of motivation for these social tendencies. But the current views still tend to derive social tendencies from needs people have for themselves. For example, we described in Chapter 9 how Maccoby explains infant attachment as resulting not only from the provision of comfort by the caretaker when the child is distressed but also from the aid which the caretaker gives the child in mastering the environment.[39] According to Maccoby, it is not only the caretaker's ministering to biological needs that accounts for the development of attachment but the caretaker's ministering to the child's needs for mastery or competence as well. Mastery and competence, however, are still needs for the self: the goal is the child's own effectiveness, power, being in control.

Veroff and Veroff have another way of accounting for attachment that similarly derives from more than the child's physical needs but still from the child's own needs.[40] The growing infant, with ever-increasing cognitive skills, is highly subject, in their view, to cognitive distress from overstimulation, and the familiar adult provides a kind of secure anchor, which can alleviate such distress. What is seen as underlying attachment by the Veroffs is the need for avoiding overstimulation. (We might note that while excited infants certainly can be made more calm and subdued in their mothers' arms, calm infants also can break out in excited delight when, for example, their mothers appear in the morning or after a nap.) A similar presumption of needs for the self underlying motivation with regard to others can be seen in the way the Veroffs discuss affiliation with one's peers. Drawing partly on Schachter's[41] finding that many people prefer to be with others when in situations of anxiety, they hold that what triggers joining other people like oneself is uncertainty. Fundamental to affiliation in their view is a need for approval from others similar to oneself—a need to receive assurance of one's own acceptability.

The lengths to which psychologists can go in attributing behavior toward others to self-directed needs may be illustrated by a moving biographical vignette McClelland[42] presents of his mother-in-law. He offers a marvelous and deeply appreciative description of a very strong, warm, and impressive woman. She had no thoughts of a career, although she taught kindergarten for a time, and was much involved in attempts to improve race relations and oppose war. She was highly active in counseling and giving emotional support to her large family. When her children were grown, she contributed to the formation of a marriage council in Philadelphia and provided counseling to many young couples as well as to other troubled young people. Even in her eighties, she wrote that teenagers " 'just keep calling me up and telling me they want to come over and talk.' "[43] A devout Quaker, she firmly believed that the resources and strength of which she gave so generously came to her directly from God.

What is startling is that these active, energetic efforts that his mother-in-law made toward helping others are attributed by McClelland to the need for power. His aim is to show that this need doesn't necessarily express itself in the competitive, manipulative domination of one person over others with which it is largely associated in Western thinking. According to McClelland, in "the most advanced stage of expressing the power drive . . . the self drops out as a source of power and a person sees himself as an instrument of a higher authority which moes him to try to influence or serve others."[44] But is it a need to feel strong, as McClelland defines the need for power, that underlies in any form these activities of his mother-in-law? Must we assume that she really undertook them for the sake of feelings about herself or to satisfy needs of her own?

The assumption that motivation is ultimately based on self-directed needs has been so broadly taken for granted that it has become almost a tautology. Even the tender-minded have not escaped it. Despite the potential problems of inconsistency with their stress on genuine, other-directed concern, the neo-Freudians derive our behavior with regard to others from needs of our own for security or relatedness. And Maslow and Rogers—again wanting genuine concern for others—paradoxically view what they describe as our natural, spontaneous caring and helpfulness as a derivative of the need to actualize ourselves.

To be sure, Maslow himself felt strongly that people were not always behaving instrumentally—doing something to gratify needs. They could be metamotivated, as when admiring one's grandchild or a landscape. But in that case one was not striving for anything, just passively being: appreciating, yielding. Not to be striving to satisfy one's needs seems to mean not to be striving or motivated at all.

In sum, almost all psychologists for the past half century have tended to regard motivation as based upon a person's needs. This outlook emerged from the conviction that there had to be something inside the organism to account for purposive, goal-directed behavior. Innate purposes or goals seemed mysterious and metaphysical; an explanation in terms of internal bodily conditions produced by biological needs seemed to be the answer. Activity could be instigated by these conditions and their cessation would provide rewards; the organism could learn to repeat the behaviors that led to satisfaction of its needs. No mysterious inborn purposes or goals had to be called upon, and the account was firmly in line with evolutionary thinking. Although cases of motivated activity then came to psychologists' attention that did not appear to depend on biological needs, further kinds of needs were postulated to account for these. The problem of what leads to purposive striving seemed to have been solved, and the possibility that we could be motivated by anything other than our needs was almost entirely ignored.

Motivation Not Based on Needs

The aforementioned possibility, however, is a very real one. There is good reason to believe that purposive behavior does not always depend on needs. Rather, such behavior, as proposed several decades ago by Leeper[45] and Young,[46] often seems to be a consequence of the affective reactions that many environmental stimuli seem to evoke in their own right. We may be born with predispositions to respond positively or negatively to certain kinds of stimulation, and motivation may frequently be based on such reactions quite apart from our needs. Actually, this is already suggested by findings that appetizing foods often will be obtained and consumed although people are not really hungry and that rats will press a bar that leads to their obtaining saccharine immediately after they have been fed. The problems such observations pose for the traditional views of motivation strongly resist the solution of merely adding further needs.

There is solid experimental evidence that animals are attracted by and willing to work for a great diversity of sensory stimulation. Interpretation of much of this evidence seems highly forced, if not impossible, in terms of need satisfaction or association with need satisfaction.[47] Rats have pressed levers when increases in illumination and also sometimes when decreases in illumination were the reward. Deer mice given two levers, one leading to an increase in illumination and the other to a decrease, even maintained alternating periods of light and darkness much as they would normally experience day and night. If certain kinds of stimulation are, as they seem to be, directly rewarding to lower animals without providing or having provided satisfaction for their needs, is it not likely that this is the case with human beings as well? Predispositions to positive or negative reactions to stimuli can serve as the basis for all sorts of adaptive learning (as we will expand on later). Given that the action patterns of humans tend to be far less fixed than those of lower organisms, and our adaptation far more dependent on learning, it actually would seem all the more likely that such predispositions should have evolved in humankind.

Although unlearned predispositions to positive or negative reactions may exist, can they provide a basis for motivation? What about the energizing of behavior? Aren't needs, in contrast to mere affective reactions, required in order to provide the energy for activity—to give it drive, to get it going? Although this is indeed (in spite of the efforts of Tomkins[48]) the traditional conception, needs seem to have no advantage over affective reactions here. First of all, needs clearly do not literally provide the energy for behavior in a physical sense. A need for food means that there is less, not more, physical energy available to the organism. What is usually meant in speaking of needs as energizing behavior is rather that they "arouse" the organism, perhaps "releasing" energy, and thereby lead to activity. We have already seen that the early evidence that seemed to suggest that needs instigate general activity has not held up. Animals frequently do not engage in greater amounts of overall activity when they are more deprived.[49] On the other hand, needs do, of course, "activate" particular behaviors in particular situations. An animal that has been provided with food pellets when it presses a bar, for example, is likely to press the bar when it is hungry. But this kind of activation can also be provided in the absence of need by stimuli to which the animal is attracted—or the expectation of such stimuli—as the learning of behaviors to obtain candy by humans who are not hungry and to get saccharine by well-fed rats makes evident. The energizing of activity thus does not seem to require that we postulate needs.

In the previous section, we have seen that it was originally thought necessary to introduce motivational concepts into psychology because environmental factors seemed clearly insufficient to explain purposive, goal-directed behavior. Recall McDougall's description of how the guinea pig when taken out of its hole, unlike a billiard ball, does not remain immobilized in the absence of external forces, but runs back to its nest, circumventing obstacles as it goes. Woodworth noted how the hunting dog's seeking for its prey, "not being evoked by any external stimulus (but rather the absence of an external stimulus), must be driven by some internal force." Such behaviors could not be explained simply in terms of what was outside the organism; they had to have a determinant within. It indeed does seem that an internal determinant is called for here, that there must be something like a desire, a want, a motive, or perhaps, as some would put it, some kind of a reaction tendency. There is no requirement, however, that this internal determinant be a need or derive from a need.

Why shouldn't a motive, wish, or reaction tendency be directly related to the positive or negative effects of situations in themselves (or their cognitive representations)? If a state of affairs is evaluated negatively or produces negative affect—as seems to be the case for the guinea pig when it is removed from its nest—that in itself, apart from a need, could be sufficient to make the animal want to change that situation. In other terminology, it could be sufficient to strengthen such reaction tendencies that would lead to change. There seems no necessity to call upon needs in accounting for the guinea pig's behaving in a way it has learned will bring it back to its home. Similarly, if we like or positively appraise an existing situation, that could be sufficient to make us desire to maintain it or to strengthen reaction tendencies that promote its maintenance. We do not seem to have to call upon needs to explain a child's wanting to keep on playing an exciting game and resisting efforts to get him or her to stop and do something less appealing, like go to supper. In the same manner, to think of, or represent to ourselves, a potential state of affairs that we evaluate positively or negatively, could well be sufficient to lead to our wanting, respectively, to bring that state of affairs about or to avoid it or to the strengthening of reaction tendencies that would have these consequences. Needs, or something derived from needs, are simply not the only possible internal motivational determinants that can operate. Motivation can be based on affective reactions just as well as on needs.

Apart from considerations of energy and internal determinants, what was probably particularly important in making needs seem necessary for motivation was their presumed evolutionary role. Insofar as purposive behavior is a function of animals' needs, insofar as what they seek or like, or find rewarding or reinforcing, is what satisfies their needs or has been associated with such satisfaction, motivational processes could be understood on the basis of natural selection. An animal that failed to meet its needs would not survive and reproduce. However, as we mentioned earlier, evolution does not in fact favor the development only of motivation related to the organism's own needs. We wish to make several points here.

First of all, the evolutionary function of behavior should not be confused with its current cause. Although presumably rats' liking for a sweet taste has served the function of contributing to the satisfaction of their need for food, with resulting benefits for survival, it is not this need that motivates a rat that has just been fed to press a lever for saccharine. Such a rat is currently not in need of food, and saccharine would not serve this need if it were. Predispositions to be positively affected by certain kinds of stimulation, and negatively affected by other kinds, are just as likely to have evolved on the basis of natural selection as predispositions to be motivated by current needs. Infant monkeys' liking for soft, furry substances plays an obvious evolutionary role in keeping them in the vicinity of their mothers.[50] The rewarding effects of stimulus change and novelty would similarly seem easy to understand as the result of unlearned predispositions that would be adaptive in most expectable environments, as in the case of animals foraging for food with greater success in locations not yet depleted.

Of particular importance to us is the likelihood that natural selection promoted the evolution of certain unlearned bases of concern for others, of some innate tendencies to be responsive to their outcomes as well as one's own.[51] It is not only predispositions likely to contribute to the survival of the individual that should be expected on the basis of natural selection. Rather, as noted earlier, natural selection is conducive to the development of tendencies that will contribute to the perpetuation of an individual's genes. A mother's looking out for the welfare of her offspring obviously contributes to the propagation of her own genes. Aid provided by any relative to another can have the same effect. And since someone's being familiar or in one's neighborhood has, in the course of evolution, probably been closely associated with genetic relatedness, concern for others whom one knows could also well have contributed to the perpetuation of the individual's own genes.

Another reason why natural selection would seem likely to have led to the evolution of certain forms of unlearned concern for others is that aid to others often contributes indirectly to the welfare of the individual himself or herself. Most organisms benefit enormously from the groups of which they are members, in terms of the opportunities these provide for protection, obtaining necessities, and learning. Systems of cooperation and of mutual aid exist as well. Current psychological thinking tends to interpret behavior apparently directed towards others' interests as actually motivated by expectations of this kind of indirect benefit for the individual himself or herself. No doubt sometimes this will be the case. But indirect benefits to the individual would also seem to present strong further grounds for natural selection to have led to the evolution of *unlearned* forms of responsiveness to the interests of others. In light of such possibilities as those here considered, perhaps it is not surprising that evidence is beginning to emerge that suggests that empathic concern may be a heritable human characteristic.[52]

There is a great deal of ferment and dispute currently on the "evolution of altruism."[53] Until the past decade, biologists often held that not only individual but also group advantage could play a significant role in natural selection. This notion is now widely doubted. Some current thinkers both in biology and psychology are highly skeptical concerning the degree of self-sacrificial altruism to be expected among human beings toward other than one's closest relatives. But note that these controversies do not affect the points we have just made. Our arguments are in terms of individual, not group, advantage, and the existence of unlearned responsiveness to others' outcomes as well as one's own does not necessarily mean the occurrence of appreciable self-sacrifice. There has never been any doubt that an evolutionary basis exists for at least some innate predispositions toward concern for others. No one has ever denied that natural selection is conducive to caring about offspring or other close relatives. But why, then, should behavior always have to be motivated by one's own needs?

We will close this chapter with a few brief illustrations of what seem exceedingly likely to be unlearned dispositions toward caring about other individuals. One is the almost universal appeal of babies and young children and the way in which almost everyone enjoys their smiles and other signs of pleasure and is disturbed by their crying. The role of such tendencies in motivating behavior that aids others who may carry some of one's own genes and cannot yet care for themselves seems evident. The babies' own reactions to social stimulation fit right in. Already in the first hours of life, a newborn turns its head toward a human face and toward the sound of a human voice.[54] It has been repeatedly shown that the young infant not only takes part in "a dance-like synchrony of movements, facial expressions and vocalizations"[55] but also becomes visibly distressed if the infant's partner becomes unresponsive.[56] As Emde, Gaensbauer, and Harmon have said: "There is little in life more quietly dramatic than a mother's moment of discovery that her baby is beaming at her with sparkling eyes."[57] The extreme difficulties that can attend the care of an infant whose social responsiveness is attenuated are movingly described by Emde, Katz, and Thorpe.[58] In the face of data and considerations like these, doesn't it seem exceedingly probable that human beings have evolved in the direction of affective responsiveness not only to their own internal states but also to specific—and particularly social—stimuli outside themselves? Isn't it likely that such unlearned forms of responsiveness to external events, not just their own needs, serve as a basis for their motivation?

Neither energy requirements, the importance of internal determinants, nor considerations of evolution support the idea that motivation is always a function of our needs. It seems, rather, extremely likely that it is often a function of unlearned predispositions that we have to be affected by various kinds of events outside of as well as internal to ourselves, including, in particular, certain matters having to do with other people and their welfare. The sorts of concern that human beings show for one another do not have to be explained away as derivative from individuals' needs for themselves. Needs do not seem to offer the only available basis for motivation, and the egoistic assumption appears to be wrong.

Notes

1. Campbell, 1975.
2. See, for example, Milo, 1973, for selected philosophical writings.
3. See, for example, Aronfreed, 1970; Krebs, 1975; Wispé, 1978; Batson and Coke, 1981.
4. For example, Hoffman, 1977, 1981.
5. McDougall, 1908, p. 16.
6. McDougall, 1908, p. 20.
7. See, for example, McDougall, 1923, p. 48.
8. This critique was advanced, for example, by Bernard, 1924.
9. Woodworth, 1918, p. 41.
10. Cannon, 1915.
11. Dashiell, 1925; Richter, 1927.
12. Dashiell, 1928, pp. 233–234, italics his.
13. For example, Warden, 1931.
14. For example, Hull, 1943.
15. For example, Cannon, 1932.
16. For example, Morgan, 1943.
17. Sheffield, Wulff, and Backer, 1951.
18. Fisher, 1962.
19. Dewsbury, 1981.
20. Sheffield and Roby, 1950.
21. Carper, 1953.
22. Dashiell, 1925; Richter, 1927.
23. See, for example, Cofer and Appley, 1964, chap. 6; Bolles, 1975, chap. 7.
24. Butler, 1953.
25. Harlow, Harlow, and Meyer, 1950.
26. Montgomery, 1954.
27. Bexton, Heron, and Scott, 1954.
28. Harlow and Zimmermann, 1959.
29. Suomi, Harlow, and Domek, 1970.
30. See Hunt, 1971a, 1971b, and Deci, 1975, for reviews.
31. White, 1959.
32. Hartmann, 1964c.
33. de Charms, 1968.
34. Deci, 1975, 1980; see also note 31.
35. See Koch, 1956.
36. de Charms, 1968.
37. Deci, 1975, p. 61.
38. Deci, 1975, p. 100.
39. Maccoby, 1980.
40. Veroff and Veroff, 1980.
41. Schachter, 1959.
42. McClelland, 1975.
43. Quoted in McClelland, 1975, p. 114.
44. McClelland, 1975, p. 20.
45. Leeper, 1948, 1965.
46. Young, 1952, 1959.
47. See, for example, Hinde, 1970, pp. 594–603.
48. Tomkins, 1962.
49. See, for example, Cofer and Appley, 1964, chap. 6; Bolles, 1975, chap. 7.
50. See Bowlby, 1969.

51. See Ainsworth, Bell, and Stayton, 1974; Hoffman, 1977, 1981.

52. Matthews, Batson, Horn, and Rosenman, 1981.

53. See, for example, Campbell, 1975, 1978; Dawkins, 1976; Wispé and Thompson, 1976; Davies and Krebs, 1978; Wilson, 1978; and Ridley and Dawkins, 1981.

54. Brazelton, 1973.

55. Hofer, 1975, p. 309.

56. Brazelton, Tronick, Adamson, Als, and Wise, 1975; Trevarthen, 1979.

57. Emde, Gaensbauer, and Harmon, 1976, p. 3.

58. Emde, Katz, and Thorpe, 1978.

11

Must Psychology Promote Selfishness? Therapeutic Benefits from Turning Outward

We have been questioning the presumed scientific basis for what turns out to be psychological advocacy of selfishness in one or another form. One consequence of the widespread scientific acceptance enjoyed by the assumption of egoism—an acceptance that Chapter 10 argues is unwarranted—has been support for therapeutic encouragement of clients' learning to concentrate on seeking their own interests. If the scientific basis is lacking for this emphasis, the situation is one in which scientific auspices are accorded to what really is a value position.[1] Especially in view of the scientific case against egoism, alternative therapeutic directions deserve a closer look. They may be more in tune with our real natures.

The range of what psychotherapy has to deal with these days is vast. Among other things, there are interpersonal difficulties that can ramify into symptomatic disturbances such as phobias, obsessions, attacks of anxiety, insomnia, inability to concentrate, impotence, or frigidity. And there are complaints that are harder to define, such as being empty, bored, dissatisfied, without zest, cast adrift, the sense that life is meaningless, that nothing is worthwhile. If anything, the historical trend seems to be away from the more definable symptoms and toward the latter kind of "existential sickness"—a sense of meaninglessness and anomie.[2] Ironically, this growing complaint of meaninglessness with which therapists are confronted may itself be an effect of the freedom and liberation that much of psychology has urged in the name of mental health. Lowenfeld and Lowenfeld, who are Freudian psychoanalysts, diagnose this widespread sense of meaninglessness as coming from a permissiveness that downplays guilt and responsibility, although the Lowenfelds seem less to view psychology itself as a contributing factor in what they deplore than simply to pin the blame on the "social climate."[3] Downplaying guilt and responsibility is, of course, a trend that some would trace to Freud.[4]

At least three traditional domains of meaning for people that psychology may have had a hand in eroding are those of work, marriage, and children. The direct fulfillment emphasis leads people to require that work provide inherent, creative forms of satisfaction it probably can't be expected to give everybody.[5] But to find meaning in work for its contributing to the welfare of others, such as one's family and members of a larger community, is undermined as well, since personal satisfaction presumably calls for one's freedom from such sources of constraint and control. A comparison of short stories published in American magazines in 1955 with those that appeared in 1890 reveals that story characters in 1955 show substantially greater dissatisfaction with their work.[6] Focus on the self may well be part of the reason for this change. Perhaps for the same reason, marriage and parenthood are substantially more likely to be reported as sources of dissatisfaction—burden-some and restrictive—in 1976 compared with 1957.[7]

The psychological emphasis on fulfillment and free-dom—on what the individual wants and feels—thus may be counter to much of what helps to give people a sense of meaning in their lives. Meaning may depend to a large degree on assuming and carrying out responsibilities for one another. Having social purposes beyond ourselves may be relevant to our mental health, with contributions to meeting the needs of others a source of our own satisfac-tion. And that satisfaction may, if anything, be all the more likely to elude us, the more we pursue it directly, as we will discuss later. Self-determination and self-fulfillment as goals may function most clearly to loosen the interconnec-tions among people; the sense of our interdependence be-comes weakened as what we do for one another is dis-paraged as allegedly bringing more by way of resentment than satisfaction. Rather than benefiting us, this outlook may be helping produce people's troubles.[8]

Some therapists understand such points very well and have not let egoistic assumptions get in their way. Pro-ceeding mostly from intuition, their own values, and prag-matic clinical sensibility about what works, they counter the general trend. Thus, for example, Yalom[9] is convinced of the therapeutic importance of clients' being able to step outside of themselves and care for another human being for the other's sake, with no thought or expectation of re-turn. He recognizes that clients who have trouble finding friendship and love usually are unable to relate to others in a manner genuinely focused on knowing and experi-encing the other person. The self in these instances keeps interfering, maintaining some kind of balance sheet and seeking some kind of quid pro quo. An illustration is Yalom's description of a male patient whose intense anxiety in relation to women turned out to hinge on the patient's covert understanding that his interest in the other person was manipulative, not genuine. Yet when it comes to theoretical grounding for his encouraging a patient toward selflessness, Yalom draws upon Maslow and Fromm, seeming not to recognize the ways in which such a basis is, as we have seen, a shaky foundation that weakens his case.

Bergin in turn has eloquently argued for the therapeutic significance of acting to be of service to others in selfless ways, of commitment to spouse and family, and of acceptance of guilt, suffering, and contrition, all of which he considers to be contrary to the customary clinical beliefs that are held by therapists and influential in their work with clients.[10] Bergin points out that the forms of conduct he often finds therapeutically beneficial for clients not only run counter to major currents of clinical thought but also are prominently associated with religion. Such conduct includes primary concern for other people rather than oneself, making commitments to service and sacrifice for others' sakes and abiding by these commitments rather than attending to one's own sense of gratification, and an attitude of forgiveness rather than ventilation of hostility toward those who cause us distress. Bergin therefore urges therapists to be more tolerant within therapy of the implications of the religious outlooks held in one degree or another by many of their clients. He believes that the prescriptions emerging from these religious outlooks possess psychological wisdom that therapists are predisposed by their training to disregard. The argument of the previous chapter suggests that science as well as religion may well be consonant with what a therapist like Bergin urges.

Others, too, have pointed to the therapeutic benefits that can follow from religious teachings of service and self-sacrifice. Allport, for instance, comments on how religious ideals if deeply felt can guide a person in ways that yield greater mental health as a by-product.[11] Mowrer urges that we take more seriously the religious view of the reality of the values that conscience represents.[12] He advocates that therapists should support the directives of conscience found in their clients; in his experience, inducing clients to live in congruence with these values heals psychological wounds. What conscience objects to, according to Mowrer, is the rupturing of a person's social embeddedness that comes from putting oneself first. Since Mowrer's work with patients suggests that we fail to heed the voice of conscience at our psychological peril, he concludes that the formula for achieving mental health must take us beyond "mere biology." Biology, to him, can do no more than support a focus on fulfillment of personal wants. According to what is argued in Chapter 10, Mowrer's therapeutic outlook may, however, be congruent not only with religious conviction but with biology as well.

In a vein similar to Mowrer, Menninger notes how various major religions teach that egocentricity or self-centeredness is the fundamental human problem, and love is the means for overcoming it.[13] His clinical experience leads him to agree that therapy becomes more beneficial to the extent that it implements the widespread religious sentiment that we need to reach out toward union with others, replacing self-love or self-aggrandizement with responsibilities beyond ourselves.

Sometimes personal phenomenology is invoked as a rationale for why this kind of therapeutic advice should be offered. Frankl,[14] for example, argues for a therapist's directing clients away from themselves on the grounds that meaning is objective, not subjective. He points to the way in which our language refers to meaning as something to be found or discovered, not something we merely invent or impose. If meanings were no more than arbitrary projections, he says, they would lose their character of challenging us and making demands upon us. The apparent objectivity that meanings possess does not seem in itself a convincing warrant for directing clients outward. Much clinical work has, after all, been fruitfully based on the possibility that what seem like demands from outside us really are projections of wishes. Yet we see that there are various clinicians who believe that directing clients outside of themselves can be extremely helpful. Contrary to most approaches, they attempt to diminish self-concern and encourage attention to values and to other people. The previous chapter suggests that this is consonant with science. Here we consider some of the therapeutic activities that seem to have this kind of thrust.

What psychotherapy might be able to do on this side becomes all the more interesting to explore when we consider how often it tends to be judged as inevitably or necessarily pushing for selfishness. Thus, Albee calls attention to Benjamin Franklin's list of virtues that included moderation, frugality, humility, justice, and industry. "These virtues, of course, were demanded by a religious doctrine that promised one's salvation in return."[15] Albee, a psychotherapist himself, seems rather automatically to view such virtues as tied in with people's acceptance of religion and belief in some kind of ultimate reward. Psychotherapy, to him, points elsewhere. He is pessimistic about the future in America perhaps precisely because he doesn't recognize the extent to which therapy and counseling can support in the individual's best interest many of the virtues on Franklin's list—rather than these virtues requiring a religious tradition that Albee considers on its way out. Where psychotherapy ends up standing on such matters will be of no small importance, of course, since, as Garfield notes, "At the present time psychotherapy is provided to more people by more therapists than ever before in our history, and all kinds of professional and nonprofessional workers are busily engaged in delivering such services."[16]

Detaching from Self-Oriented Experiences

Two major groups of recommendations and practices can be discerned in much of the therapy that directs clients outward: achieving detachment from self-oriented experiences, and furthering something beyond oneself. These are far from mutually exclusive considerations; indeed, they often are intertwined. They are at least partly separable, however, and for this reason we take up first one and then the other in what follows.

The patient's achieving detachment from self-oriented experiences turns out to be an ingredient common to the work of a number of therapists who seem to have come to it from diverse starting points. For example, Freud's former disciple Alfred Adler arrived at the view that the therapist must act to undermine the significance that the neurotic attributes to his or her symptoms.[17] The neurotic's concern about the symptom is understood as a kind of self-preoccupation that keeps the patient unhealthily focused on internal states and feelings rather than acting in the world. It is necessary to induce the patient to make light of the symptom rather than to be locked in mortal combat with it, trying to overcome it by brute force. Thus, Adler might tell an insomniac to stop trying to fall asleep. Instead, the insomniac is to accept the sleeplessness and put the time to constructive use such as by thinking of ways to please others the following day. Pulling the rug out from under the symptom in this way by debasing the symptom's disturbance value can incur the patient's wrath. But, according to Adler, sometimes the patient's accepting sleeplessness as instructed makes the patient unable to maintain it.

Another instance of Adler's maneuvering patients away from their preoccupation with themselves is his account of how he would prefer to handle the case of an 11-year-old girl who disrupts her family every morning of a school day with anxiety over going to school. After assuring himself that the approach could be risked in the case at hand, he would want to tell the girl: " 'School is the most important thing in the world, and if I were you I would make even a greater fuss about it.' "[18] He would expect this instruction of symptom exaggeration to make the symptom more difficult to maintain by functioning as a reductio ad absurdum, offering a less self-involved perspective from which the symptom is taken less seriously. Adler discussed this paradoxical prescribing of symptom intensification in a 1929 publication; along with the idea of symptom acceptance, it has been very important in work by others as well.

Frankl, too, believes the neurotic's basic problem to be self-centeredness. Over a number of years, Frankl has argued that a great deal of therapy, quite the opposite of what is needed, in effect invites the neurotic to focus more attention on his or her own feelings and sensations.[19] Introspection about how one really feels, on whether one is happy or actualized, is viewed by Frankl as counterproductive. To pursue positive affective states and the avoidance of negative affective states directly will fail because these are not normal human goals. Our normal goals are outside of ourselves and in the world in tasks and other people we care about. Self-referent states like happiness and fulfillment can never usefully be our direct objectives; to aim at them will be to miss them. As Frankl puts it, they must "ensue," or be by-products; they "cannot be pursued." Frankl wants us to let the feelings take care of themselves.

For example, in describing how he would approach someone who suffers from feelings of inferiority, Frankl argues that it will not help for such a patient to try to overcome them by direct confrontation.[20] That just makes them worse. Instead of brooding over and trying to fight these inferiority feelings, the person should aim at carrying out activities in spite of them. Attention should be focused on the activities that need doing, with the feelings accepted and left alone. Frankl is fond of using the analogy of the healthy eye and the sick eye: an eye when healthy is an unobtrusive instrument for seeing the world, but when sick gives forth effects it produces itself, which are then seen instead of the world. It is not in our interest, Frankl asserts, to observe and analyze self-generated effects.

One way in which Frankl gets patients to stop attending to their feelings and symptoms is by directly countering their usual assumption that they should be doing so. Instead, by one ruse or another he imposes the requirement that they must not. The client is supplied with an excuse that lets him or her off the hook of self-attention. For instance, a husband with an impotence problem may be told it is imperative for the treatment that he and his wife not have intercourse, but they are permitted to lie naked in bed and caress each other. This frees the husband from concern over his own sexual performance, and instead he pays attention to his wife. The result can be an apologetic report that he couldn't stop himself from having intercourse and an orgasm. Or a woman who is very concerned about not being able to attain orgasm may be given the benign deception that Frankl can't treat her right away. While on a waiting list, she is required to prepare herself for the ensuing treatment by clearing her mind of concern over her frigidity. Instead, she is to concentrate on what it is about her partner that makes her fond of him, in order to report this when treatment starts. The frigidity problem may dissipate as a result.

Another way in which Frankl breaks the hold that symptoms can exert is by having the patient welcome and even try to exaggerate them. The stutterer is asked to try to stutter rather than resisting it, the obsessive should dwell on thoughts even more obsessively. An insomniac will be asked not only to accept the insomnia but also to go to bed and try to stay awake all night. Someone who is phobic about public places is asked, when feeling the fear coming on, to try to magnify the panic, to sweat and tremble even more, to respond with even more dizziness, to give a consummate demonstration of what an extreme panic reaction looks like. By such paradoxical instructions, neurotics are jolted out of their accustomed stance of fierce opposition to their symptoms, and perspective is introduced. They come to view their symptoms as less monumental, even a matter of humor. To be wrapped up in them takes on a certain absurdity; their liabilities come to outweigh their advantages. Robbed of its power to inspire anxiety, the symptom has had the wind taken from its sails, making it more likely to recede.

Similarly paradoxical requests to intensify or exaggerate symptoms are found in the therapeutic practices of Milton Erickson, along with those of others, such as Haley, who have studied Erickson's work.[21] Again the aim is to induce detachment and distance from self-involvement by welcoming and extending, instead of opposing, the symptom until it takes on comical or absurd properties in the patient's eyes or becomes too bizarre even for the patient to take seriously. For example, Erickson's approach to a child's thumb sucking problem might be to ask the child to sit near its parents and suck not only the thumb but the rest of the fingers as well. Moreover, the child will be requested to watch the clock and make sure each finger gets sucked for a specified amount of time. Carried to sufficient extremes as a duty, finger sucking becomes an onerous burden interfering with what the child wants to do.

As another example, Erickson worked with a young man who had a phobia about driving beyond the city limits. Driving his car to the edge of town would make him nauseated and he would vomit and faint. Trying to keep going would only result in his fainting again. Erickson got the man to promise, despite vigorous protests, to drive to the city's edge at three in the morning in his best clothes. Upon reaching the city limits, he was to park by the side of the road, jump from the car, and spend at least 15 minutes lying on his back in the drainage ditch. Then he was to return to the car, drive a car length or two further, return to the ditch to lie there for another 15 minutes, get back in the car and drive another car length or two, return to the ditch, and so on. He was to creep along in this manner from one telephone pole to the next, returning to the ditch at the first sign of his symptoms. As he reported later to Erickson: " 'I thought it was a damn-fool thing you made me promise to do, and the more I did it the madder I got. So I just quit and began to enjoy driving.' "[22] Thirteen years later, the driving phobia still hadn't returned. Erickson had apparently managed to maneuver the man away from being wrapped up in and concerned about his symptoms by the absurdity and aversiveness of the exaggeration.

Another case of Erickson's was a young woman preoccupied with a slight gap between her front teeth, which she would hide with her hand as she talked. Viewing it as a blight on her appearance, she had lost all confidence, was reclusive, felt herself too homely to get married, and was contemplating suicide. At the office where she worked, a young man seemed to correlate his turning up at the drinking fountain with her being there, but she was too ashamed and concerned over her physical defect to encourage him. Since she felt her life was over anyway, Erickson was able to secure her cooperation in the apparently zany task of learning to squirt water expertly through the gap in her teeth, and then in the even greater absurdity of using her new skill in order to squirt water through her tooth gap at the young man when he showed up at the drinking fountain. The result of her practical joke was that he chased after her and kissed her. When on the following day she approached the fountain for a drink, the young man sprang out from hiding and sprayed her with a water pistol. The day after that they went out on a date and soon were married. The woman's preoccupation with the gap between her front teeth had been amplified by Erickson and made the cornerstone of renewed social involvement. Erickson had gotten her to exaggerate her focus on it in ways that made sustaining her shame difficult; from the new perspective in which her dental defect was placed, it just couldn't be taken so seriously any longer.

Moving patients to a perspective from which they stop focusing on themselves thus can be of therapeutic value. Sometimes a tragedy accomplishes this; Yalom describes a therapy patient of his who suffered from disabling interpersonal phobias. The phobias rapidly disappeared after she found that she had cancer. Her explanation of why her phobias had ended was: " 'Cancer cures psychoneurosis.' "[23] From the vantage point of anticipating death, what had preoccupied her before and brought about her interpersonal phobias now could be seen as out of proportion.

Similarly—but in a lighter vein—Yalom himself, worried that he would have insomnia on a trip that was in the offing, sought help from a behavior therapist who tried customary behavioral techniques, to no avail. Leaving the behavior therapist's office after a session, however, the therapist remarked to Yalom that he should remember to include a revolver when packing his bag for his trip. When Yalom asked why, the therapist replied that if Yalom couldn't fall asleep, he could always shoot himself. In contrast to the behaviorial techniques, this offhand humor proved quite beneficial. It helped, apparently, by bringing home to Yalom that he had allowed his insomnia to assume disproportionate significance; he had taken it too seriously.

Withdrawing attention from one's feeling states and symptoms comes up as a theme in other therapeutic work as well. Thus, not unlike Frankl, Mowrer argues that it is relatively fruitless to try to change feelings directly, but that patients often feel better—less anxious or emotional, for example—as an effect of their changing their behavior in the direction of contributing to others'welfare.[24] In a related way, the psychiatrist Glasser finds it counterproductive to focus on how patients are feeling and the symptoms they experience, for he considers such a focus as reinforcing of the "self-involvement" that constitutes the problem.[25] "Talking at length about a patient's problems and his feelings about them focuses upon his self-involvement and consequently gives his failure value."[26] The aim instead should be to induce commitment to more useful activities in the world, regardless of one's feelings. With involvements outside replacing self-involvement, Glasser, like Mowrer, finds that feelings often change for the better. And a clergyman who describes his counseling work makes the same point. Rather than trying to deal with a troubled person's feelings directly, Anderson finds it more helpful to bypass them—not to ruminate with the client, but to encourage behavior that is considerate of significant others in the client's life.[27]

Detaching from self-oriented experiences also plays an important role in a therapeutic approach developed thousands of miles away from any of the work considered thus far. The Japanese psychiatrist Shōma Morita was influenced in the forming of what came to be called Morita psychotherapy by his own neurotic difficulties. As an adolescent before the turn of the century, Morita was beset by so-called neurasthenic symptoms such as headaches, fatigue, and anxiety attacks with which he tried to cope by means of various medical interventions. What finally helped him was the shock, while a medical student, of sudden financial exigency.[28] Reminiscent of Yalom's patient who developed cancer, Morita literally could no longer afford his concern over his symptoms, stopped his medicines and therapeutic regimens, and threw himself into his studies. The symptoms abated.

As Morita's psychiatric work evolved, he came to view much neurotic trouble as stemming from obsessive self-consciousness—preoccupation with anxiety, unhappiness, pain, or with some other negatively experienced symptom or state, coming to stand in the way of a person's attending to outside events. With a formulation that could have come from Frankl, Morita pointed out that the more the person tries to struggle against these negative experiences, the more central they become, in a vicious circle of increasing sensitivity. Again the emphasis is on strategies to redirect attention away from oneself.

Inpatient treatment at a Morita-style psychiatric hospital in Japan lasts about one to two months and is divided into four phases.[29] First comes a week of absolute bed rest. Although far from a condition of sensory deprivation, the patient is to lie quietly, alone in a room, without reading, talking, or any kind of pastimes or amusements. The patient is to accept thoughts and feelings as they are—not to resist or struggle against them. In a manner related to symptom exaggeration, self-focus thus is welcomed and amplified; indeed, the patient has nothing to do but wallow non-stop in his or her feelings, symptoms, and obsessions. Typically, this intensified self-focus becomes a burden as the week progresses. The patient becomes eager for permission to put inner states aside and engage the environment. Being allowed to sweep out one's room at the end of the week becomes a fresh, rich activity. As with Milton Erickson or Frankl, the neurotic has been maneuvered away from fixation upon self-oriented experiences.

After the bed-rest phase comes a second phase in which, for about a week, the patient is allowed to undertake light work. Most of the tasks assigned are contributory to others in the hospital community such as raking leaves, washing clothes, or helping with cooking. The tasks are to be carried out purposefully and carefully. No casual conversations, reading, or visitors are permitted. Starting with this phase, the patient keeps a diary, which the Morita therapist annotates. The diary is not to concern symptoms or feelings, but what one saw and did during the day and particularly the work that one has accomplished. As the initial euphoria at the wonder of the world's beauty and one's own simple actions in it declines with time, the diary annotations keep reminding the patient that feelings come and go, are hard to control, and should be left alone; what matters is carrying out meaningful tasks regardless of how one feels.

A period of heavy work, also lasting about a week, then follows. The tasks now undertaken—again socially useful forms of work—are more demanding physically. Carpentry may be assigned, for example, or chopping wood, clearing gutters, or gardening. The patient is also expected to find what needs doing in the environment and take care of it, for instance, if there is a puddle on the path in the hospital garden, to fill it in, if a chrysanthemum stalk is falling, to arrange a support for it. By losing oneself in the work to be done, the patient comes to "notice" symptoms less and in any case keeps being reminded through diary annotations that feelings should be taken as they come. We should fulfill our purposes while letting our feelings and symptoms be however they may. And as Mowrer or Glasser would say, a Moritist, too, will point out that if we engage in constructive actions, we may well come to feel better as a by-product.

During the last phase of treatment, finally, the patient gradually undertakes more and more of the privileges and responsibilities of normal life. The emphasis always is maintained on carrying out tasks for their own sake, doing what needs doing in the world, regardless of how we feel. For example, if a patient indicated that going for a loaf of bread to the store had changed from something that was dreaded to a really enjoyable experience, the therapist's response would point out that getting the bread should be what the patient is most thinking about, not enjoyment. The patient must be resolved to go to the store for the bread even when feeling depressed.[30] Or a patient with a phobia about riding on trains would be expected to ride the train for the purpose of carrying out errands that require a train ride, not for the purpose of reducing one's fears. Although a patient might be encouraged to look around for such errands, the emphasis is to remain on doing the task for its own sake, not for the sake of conquering the symptom.[31] The symptom may, indeed, abate, but the patient learns to be responsible for getting the job done whatever his or her feelings. The patient becomes able to put symptoms and feelings aside, to take them less seriously. When considered ready for discharge, the patient thus may still experience some anxiety or other symptoms, but has learned nevertheless to pursue an active life.

It would be Moritist advice, for example, not to wait until feeling like getting up in the morning before doing so, but to get out of bed regardless and then one is more likely to want to be up. Or to encourage a jogger who doesn't feel like jogging on a given day to go out and jog with involvement anyway. The jogging is a necessary activity for that person, and the desire to jog may emerge while one is doing it. And a typical Moritist illustration might be to mention, in the case of an outpatient who comes in complaining of a nagging, continuous headache, that one's nose is always visible in one's visual field, and yet we go about our business with little awareness of it. The result, of course, is that the patient now becomes highly conscious of this peripheral visual phenomenon. The therapist then points out—and is usually right—that at the moment the patient's attention focused on the visibility of one's nose, the patient's awareness of the headache diminished. The patient has to come to treat the headache as we normally treat the visibility of our nose.[32]

When we are immersed in our tasks, aversive feelings or symptoms lose their hold on us. They may improve, but in any case we learn to ignore them. We learn to let feeling states, both positive and negative, take care of themselves.

As we have already seen, the kinds of nonmainstream therapeutic work here considered often seeks not only to detach clients from self-oriented experiences but also to encourage engagement in tasks and purposes outside oneself. Next we take a closer look at this second point.

Furthering Something Beyond Oneself

The therapeutic utility of involving patients—or a society's members in general—with what is outside themselves has been sensed and applied in various ways both outside and within formal psychotherapy. It can be present, for example, as an element in primitive healing rituals when the patient is called upon to perform services for the group. Thus, a 63-year-old Guatemalan Indian woman suffering from depression is asked by the healer to make the elaborate preparations needed for a large feast to take place during her curing session, as described by Frank.[33] And in the religious healing ceremonies at Lourdes, Frank points out that "the emphasis is on self-forgetfulness and devotion to the welfare of others. The pilgrims pray for the sick and the sick for each other, not themselves."[34] Again, the sick are made to feel useful through their carrying out acts of service for others. Similarly to Lourdes, an account of a contemporary Japanese religious sect's therapeutic activities indicates that the participants pray not for themselves but for one another: "They stand facing each other and pray that one another's unhappiness will diminish."[35]

Part of the power of group psychotherapy may consist in the same sort of opportunity it provides for the patient to help someone else. Group members, who may have felt worthless and a burden to others, discover that they can contribute meaningfully to others in the group by helping them with their problems.[36] Mowrer likewise has made the observation that finding one can be of benefit to other group members is a powerful source of therapeutic effectiveness in self-help groups like Alcoholics Anonymous.[37] Service and help to others in the group is, according to Mowrer, itself therapeutic—a doing of "good works" that restores to a state of human community someone who has been alienated. From his work in group therapy Yalom also concludes that a source of its effectiveness seems to be the opportunities it presents for the patient to help others.[38] Finding that they were of help to other group members is often viewed by patients as contributing to their own improvement. Yalom thus will urge a lonely, socially isolated young woman who has group sessions with him to stop focusing on herself and her reactions and instead " 'try to extend yourself to others in the group. Try to enter their experiential world.' "[39]

The potential benefit to the individual of being engaged by concerns outside oneself seems to have gained particular notice in relation to troubles like depression, alienation, anomie, or a sense of meaninglessness, but may well be relevant to other problems also. The significance of inducing engagement is clearly felt by Yalom, whose intuition is that as therapist he must figure out how to free the given patient from obstacles that impede losing oneself in commitments to people and to tasks. He considers it important, for example, to explore with patients not only what they seek from others but also what contributions they make to others' lives. When a 30-year-old dentist laments that he is alienated from his father, always fights with him, isn't able to communicate with him, Yalom advises him to take the responsibility of writing his father a letter. When the patient, stunned by the suggestion, objects that his family doesn't write letters, Yalom won't let him wriggle out of it but keeps prodding him toward engagement. The patient writes his father, and while he is doing so, his father phones him. As a result, they are able to make contact.

Prodding patients toward concerns that take them out of themselves can sometimes help in more extreme situations too. In one of Erickson's cases, a businessman hospitalized for depression after losing his fortune would spend his time weeping and moving his hands in a compulsive fashion.[40] Erickson managed to put the hand movement to work by placing a piece of sandpaper in each hand and a rough board between them, so the hand movement would have the effect of sanding and polishing lumber in the hospital workshop. Finding himself doing something productive, the patient stopped crying. Then he took up carving chess sets in wood and selling them. He continued to improve thereafter. Erickson had managed to change the arm movement symptom from something patient-centered to a means of getting the patient to fulfill a task. He had gotten the patient to accept, in place of crazy symptoms, what Glasser would characterize as "a good plan to do some worthwhile work."[41]

In another of Erickson's cases, a young man, hospitalized for acute depression, would stand wherever placed, stubbornly refusing to move. An expert cardplayer, he had played incessantly before hospitalization, but now was depressed into sullen immobility. Erickson prodded him into engagement by standing him next to a card table. At the table Erickson assembled four patients who were deteriorated to the point that they didn't quite know what was going on. Erickson describes the resultant card game: "One would be playing poker, another bridge, another pinochle. One would say, 'What's wild?' the other would reply, 'I'll bet you two trump.' They put one card on another with no reference to each other."[42] Erickson would stand his patient next to each player in turn. After several evenings of this, his patient capitulated. He agreed to play cards if Erickson would get him three players who knew what they were doing. The affront of having to witness a Mad Hatter type of card game had needled this good cardplayer sufficiently to bring him out of himself, no longer able to maintain his disengagement. He cared about the game and wanted it played well.

The mental health significance of attention to goals beyond ourselves is what the psychiatrist Angyal meant to convey in his use, in the early 1940's, of the phrase "trend toward homonomy." Angyal felt that the healthy person "wishes to share and participate in something which he regards as being greater than his individual self."[43] The philosopher John Rawls argues, in turn, that most of such commitments beyond ourselves have a social element, because they involve larger units that can be furthered and take on meaning to the extent that others make their contributions too.[44] Rawls gives the example of an orchestra. Its various musicians each could have learned different instruments than the ones they did, but depend on a division of labor that creates the music no one of them could have realized alone. The successes and skills of the other members are necessary for any one member's well-being or good. Recall, by contrast, our earlier mention of Fellini's film *Orchestra Rehearsal,* in which a situation of orchestral anarchy is depicted as the members each do their own thing. Anarchy works no better in an orchestra than in the chaotic card game that Erickson created to goad his depressed, immobile patient into action. Our own well-being, Rawls would tell us, is tied in with what we can do to further others—not because of mutual back-scratching but because one cares directly about something larger than oneself: a good play of the game, a sensitive rendering of the symphony, talents one appreciates without possessing.

We inevitably live partly through others, Rawls says, unless we are hermits. Consider again from this point of view Sampson's critique, noted in Chapter 1, of psychological androgyny as an ideal—the presumed desirability of each person trying to become a full exemplar of the masculine and the feminine.[45] Or, more generally, take the individualistic goal of trying to become complete in oneself, to be all desirable things, and thus less tied to others for completion. To stake our satisfaction on such an aim, according to Rawls, is to ensure our grief. For what we can envision and appreciate, what can inspire and psychologically nourish us, is far greater than our own individual skins are able, even in principle, given mortality, to contain. Our necessary incompleteness means that "the self is realized in the activities of many selves."[46] We overcome our incompleteness not by trying to become everything but by contributing to larger wholes whose results are part of our own contentment.

In light of these considerations, recent findings by Lubinski, Tellegen, and Butcher are of some interest. They found that, even in this culture's strongly individualistic orientation, the tendency to be psychologically androgynous was not associated with signs of well-being or mental health. Lubinski and his colleagues felt that their "evidence casts doubt on . . . the appropriateness of developing 'psychotherapeutic' techniques that attempt to change both masculine and feminine sex-types to a more androgynous orientation."[47] Nor would Rawls be surprised at what was found in studies by Brown and Harris on the kind of events associated with the onset of depression in women. Change as such or long-term health difficulties for oneself or another, no matter how severe, did not increase the likelihood of depression. What seemed most critical was loss of something vital to a person, and the majority of these losses concerned a close relationship with another person. Thus, a life-threatening illness to someone close will provoke depression, while a long-term health difficulty for that same person will not. Indeed, it seemed to the authors that, in the absence of a life-threatening crisis, the very act of caring for someone close who had a long-term health problem "gave women a sense of purpose which might even have reduced risk of depression."[48] Commitment to others seems itself psychologically healthy; its loss undoes our happiness.

That "the self is realized in the activities of many selves" suggests the extent to which the isolated self may be an impossible abstraction that denies a social context from which the self is all but inseparable.[49] What is best for the individual therapeutically may then become easier to identify with furthering what is beyond ourselves than has often been the practice, since what is "beyond" ourselves is not separable from ourselves.

This is a point of some familiarity within the traditions both of historical and comtemporary China. Westerners often are impressed by what seems like less alienation and greater self-discipline and dedication in the People's Republic of China when they make rough comparisons to life as they know it at home. An example is Munro, who tried to answer for himself the question of where this discipline and relative lack of alienation come from.[50] One of its sources, he came to feel, is the great effort made in contemporary China to elucidate the positive bearing of people's work and tasks on the broader values and goals they already consider worthy. Large segments of the Chinese population are able to see the connection between what they do and the larger purposes that matter to them. They are shown how their day-to-day work has the meaning of contributing to what they want to have happen in the world, what they believe in. And these goals in turn are nothing new, but continuous in important respects with the historical tradition of Confucianism, which emphasizes the desirability of contributing to the welfare of the larger social group of which one is part. Not unlike Rawls, the Chinese have long understood that our satisfaction is partly dependent on contributing to something beyond ourselves that we appreciate and wish to further. Attention in China to showing how what we do can make a difference to what we value seems to result in the relatively high dedication and low alienation that can surprise Westerners. As we shall see, Frankl, too, emphasizes helping people to see the meaning of their situation and their work, in terms of larger goals that they already hold.

Westerners have shown comparable surprise in observing children in the People's Republic. A team of visiting American child development experts was struck by the discipline and control shown by Chinese kindergarteners, for example, spending two 20-minute periods each week testing flashlight bulbs from a nearby factory, folding cardboard forms for packing the bulbs, and inserting them with impressive dexterity one by one in the holes in the forms.[51] They did this without becoming anxious, inhibited, and distressed as a result, but showing themselves rather to be capable of spontaneity and animation. The kindergarteners packing the bulbs for shipment knew that this was real work, not exercises; they were performing a needed task and were proud of the fact.

When, in turn, the kindergarteners performed songs and dances, with some of them inevitably singled out for lead roles, they were given to understand that their selection was for the purpose of doing a service for their school, not bringing attention to themselves; the children would change leads in different performances. Their level of skill in dances, songs, and skits was impressive to the observers, along with the confidence of their demeanor on stage. Again the visitors were struck that the discipline and high standards did not seem to come at a psychological cost; the children showed little distress, anxiety, or tension. Perhaps the reason once more has to do with the children being given to understand that what they did was not so much for themselves as for purposes beyond themselves—the school, the nation.

In observations of primary school children as well, the Americans kept being surprised that the relatively high levels of discipline and demands that prevailed—and were fulfilled in skilled academic and other work—were not gained at the price of spontaneity, initiative, or positive affect. On the contrary, the children appeared confident, expressive, and cheerful. As with kindergarteners, "Obvious signs of tension, depression, or apathy were rare compared to those in groups of Western children."[52] Where the visitors were "unnerved" to find the combination of discipline and concentration with happiness and exuberance in these children, however, the answer might well be the extent to which the children understood what they did as in the service of larger goals that had their allegiance. And, as pointed out before, these goals were integrated into a long Chinese heritage. Like the adults whose self-discipline and dedication impressed Munro, these children, too, were shown how what they did played a part in furthering what mattered to them. They would paint toys for other children to use. They would assemble and package badminton birds; not only were the products meaningful per se as contributions to others in the society but also the factories would pay the school workshops so the schools could purchase needed medicines or sports equipment.

Doing things for the sake of others and seeing that they benefit from one's contributions seems, in the case of such children and adults, to facilitate one's own well-being. The essence of such an effect is put this way by Kaswan: "If people do not need one another for essential aspects of their lives, then what they do for one another loses importance, their sense of worth decreases, and their actions have little meaning beyond the moment."[53] When, in turn, mainland Chinese are urged to engage in self-criticism, the aim—at least in principle—is not coercion as much as persuasion based on engaging the person's own values and "consciousness raising" (a term from communist China, as Barlow indicates) about what those values imply.[54] Thus, kindergarteners selected for lead roles in songs and dances will not only be reminded that they are performing to serve their school, but they may be asked to undertake self-criticism against making the performance into an occasion for self-admiration.[55] Such self-criticism appeals to already shared values, indeed, values deeply embedded in Confucian thought. At least judging from the visiting American group's observations, a group looking for psychological costs, the effect on the children was not oppression into surrender and apathy. Instead, they may have been liberated from a major source of anxiety.

Although contemporary Chinese self-criticism toward reduced selfishness and increased social connectedness comes out of a Confucian heritage, it has its affinities to the Christian confession of sin. To Mowrer, therapy needs to follow a Christian confessional model in which he views conscience as standing for what connects us to others.[56] Like self-criticism, confession and atonement deal with consciousness raising about how to conduct oneself in ways that will be more consistent with the concern for others that is part of one's own values. The effect should be to lessen psychological disturbance. The reason why violating our sociality is bad for us comes for Mowrer, as also for Menninger,[57] from religion—our sense of connectedness to others is God working within us. But, as we have seen in Chapter 10, naturalistic reasons can be provided also. In any case, therapeutic benefits are felt to accrue from criticizing one's selfish tendencies and seeking to act in ways that serve others.

An example within the Christian tradition is the auto-biographical (though third-person) account by Clark, a minister who found himself unable to shake off self-consciousness about his own competence and standing as he tried and failed to carry out his work.[58] What finally helped him was coming to function not with an eye to his own accomplishments but as an instrument of God through whom purposes Clark considered worthy could be fulfilled. He became free of his "prison of self" and able to act as a means through which beneficial effects could flow to others. Thus, after winning his way to this sense of functioning in the service of what he values, he was preaching one Sunday when a new line of thought occurred to him. Since it seemed to Clark to be what God wanted him to develop, he abandoned his carefully prepared sermon outline and extemporized to a very different conclusion. After the service, a member of the congregation told him the sermon was wonderful, and he found himself enthusiastically agreeing: " 'It *was*, wasn't it!' " When the person making the compliment looked horrified, he explained that "it was God's achievement instead of his, and therefore *was* wonderful."[59] As with the Chinese children encouraged to think of their lead roles in songs and dances not in terms of implications for themselves but of service to others, so with his sermon Clark forgot himself.

Quite in line with the Chinese emphasis on showing people how what they do serves to further already shared values, Viktor Frankl's therapy makes a point of interpreting people's activities and lives to help them discover larger purposes or goals that matter to them and are served thereby. For example, Frankl describes the case of an elderly widower, depressed since his wife died, who came to see him.[60] Frankl asked him what would have been the situation if his wife had survived him; the man replied that she would have suffered greatly. This let Frankl point out that, by her dying first, she was spared such suffering. One of them had to die before the other; his present situation means that he is suffering for her sake: the price of saving his wife what she would have gone through if the order had been reversed. Thus, what the man was going through had a purpose he endorsed, and seemed to become more tolerable as a result.

Similarly, Frankl found—for himself when interned at Auschwitz and Dachau by the Nazis and for other concentration camp inmates—that what helped them keep going was a sense of some purpose outside themselves and of significance to them that drew them forward.[61] Frankl helped one would-be suicide by underscoring that he owed it to his child to survive; the child was waiting for him in another country. He helped talk another out of suicide by emphasizing the man's responsibility to some uncompleted scientific work. In each instance, the inmate's consciousness could be raised, as it were, to the effect that their own acknowledged responsibilities implied they had to keep going. What seems to work in such cases is being guided toward the understanding that one's activities or life patterns or travails are not gratuitous but rather are in the interest of goals or commitments beyond oneself to which one subscribes. And this engagement by something beyond oneself can take place in small ways as well as large—as when, for example, Frankl quotes a patient suffering from a sense of meaninglessness: " 'Sometimes in order to get relief I need only to turn to the immediate tasks confronting me.' "[62]

In his concept of "social interest"—or, literally, "feeling of community" (*Gemeinschaftsgefühl*), Adler seemed to have

a related point in mind.[63] He found it therapeutically beneficial for his patients if they could immerse themselves in
interests and concerns directed toward others and toward
task involvements. Adler would point out to patients the
selfish implications of their symptoms—for example, that
a wife with phobic fears of harming her son and hitting
strangers on the street forces her husband thereby to be
at her beck and call. She is in this way neglecting her
responsibilities toward him. Again we see the operation of
consciousness raising: clarifying the selfish implication is
expected to enlist the patient's cooperation toward change
because of shared values against selfishness. So too, neurotic anxiety over failure is understood in terms of the self-
boundedness that makes failure into a personal defeat.
Adler thus will want to show patients that sufficient involvement with purposes beyond oneself will remove this
kind of personal onus from one's performance. This is not
unlike the visiting American group's observations of Chinese
children showing great skills with quiet confidence rather
than anxiety with their focus on performing for the benefit
of others, not on themselves. The point is to show patients
that much of their disturbance is linked with an exploita-
tive attitude—"wanting to take and not wanting to give"[64]—
that Adler assumes the patients themselves will want to
disavow and counter because of the feeling of community
that is also there to be supported. The "moral treatment"
approach that seemed to work with some effectiveness in
rehabilitating mental patients in the nineteenth century looks
in these terms rather Adlerian; it was based on involving
the patients in activities that would direct their interests
outward to people and pursuits in the world and away
from themselves.[65] Morita's approach also shows similarities.

Crandall looked at contemporary American beliefs about
the significance of the kinds of traits Adler conceptualized

in terms of social interest or feeling of community—traits like helpfulness, sympathy, and tolerance, indicating the presence of concern for others.[66] As might be expected from what psychology tends to teach about the self-focused sources of mental health, respondents did not seem to expect greater psychological well-being to be associated with such traits. Yet, perhaps all the more intriguing in light of this belief, Crandall found that scores on a scale he developed to assess social interest in the sense of concern for others were correlated with a variety of different indicators of mental health. In one study, presence of food aversions turned out to be associated with lesser social interest or concern for others. The tendency toward food aversions—disliking foods so much one would refuse to eat them—has been found in other work to be more frequent among neurotics than normal people.

In another study reported by Crandall, self-appraisal was examined before and after participants underwent a contrived failure experience on a task involving problems to be solved. Those with less social interest tended to show large positive or large negative shifts in self-appraisal in response to the failure experience—defensive self-aggrandizement in reaction to failure on the one hand, severe self-derogation on the other. Those with greater concern for others, by contrast, tended to show less lability of self-appraisal. This latter result does not seem to be a product of denial of failure since the two groups rated their failure as comparably severe. The evidence seems to suggest "greater stability and feelings of security on the part of those with strong social interest."[67] This is, of course, what Adler would expect; as noted before, they should be less inclined to interpret the failure as a personal defeat.

Morita psychotherapy too, as we have seen, is strongly organized around the theme of turning the patient's attention away from self and toward tasks to be carried out and social responsibilities to be met. This begins in small ways after the period spend in isolated bed rest when the patient is assigned light work to do, followed later by heavier work. The idea of socially constructive activity is emphasized—most of the work serves to maintain and beautify the hospital. The patient then gets increasingly weaned to the outer world, with purposeful living for others maintained as the new focus of the patient's attention. The patient learns to redirect attention away from the self, feelings and symptoms, and toward tasks that need doing, a major component of these tasks being that they are expressive in various ways of concern for others in a shared social environment. Valid goals and purposes according to the Morita approach are ones that involve a strong contributory component toward others' welfare.[68]

Another form of therapy also practiced in Japan relevant to the present subject is naikan therapy. "Naikan" means introspection, and in this form of therapy the client is to follow a prescribed pattern of intensive all-day meditation during a week's stay at a naikan center, followed by some daily meditation along similar lines at home.[69] The therapist guiding a client's meditation assigns different significant figures to meditate about, such as the patient's mother, father, siblings, teachers, and spouse, and different chronological periods of one's life within which to consider the particular person, from the years of early childhood to the present. The focus of one's thinking is to be specific, concrete experiences. For a given person and period of life meditated about, the client is expected to divide the meditation time, giving about 20 percent to the themes of the kindnesses and benefits received from the other person, 20 percent to what the client returned to that person, and 60 percent to the troubles that one has caused the other person. The expected way of meditating is one in which the client reports receiving much kindness from the other person, returning little, and causing the other much trouble. The typical effect as the week progresses seems to be that the patient comes to experience a growing sense of gratitude and guilt, leading to the wish to make restitution through serving others. What seems to happen is the patient's "realization and confrontation on a conscious level of actual violations of essential moral values in regard to a particular person."[70] Patients are brought to see that, in terms of their own values, they have acted badly to significant others. Again, then, we seem to find a kind of consciousness raising taking place in regard to the conduct implications of one's own already held values. Presumed consequences are acting in ways more regardful of others, and feeling less alienated from others.

Various forms of therapeutic activity can be glimpsed, then, that seem to operate in terms of detaching individuals from self-preoccupation and orienting them beyond themselves. Benefits to well-being are expected as a result. The great diversity of starting points and belief systems reflected in these therapeutic practices outside the mainstream support the possibility that their common concern with directing people outward yields genuine psychological benefits. Psychotherapy need not be cast in forms that encourage selfishness. Other forms are possible.

Notes

1. Smith, 1961.
2. See, for example, Maddi, 1970; Lowenfeld and Lowenfeld, 1972; and Yalom, 1980.
3. Lowenfeld and Lowenfeld, 1972.
4. For example, Mowrer, 1961.
5. Klinger, 1977.
6. Martel, 1968, reports these story character findings.
7. Bernard, 1981, describes the marriage and parenthood evidence.

8. See Thom, 1979.
9. Yalom, 1980.
10. Bergin, 1980.
11. Allport, 1969.
12. Mowrer, 1961, 1964.
13. Menninger, 1978.
14. Frankl, 1962, 1970.
15. Albee, 1977, p. 157.
16. Garfield, 1981, p. 175.
17. Adler, 1979; Ansbacher and Ansbacher, 1964.
18. Adler in Ansbacher and Ansbacher, 1964, p. 398.
19. See, for example, Frankl, 1962, 1970, 1979.
20. Frankl, 1979.
21. See, for example, Haley, 1973.
22. Haley, 1973, p. 70.
23. Yalom, 1980, p. 160.
24. See, for example, Mowrer, 1964, 1972.
25. Glasser, 1975a, 1975b.
26. Glasser, 1975b, p. 81.
27. Anderson, 1967.
28. Kondo, 1976.
29. Reynolds, 1976, 1980.
30. Reynolds, 1976, p. 214.
31. Reynolds, 1976, p. 140.
32. Reynolds, 1976, 1980.
33. Frank, 1974.
34. Frank, 1974, p. 69.
35. Sasaki, 1976, p. 245.
36. Frank, 1974.
37. Mowrer, 1964.
38. Yalom, 1980.
39. Yalom, 1980, p. 396.

40. See Haley, 1973.
41. Glasser, 1975b, p. 223.
42. Quoted in Haley, 1973, p. 290.
43. Angyal, 1972, p. 172.
44. Rawls, 1971.
45. Sampson, 1977.
46. Rawls, 1971, p. 565.
47. Lubinski, Tellegen, and Butcher, 1981, p. 729.
48. Brown and Harris, 1978, p. 276.
49. Smith, 1978, 1980.
50. Munro, 1977.
51. Kessen, 1975.
52. Kessen, 1975, p. 142.
53. Kaswan, 1981, p. 296.
54. Barlow, 1981.
55. Kessen, 1975.
56. Mowrer, 1961.
57. Menninger, 1978.
58. Clark, 1967.
59. Clark, 1967, p. 350, italics his.
60. Frankl, 1962.
61. Frankl, 1962, 1979.
62. Frankl, 1970, p. 96.
63. See, for example, Adler, 1979.
64. Adler, 1979, p. 304.
65. Bockoven, 1967.
66. Crandall, 1980.
67. Crandall, 1980, p. 491.
68. See Reynolds, 1976, 1980.
69. See Reynolds, 1976, 1980.
70. Murase, 1976, p. 268.

12

The Place of Ethics

Traditional wisdom, as reflected in many religions, in the sages of many cultures, and in some of the psychotherapeutic ideas described in Chapter 11, urges concern for others and for ethical principles and ideals. Much psychological thinking, as we have been documenting throughout this book, pushes in a different direction.

The neo-Freudians, Maslow, Rogers, and others concerned with freedom and authenticity—and probably to some degree most contemporary clinical psychologists— oppose prescriptions and restraints, and encourage us to aim fundamentally at our own development and fulfillment. On the one hand, we can find this in a psychoanalytically oriented clinician like Erik Erikson, who interprets in the self-referent terms of finding an identity and need for identity young people's search for ideals to live by and valid work to do.[1] They are understood as seeking self-definition. On the other hand, we can find it in practitioners of behavior modification like Galassi and Galassi, who urge us to base our behavior on assertive implementation of our own wants and preferences rather than letting our behavior be ruled by "shoulds," "musts," or "oughts."[2]

None of these psychologists intends to promote selfishness. As Waterman argues, they value respect for the integrity of others and the viewing of persons as ends in themselves and not as means toward the fulfillment of one's own interests.[3] They believe, as Waterman does also, that accepting oneself and gratifying one's own needs do not prevent but rather make possible the occurrence of cooperation with and helpfulness to others. Although cases exist in which a person will be better able to aid others if he or she first recognizes and accepts something about himself or herself, focusing on one's own needs and development cannot help but lead away from other-directed concern. Maslow's recommending that the environment, which includes other people, be primarily a means to our own self-actualizing ends and Rogers' thinking that the only real criterion for an individual is his or her own development (and thus not anyone else's) follow directly from their view of self-realization as the fundamental objective. The fact that psychologists who advocate something like this as the primary aim hold contrary values as well and do not wish to spur selfishness cannot (Waterman's claim to the contrary notwithstanding) keep their encouragement to focus on ourselves from doing so.

There are other psychologists who, rather than opposing prescriptions and restraints and urging self-realization, strongly object to such tendencies and continue, as did Freud, to insist on the necessity for constraining ourselves, for explicit consideration of others, and for sublimation. We have seen how, for example, Campbell,[4] Kanfer,[5] and Rushton[6] believe it is of the first importance that our society attempt to foster greater altruism. They concern themselves with suggesting means by which this may be done, such as increased attention to the provision of social approval for conduct helpful to others, demonstration of rewards accruing to people who behave with consideration for others, and getting us to reinforce ourselves for such behavior.

But these psychologists—and probably the vast majority of psychologists altogether—counter traditional ethical wisdom once again, albeit in a different way. They do so by virtue of their assumption of the ultimate egoism of all motivation. If all that can ultimately matter to you is your own good—the fulfillment of your needs and desires for yourself—then to aim at anything other than what will accomplish this is simply to be irrational. To be sure, it may be useful to take the wants of others into consideration, since they are likely to treat you better if you do, and your own conscience may give you a hard time if you attend too little to its precepts. But concern for others or for principles is now at most a means for gaining your own ends. What will be best for you, as social exchange theorists like Kelley and Thibaut[7] make explicit, is to arrange things so that you get maximal returns from others while going out of your way as little as possible.

We have seen how Freud, although urging restraint and the diversion of our energies toward socially useful ends, at the same time implied and even stated explicitly that what would actually be best for each of us is the greatest possible direct gratification of our needs. We would be better off if only we could be less good. For social learning or social exchange theory as for Freud, what is outside ourselves ultimately matters to us only insofar as it relates to our own personal needs and satisfactions. Although the existence of internalized standards means that we can expect to suffer if we too strongly go against the wants of others or ethical principles, again the implication is that we would be better off if only we could be less demanding of ourselves. And this is true with all the many other thinkers who make the assumption of our basic egoism—even those, like Hogan, Johnson, and Emler[8] or Baumrind,[9] who conceive of human nature as intrinsically social and oppose the individualism of our culture. As long as what motivates my concern for others is my own need for social approval or other needs for myself, it still will be irrational for me ever to aim at any objectives other than ones that provide me personally with the greatest possible long-run gain.

The psychologists who urge the importance of promoting ethical and altruistic behavior while at the same time maintaining that we can be motivated only by what relates to our own needs seem surprisingly oblivious of the discrepancy between what they are trying to encourage and where their assumptions lead. If all that you can ultimately care about is yourself, then it will only make sense for you to take other people or ethical principles into account insofar as doing so will serve to benefit you. Trying to get you to give consideration to such matters beyond this point cannot be anything other than an imposition that you would do well to resist.

Both encouraging something like self-actualization as our fundamental goal and assuming the necessary egoism of all motivation thus push against traditional ethical conceptions. Either trend, as well as the effect of both together, tends to vitiate the legitimacy of any ultimate considerations outside the self. Given this sanction for pursuing personal advantage, most ethical ideas face dim prospects.

Are Ethical Values Irrational?

The erosion of ethical conviction in our civilization is of course not to be laid at the door of psychology alone. Apart from the huge changes in our world outside the realm of ideas—technological revolutions and growing bureaucracies, for example—there have been crucial developments in thinking about God and the nature of knowledge and in studies of cultures very different from our own. Not so long ago, the vast majority of people felt fairly clear that what was good was what was asked of them by God and had few doubts. This is hardly the case any longer. Knowledge has come to be almost entirely identified with science; what is neither a matter of logic or mathematics nor founded on publicly verifiable empirical evidence is widely regarded as outside the knowable. Further, the widespread realization that other societies condone or even encourage what in ours is regarded as evil—for example, one man marrying several women, families permitting their older members to die from starvation and exposure to the elements—has made it difficult for us to continue taking for granted the virtues of our ways. If God is dead and human beings disagree with one another on the good, if scientific method is our only route to knowledge, it is perhaps small wonder that our ethics crumble.

It is probably, at least in part, because ethical doubt and skepticism seemed inevitable with a scientific outlook, that psychologists have tended to pay so little attention to their own contributions to this doubt and skepticism. Most psychologists—as perhaps the majority of the more educated people in our culture altogether—essentially take for granted that ethical judgments have no claim to any kind of validity as such. Existentialists speak of our creating or inventing our values in ways that are ultimately arbitrary and irrational; philosophers in the positivistic tradition consider what we are doing when we make judgments of value as expressing approval or disapproval and perhaps trying to induce others to agree with us. Indeed, to say of an assertion that it is a value judgment is widely regarded as tantamount to ruling it out of the realm of rational discourse—a way of trying to close off discussion.

On the other hand, within the past few years a number of philosophers have been concerned to counter this trend.[10] They have pointed out that the existence of differences of opinion and difficulties in their resolution are not unique to the area of value judgments, but occur even within the sacred precinct of science itself. They remind us that we do argue with one another (and with ourselves) regarding value issues and sometimes change our minds, concluding that we have been wrong. And they themselves present us with rational argumentation intended to convince us of certain answers to ethical dilemmas confronting our society on such issues as abortion, euthanasia, and the distribution of resources.

Let us consider a little further these efforts to rescue ethics from radical subjectivism—from the realm of the "merely emotional," irrational, and arbitrary. The existence of differences in valuations does not necessarily imply that valuation is an irrational process or devoid of all objectivity. That the existence of valuation differences fails to prove subjectivism is rather obviously the case when different valuations are being made of the "same" act in different situations, although even such differences are sometimes regarded as demonstrating the lack of any possible claim to validity in the domain of values. Our willingness under some circumstances to, for example, regard breaking a promise or lying as justified means only that it is possible for other considerations to outweigh those of keeping promises and telling the truth, not that our evaluation of these is irrational or merely a matter of subjective preference.

Differences in valuation of various practices among different cultures are often related to different circumstances or to different beliefs about what the circumstances are. As Asch wrote some decades ago, we too would evaluate differently allowing one's parents to die of exposure or even killing them, if there were no means available to care for them or if we believed that they would continue forever in the next world with the level of health and vigor that they possessed when they died.[11] Perhaps this point may be brought home to the reader by consideration of the issue of mercy killing. Is it entirely obvious that it is always better to prolong life, even if this means continuous intolerable pain without hope of recovery? But if we do not believe it is always better to prolong life, does this make the prizing of life an arbitrary value for us?

In addition, it has frequently been pointed out that despite the great variety in cultural practices, there are ethical codes in all known societies, as well as certain commonalities in all these codes. Some kind of provision always seems to be made for consideration—at least within some group to which the individual belongs—of others than oneself, and for matters such as honesty and impartiality in the administration of justice. As Singer mentions, now and then it is claimed that a group has been observed whose members live in blatant dog-eat-dog fashion, without any ethical code whatsoever.[12] Recently Turnbull has held that the Ik—an originally nomadic tribe in northern Uganda that he studied, whose society collapsed when their hunting grounds were taken from them and they were overcome by drought and famine—constitute such a group.[13] The strong would steal food from the weak; parents would turn their young children out on their own.

But even the Ik, as Singer points out on the basis of Turn-bull's report, still regard stealing from one another as wrong, strictly prohibit a tribe member's killing or even drawing blood from another, and engage in pacts of mutual assistance whose obligations are invariably carried out.

There are, then, commonalities in valuations across widely varying groups, and some differences in valuations can be attributed to variations in circumstances or variations in what the circumstances are believed to be such as different views regarding what happens after death. But there are also differences in valuations that cannot readily be so interpreted. Although it is difficult to remove the effects of disagreement on matters of fact in value controversies, it seems unlikely that such disagreement is the sole source of different views on questions about, for example, the appropriateness of affirmative action, abortion, or socialism. If there are differences in valuations that are not a function of variations in factual beliefs, are such differences subject to rational consideration? Or does the recognition now force itself upon us that—apart from factual issues within some value controversies—our valuations are irrational and arbitrary? It is widely believed that once people attempting to resolve value differences have made clear what they mean by the terms they are using and have agreed on relevant matters of fact, there is nothing left for them to do but express their own attitudes or preferences and urge them upon one another.

Consider, however, what actually happens in ethical controversies. In actual practice, not only do we never seem to come to an end of possible things to say about factual matters or the meanings of words, but we also call upon principles and attempt to get one another to agree about them and about their application. Thus, for example, it would generally be agreed that, at least in the absence of extremely strong considerations to the contrary, innocent persons should not be seriously harmed.[14] Anyone advocating a course of conduct that appears as if it may result in such harm is thus obliged to argue that there would not in fact be serious harm, or that what is to be gained is so significant that it outweighs the harm, or that the persons at issue are not really innocent. And in so arguing, he or she would have to take into account further principles, such as that persons known to be innocent should not be declared guilty (again, at least in the absence of extremely compelling considerations to the contrary). A different kind of principle that seems important in all ethical reasoning (as well as other kinds of reasoning) is the absence of bias. If you can show a male disputant in a debate on abortion that the views he has been expressing are partly a function of his gender—if you can demonstrate to him that he has been inappropriately weighting the point of view of the sex he represents—then it becomes incumbent upon him to reconsider and to attempt to reason in a less biased manner. Far from there being no possibility of rational discourse apart from issues of fact or the meanings of terms, it would seem that a great deal of such discourse—with ourselves as well as with others—consists of bringing up principles and questions of their application for consideration.

Existentialists sometimes take the position that general principles cannot really serve to guide us. To illustrate his conviction that we must "invent" our own morality, Sartre tells the frequently cited story of a French student who came to him for advice during the German occupation of France in World War II.[15] The Germans had killed this student's older brother; his father was quarrelling with his mother and collaborating with the Germans. The mother resided alone with the student and depended entirely upon him. He desperately wanted to join the French resistance and avenge his brother, but he was also extremely aware of the grim implications for his mother if he should leave and perhaps even die. The student, as Sartre noted, was confronted by a choice between two very different kinds of action: one directed at a single other person, the other directed at a much larger end, but by the same token one that was much more ambiguous and uncertain of success. No principles seem to resolve the dilemma of what should be done. Is it better to fight for the larger group, or more clearly to help one particular person to live? Is it better to focus one's aims on one's mother or on one's community? Sartre argued that to such questions no one can give an answer on an a priori basis. Sartre had, therefore, "but one reply to make. You are free, therefore choose—that is to say, invent. No rule of general morality can show you what you ought to do."[16]

But Sartre's example does not in fact illustrate that general principles can offer no guidance, that our values are always something we must invent for ourselves. As Bambrough points out, the presentation of the student's conflict presupposes certain values—that of supporting one's mother rather than permitting her to die of starvation or grief and that of combatting murderous oppressors.[17] It is precisely because the student already so strongly values both of these, with no clear basis for one to outweigh the other, that his dilemma is so difficult. There probably are, indeed, moral problems that rational consideration will not resolve—conflicts in which it is impossible ever to come to the reasoned conclusion that one option is clearly better than another—and Sartre's example may well be one of them. This hardly implies, however, that recognized principles or values play no role in moral choice, or that they are arbitrary inventions on our part.

It can even be plausibly suggested that the very idea of behaving ethically is tied to the idea of being able to give a certain kind of rational justification of what one does. One must be able to account for one's behavior in terms of principles or standards that are somehow universal. Or as Singer puts it, to invoke ethics is to move "beyond 'I' and 'you' to the universal law, the universalizable judgment, the standpoint of the impartial spectator."[18]

Questions of ethics do not, then, seem to be just a matter of subjective preferences. We reason about ethical problems and we call upon general principles to help solve them. But does it make sense for us to behave in this way— is it rational on our part? According to most psychological thinking, to be concerned about ethical principles or about other people only makes sense in terms of the gains that will accrue to ourselves. Insofar as following universal principles and considering others will lead to reciprocation, approval, or other forms of reward, or to the avoidance of punishment, doing so is rational; otherwise, it is against one's own interests to do so and may even cause psychological ill-health.

An Alternative View

If it is true that motivation can only be directed fundamentally toward the self, the aforementioned conclusion may be unavoidable. If you delude yourself when you think you are concerned about anything apart from what it ultimately means for you, then indeed to aim at your own good is the only reasonable option. We have argued, however, that the assumption of egoism is unwarranted and false. The general acceptance of this assumption in psychology followed from what was widely regarded some time ago as the solution to the problem of purpose. Human beings—and lower organisms as well—do not behave simply in accord with outside forces, but act in a manner that will increase the likelihood of reaching certain goals. To posit instincts did not really serve to explain such behavior; to think in terms of inborn ends or goals seemed in addition to be metaphysical. But biological needs could be expected to produce bodily conditions that would excite activity, and an organism could be expected to learn to repeat actions that satisfied these needs. Biological needs thus seemed to provide a satisfactory scientific way to account for purposive behavior.

Most psychologists today no longer think that biological needs will entirely suffice, at least for human beings. Many other kinds of needs have been proposed: for example, needs for activity, stimulation, and novelty; needs for competence, power, and self-determination; needs for security, social approval, and predictability. But that it is the individual's own needs that underlie all motivation is hardly ever questioned; psychologists have almost universally simply gone on assuming this to be the case.

Psychologists are assuming more than a trivial egoism. What is held is not just that we are inevitably motivated by our own motives, wants, or desires but also by needs that are directed toward ourselves. All we can want or desire or care about must then be the satisfaction of such needs or what will bear upon this satisfaction. What is outside ourselves can matter only in regard to its implications for ourselves. We can thus, for example, never be directly affected by something like the distress of a friend. According to the social learning theorist Bandura,[19] if such distress makes us sorry, this is because we recognize that we too might be subject to the same misfortune, or that we can now expect less by way of personal benefit from our friend. Even according to Aronfreed[20] and Maccoby,[21] with their interest in empathy, any distress on our part at the plight of a friend occurs only because in earlier situations distress from troubles of our own has become associated with signs of the friend's distress.

There has been little in the way of positive justification provided for these beliefs. They seem to be held not because of substantive data or arguments but essentially just because they are the legacy of what many years ago seemed to offer a scientific solution to the mystery of purposive, goal-directed behavior, namely, motivation from biological needs. Although the insufficiency of biological needs has been widely recognized, psychologists have for the most part simply added different, analogous needs without reconsidering whether purposive behavior really has to be explained in terms of needs or anything directed toward the self at all. We have attempted to show that this is not the only possible kind of explanation, and that, indeed, there is good reason to accept a different view.

Some kinds of stimulation appear to be rewarding and to be sought quite apart from needs, even in the case of lower organisms. Certain tastes, sights, and sounds elicit positive or negative reactions in their own right—reactions that do not appear to be learned. Predispositions to such reactions are highly likely to have evolved by natural selection, and they provide as plausible and scientific a basis for purposive behavior as do needs. The environment, then, does not seem to matter to an individual only in terms of its providing or failing to provide for satisfaction of self-oriented needs. Further, there is good reason to expect that human beings have evolved some predispositions toward social interest and concern as such. It seems in fact unlikely that we care about others and what happens to them only because of implications for or linkages with what happens to ourselves; some tendencies to such caring may rather be a quite direct consequence of our biological heritage.

If this is correct—if the major lines of psychological thinking about motivation are in error in this way—then it may not be true that behaving ethically is rational only when it leads to benefits for ourselves. On the contrary, to consider others and give weight to ethical principles may then be essential to the furtherance of what we most value. Our basic natures may be such that, across a wide range of circumstances (including ones that fall far short of ideal) much of what has the greatest importance to people will tend to be something different from themselves. There will be other people whom they care about, and social groups in whose practices they want to participate and to whose enterprises they wish to contribute. The roles and functions they fulfill for these others and in these groups will not constitute constraints or burdens to them but rather will provide a major source of meaning for their lives.

When this is the case, ethical considerations will be neither irrational nor an imposition from outside. One will be motivated to be helpful, to act justly, to speak honestly, and to uphold one's commitments, not because of what one hopes to gain by such actions—in which case one would have no reason not to cheat and every reason to cheat, if one could get away with it. Rather, one will be so motivated because of the significance to oneself of others' welfare and of the functions one is carrying out within larger social units. Only if the egoistic assumption is correct must rational self-determination mean that action is directed not only by, but for, the self.

To seek only our own good does not, as ancient wisdom recognizes, seem a likely way to find it. Aristotle argued that our good is connected with fulfilling the roles that bind us to variously defined communities.[22] As Angyal,

Frankl, Adler, Rawls, Bergin, and others have said, concerns and values regarding matters beyond ourselves may be essential to our own well-being. We do not seem to thrive when we are focused on ourselves. We seem more likely to do so if we undertake activities that are part of a larger social framework, taking on responsibilities not just for ourselves but for others as well.

If, as we have argued in this book, human beings can be motivated toward ends quite other than themselves, and it is in fact better for them when this is the case, then perhaps the usual lines of therapeutic advice might well be redirected. The problems and troubles that lead people to seek psychotherapy may derive less than is commonly supposed from not expressing themselves, fulfilling themselves, or satisfying needs directed toward themselves and more from not having a workable way of living in which they participate in and contribute to matters they care about beyond themselves.

Notes

1. See, for example, Erikson, 1968, 1975, 1980.
2. Galassi and Galassi, 1977.
3. Waterman, 1981.
4. Campbell, 1975.
5. Kanfer, 1979.
6. Rushton, 1980.
7. Kelley and Thibaut, 1978.
8. Hogan, Johnson, and Emler, 1978.
9. Baumrind, 1978.
10. For example, Fried, 1970, 1978; Rawls, 1971; Perry, 1976; Putnam, 1978; Bambrough, 1979; Singer, 1979, 1981; and MacIntyre, 1981.
11. Asch, 1952.
12. Singer, 1981.
13. Turnbull, 1972.
14. See Perry, 1976.
15. Sartre, 1948.
16. Sartre, 1948, p. 38.
17. Bambrough, 1979, p. 96.
18. Singer, 1979, p. 11.
19. Bandura, 1977.
20. Aronfreed, 1970.
21. Maccoby, 1980.
22. See, for example, MacIntyre, 1981.

References

Adler, A. 1979. *Superiority and social interest: A collection of later writings*. H. L. Ansbacher and R. R. Ansbacher (Eds.). (3rd rev. ed.) New York: Norton.

Ainsworth, M. D. S., S. M. Bell, and D. J. Stayton. 1974. Infant–mother attachment and social development: "Socialisation" as a product of reciprocal responsiveness to signals. In M. P. M. Richards (Ed.), *The integration of a child into a social world*. Cambridge, England: Cambridge University Press.

Albee, G. W. 1977. The Protestant ethic, sex, and psychotherapy. *American Psychologist, 32*, 150–161.

Allport, G. W. 1937. *Personality: A psychological interpretation*. New York: Holt, Rinehart and Winston.

Allport, G. W. 1961. *Pattern and growth in personality*. New York: Holt, Rinehart and Winston.

Allport, G.W. 1969. Mental health: A generic attitude. In M.C. Katz (Ed.), *Sciences of man and social ethics: Variations on the theme of human dignity*. Boston: Branden Press.

Anderson, P. A. 1967. Ministering to troubled people. In O. H. Mowrer (Ed.), *Morality and mental health*. Chicago: Rand McNally.

Angyal, A. 1972. *Foundations for a science of personality.* New York: Viking Press.

Ansbacher, H. L., and R. R. Ansbacher (Eds.) 1964. *The individual psychology of Alfred Adler: A systematic presentation in selections from his writings.* New York: Harper & Row.

Arkin, R. M. 1980. Self-presentation. In D. M. Wegner and R. R. Vallacher (Eds.), *The self in social psychology.* New York: Oxford University Press.

Aronfreed, J. 1970. The socialization of altruistic and sympathetic behavior: Some theoretical and experimental analyses. In J. Macaulay and L. Berkowitz (Eds.), *Altruism and helping behavior: Social psychological studies of some antecedents and consequences.* New York: Academic Press.

Aronson, E. 1980. *The social animal.* (3rd ed.) San Francisco: W. H. Freeman and Company.

Asch, S. E. 1952. *Social psychology.* Englewood Cliffs, N. J.: Prentice-Hall.

Bambrough, R. 1979. *Moral scepticism and moral knowledge.* Atlantic Highlands, N. J.: Humanities Press.

Bandura, A. 1977. *Social learning theory.* Englewood Cliffs, N. J.: Prentice-Hall.

Barlow, J. A. 1981. Mass line leadership and thought reform in China. *American Psychologist, 36,* 300–309.

Bar-Tal, D. 1976. *Prosocial behavior: Theory and research.* Washington, D.C.: Hemisphere.

Batson, C. D., and J. S. Coke. 1981. Empathy: A source of altruistic motivation for helping? In J. P. Rushton and R. M. Sorrentino (Eds.), *Altruism and helping behavior: Social, personality, and developmental perspectives.* Hillsdale, N. J.: Erlbaum.

Baumrind, D. 1978. A dialectical materialist's perspective on knowing social reality. In W. Damon (Ed.), *New directions for child development: Moral development.* No. 2. San Francisco: Jossey-Bass.

Bem, S. L. 1974. The measurement of psychological androgyny. *Journal of Consulting and Clinical Psychology, 42,* 155–162.

Berger, P. L., and T. Luckmann. 1966. *The social construction of reality.* New York: Doubleday.

Bergin, A. E. 1980. Psychotherapy and religious values. *Journal of Consulting and Clinical Psychology, 48,* 95–105.

Bernard, J. 1981. The good-provider role: Its rise and fall. *American Psychologist, 36,* 1–12.

Bernard, L. L. 1924. *Instinct: A study in social psychology.* New York: Holt, Rinehart and Winston.

Berne, E. 1976. *Beyond games and scripts.* New York: Grove Press.

Bertram, B. C. R. 1978. Living in groups: Predators and prey. In J. R. Krebs and N. B. Davies (Eds.), *Behavioral ecology: An evolutionary approach.* Oxford, England: Blackwell.

Bexton, W. H., W. Heron, and T. H. Scott. 1954. Effects of decreased variation in the sensory environment. *Canadian Journal of Psychology, 8,* 70–76.

Bockoven, J. S. 1967. Moral treatment in American psychiatry. In O. H. Mowrer (Ed.), *Morality and mental health.* Chicago: Rand McNally.

Bolles, R. C. 1975. *Theory of motivation.* (2nd ed.) New York: Harper & Row.

Borke, H. 1972. Chandler and Greenspan's "Ersatz Egocentrism": A rejoinder. *Developmental Psychology, 7,* 107–109.

Bowlby, J. 1969. *Attachment and loss.* Vol. 1: *Attachment.* New York: Basic Books.

Brazelton, T. B. 1973. *Neonatal Behavioral Assessment Scale. Clinics in Developmental Medicine.* No. 50. Spastics International Medical Publications. Philadelphia: Lippincott.

Brazelton, T. B., E. Tronick, L. Adamson, H. Als, and S. Wise. 1975. Early mother-infant reciprocity (and Discussion). In *Parent-infant interaction. Ciba Foundation Symposium.* No. 33. Amsterdam: Associated Scientific Publishers.

Brown, G. W., and T. Harris. 1978. *Social origins of depression: A study of psychiatric disorder in women.* London: Tavistock.

Brown, R., and R. J. Herrnstein. 1975. *Psychology.* Boston: Little, Brown.

Bryer, K. B. 1979. The Amish way of death: A study of family support systems. *American Psychologist, 34,* 255–261.

Butler, J. 1973. Upon the love of our neighbour. In R. D. Milo (Ed.), *Egoism and altruism*. Belmont, Calif.: Wadsworth. (Originally published 1726.)

Butler, R. A. 1953. Discrimination learning by rhesus monkeys to visual-exploration motivation. *Journal of Comparative and Physiological Psychology, 46*, 95–98.

Cagan, E. 1978. Individualism, collectivism, and radical educational reform. *Harvard Educational Review, 48*, 227–266.

Cairns, R. B., and D. L. Johnson. 1965. The development of interspecies social attachments. *Psychonomic Science, 2*, 337–338.

Campbell, D. T. 1965. Ethnocentric and other altruistic motives. In D. Levine (Ed.), *Nebraska symposium on motivation, 1965*. Lincoln: University of Nebraska Press.

Campbell, D. T. 1972. On the genetics of altruism and the counterhedonic components in human culture. *Journal of Social Issues, 28*, 21–37.

Campbell, D. T. 1975. On the conflicts between biological and social evolution and between psychology and moral tradition. *American Psychologist, 30*, 1103–1126.

Campbell, D. T. 1978. Social morality norms as evidence of conflict between biological human nature and social system requirements. In G. S. Stent (Ed.), *Morality as a biological phenomenon*. Berlin, West Germany: Abakon Verlagsgesellschaft. (Report of the Dahlem Workshop on Biology and Morals, 1977.)

Cannon, W. B. 1915. *Bodily changes in pain, hunger, fear and rage*. New York: Appleton-Century-Crofts.

Cannon, W. B. 1932. *The wisdom of the body*. New York: Norton.

Carper, J. W. 1953. A comparison of the reinforcing value of a nutritive and a non-nutritive substance under conditions of specific and general hunger. *American Journal of Psychology, 66*, 270–277.

Carson, R. C. 1969. *Interaction concepts of personality*. Chicago: Aldine.

Clark, A. W. 1967. A toad's-eye view of psychiatry and faith. In O. H. Mowrer (Ed.), *Morality and mental health*. Chicago: Rand McNally.

Cofer, C. N., and M. H. Appley. 1964. *Motivation: Theory and research.* New York: Wiley.

Coles, R. 1980. Civility and psychology. *Daedalus, 109,* (3), 133–141.

Crandall, J. E. 1980. Adler's concept of social interest: Theory, measurement, and implications for adjustment. *Journal of Personality and Social Psychology, 39,* 481–495.

Damon, W. 1977. *The social world of the child.* San Francisco: Jossey-Bass.

Dashiell, J. F. 1925. A quantitative demonstration of animal drive. *Journal of Comparative Psychology, 5,* 205–208.

Dashiell, J. F. 1928. *Fundamentals of objective psychology.* Boston: Houghton Mifflin.

Davies, N. B., and J. R. Krebs. 1978. Introduction: Ecology, natural selection and social behavior. In J. R. Krebs and N. B. Davies (Eds.), *Behavioral ecology: An evolutionary approach.* Oxford, England: Blackwell.

Dawes, R. M. 1980. Social dilemmas. *Annual Review of Psychology, 31,* 169–193.

Dawkins, R. 1976. *The selfish gene.* New York: Oxford University Press.

de Castillejo, I. C. 1974. *Knowing woman: A feminine psychology.* New York: Harper & Row.

de Charms, R. 1968. *Personal causation: The internal affective determinants of behavior.* New York: Academic Press.

Deci, E. L. 1975. *Intrinsic motivation.* New York: Plenum.

Deci, E. L. 1980. *The psychology of self-determination.* Lexington, Mass.: Lexington Books.

Dewsbury, D. A. 1981. Effects of novelty on copulatory behavior: The Coolidge effect and related phenomena. *Psychological Bulletin, 89,* 464–482.

Eckerman, C. O., J. L. Whatley, and S. L. Kutz. 1975. Growth of social play with peers during the second year of life. *Developmental Psychology, 11,* 42–49.

Eibl-Eibesfeldt, I. 1971. *Love and hate: The natural history of behavior patterns.* New York: Holt, Rinehart and Winston.

Eisenberg-Berg, N., and E. Geisheker. 1979. Content of preachings and power of the model/preacher: The effect on children's generosity. *Developmental Psychology, 15,* 168–175.

Eisenberger, R. 1972. Explanations of rewards that do not reduce tissue needs. *Psychological Bulletin, 77,* 319–339.

Emde, R. N., T. J. Gaensbauer, and R. J. Harmon. 1976. *Emotional expression in infancy. Psychological Issues.* No. 37. New York: International Universities Press.

Emde, R. N., E. L. Katz, and J. K. Thorpe. 1978. Emotional expression in infancy: II. Early deviations in Down's syndrome. In M. Lewis and L. A. Rosenblum (Eds.), *The development of affect.* New York: Plenum.

Erikson, E. H. 1968. *Identity: Youth and crisis.* New York: Norton.

Erikson, E. H. 1975. *Life history and the historical moment.* New York: Norton.

Erikson, E. H. 1980. *Identity and the life cycle.* New York: Norton.

Fairbairn, W. R. D. 1952. *Psychoanalytic studies of the personality.* London: Routledge and Kegan Paul.

Fellner, C. H., and J. R. Marshall. 1970. Kidney donors. In J. Macaulay and L. Berkowitz (Eds.), *Altruism and helping behavior: Social psychological studies of some antecedents and consequences.* New York: Academic Press.

Fellner, C. H., and J. R. Marshall. 1981. Kidney donors revisited. In J. P. Rushton and R. M. Sorrentino (Eds.), *Altruism and helping behavior: Social, personality, and developmental perspectives.* Hillsdale, N. J.: Erlbaum.

Fenichel, O. 1945. *The psychoanalytic theory of neurosis.* New York: Norton.

Fisher, A. 1962. Effects of stimulus variation on sexual satiation in the male rat. *Journal of Comparative and Physiological Psychology, 55,* 614–620.

Frank, J. D. 1974. *Persuasion and healing: A comparative study of psychotherapy.* (Rev. ed.) New York: Schocken Books.

Frankl, V. E. 1962. *Man's search for meaning: An introduction to logotherapy.* Boston: Beacon Press.

Frankl, V. E. 1970. *The will to meaning: Foundations and applications of logotherapy.* New York: New American Library.

Frankl, V. E. 1979. *The unheard cry for meaning: Psychotherapy and humanism.* New York: Simon and Schuster.

Freud, S. 1953. Three essays on the theory of sexuality. In J. Strachey (Ed.), *The standard edition of the complete psychological works of Sigmund Freud.* Vol. 7. London: Hogarth Press. (Originally published 1905.)

Freud, S. 1955a. A difficulty in the path of psycho-analysis. In J. Strachey (Ed.), *The standard edition of the complete psychological works of Sigmund Freud.* Vol. 17. London: Hogarth Press. (Originally published 1917.)

Freud, S. 1955b. Beyond the pleasure principle. In J. Strachey (Ed.), *The standard edition of the complete psychological works of Sigmund Freud.* Vol. 18. London: Hogarth Press. (Originally published 1920.)

Freud, S. 1955c. Group psychology and the analysis of the ego. In J. Strachey (Ed.), *The standard edition of the complete psychological works of Sigmund Freud.* Vol. 18. London: Hogarth Press. (Originally published 1921.)

Freud, S. 1957a. Five lectures on psychoanalysis. In J. Strachey (Ed.), *The standard edition of the complete psychological works of Sigmund Freud.* Vol 11. London: Hogarth Press. (Originally published 1910.)

Freud, S. 1957b. Instincts and their vicissitudes. In J. Strachey (Ed.), *The standard edition of the complete psychological works of Sigmund Freud.* Vol. 14. London: Hogarth Press. (Originally published 1915.)

Freud, S. 1958. The dynamics of transference. In J. Strachey (Ed.), *The standard edition of the complete psychological works of Sigmund Freud.* Vol. 12. London: Hogarth Press. (Originally published 1912.)

Freud, S. 1959. "Civilized" sexual morality and modern nervous illness. In J. Strachey (Ed.), *The standard edition of the complete psychological works of Sigmund Freud.* Vol. 9. London: Hogarth Press. (Originally published 1908.)

Freud, S. 1960. The psychopathology of everyday life. In J. Strachey (Ed.), *The standard edition of the complete psychological works of*

Sigmund Freud. Vol. 6. London: Hogarth Press. (Originally published 1901.)

Freud, S. 1961a. The ego and the id. In J. Strachey (Ed.), *The standard edition of the complete psychological works of Sigmund Freud.* Vol. 19. London: Hogarth Press. (Originally published 1923.)

Freud, S. 1961b. The economic problem of masochism. In J. Strachey (Ed.), *The standard edition of the complete psychological works of Sigmund Freud.* Vol. 19. London: Hogarth Press. (Originally published 1924.)

Freud, S. 1961c. The future of an illusion. In J. Strachey (Ed.), *The standard edition of the complete psychological works of Sigmund Freud.* Vol. 21. London: Hogarth Press. (Originally published 1927.)

Freud, S. 1961d. Civilization and its discontents. In J. Strachey (Ed.), *The standard edition of the complete psychological works of Sigmund Freud.* Vol. 21. London: Hogarth Press. (Originally published 1930.)

Freud, S. 1964a. New introductory lectures on psychoanalysis. In J. Strachey (Ed.), *The standard edition of the complete psychological works of Sigmund Freud.* Vol. 22. London: Hogarth Press. (Originally published 1933.)

Freud, S. 1964b. An outline of psychoanalysis. In J. Strachey (Ed.), *The standard edition of the complete psychological works of Sigmund Freud.* Vol. 23. London: Hogarth Press. (Originally published 1940.)

Fried, C. 1970. *An anatomy of values: Problems of personal and social choice.* Cambridge, Mass.: Harvard University Press.

Fried, C. 1978. *Right and wrong.* Cambridge, Mass.: Harvard University Press.

Fromm, E. 1947. *Man for himself: An inquiry into the psychology of ethics.* New York: Fawcett.

Fromm, E. 1955. *The sane society.* New York: Fawcett.

Fromm, E. 1956. *The art of loving.* New York: Harper & Row.

Fromm, E. 1965. *Escape from freedom.* New York: Avon Books. (Originally published 1941.)

Fromm, E. 1973. *The anatomy of human destructiveness.* New York: Fawcett.

Fromm, E. 1976. *To have or to be?* New York: Harper & Row.

Fussell, P. 1979. Me decade antidote. (In defense of the Boy Scouts.) *The New Republic,* May 19, 20–21.

Galassi, M. D., and J. P. Galassi. 1977. *Assert yourself! How to be your own person.* New York: Human Sciences Press.

Garfield, S. L. 1981. Psychotherapy: A 40-year appraisal. *American Psychologist, 36,* 174–183.

Glasser, W. 1975a. *Reality therapy: A new approach to psychiatry.* New York: Harper & Row.

Glasser, W. 1975b. *The identity society.* (Rev. ed.) New York: Harper & Row.

Goldstein, K. 1939. *The organism.* New York: American Book Company.

Goodwin, R. N. 1974. *The American condition.* New York: Doubleday.

Gordon, T. 1976. *P. E. T. in action.* New York: Wyden.

Gottman, J., H. Markman, and C. Notarius. 1977. The topography of marital conflict: A sequential analysis of verbal and nonverbal behavior. *Journal of Marriage and the Family, 39,* 461–477.

Haley, J. 1973. *Uncommon therapy: The psychiatric techniques of Milton H. Erickson, M. D.* New York: Norton.

Hallie, P. P. 1979. *Lest innocent blood be shed: The story of the village of Le Chambon and how goodness happened there.* New York: Harper & Row.

Harlow, H. F. 1969. Age-mate or peer affectional system. In D. S. Lehrman, R. A. Hinde, and E. Shaw (Eds.), *Advances in the study of behavior.* Vol. 2. New York: Academic Press.

Harlow, H. F., M. K. Harlow, and D. R. Meyer. 1950. Learning motivated by a manipulation drive. *Journal of Experimental Psychology, 40,* 228–234.

Harlow, H. F., M. K. Harlow, and S. J. Suomi. 1971. From thought to therapy: Lessons from a primate laboratory. *American Scientist, 59,* 538–549.

Harlow, H. F., and R. R. Zimmermann. 1959. Affectional responses in the infant monkey. *Science, 130,* 421–432.

Harrison, A. A. 1976. *Individuals and groups: Understanding social behavior.* Monterey, Calif.: Brooks/Cole.

Hartmann, H. 1958. *Ego psychology and the problem of adaptation.* New York: International Universities Press. (D. Rapaport, Trans.; original essay presented before Vienna Psychoanalytic Society, 1937.)

Hartmann, H. 1964a. Comments on the psychoanalytic theory of the ego. In H. Hartmann, *Essays on ego psychology: Selected problems in psychoanalytic theory.* New York: International Universiti˜s Press. (Originally published 1950.)

Hartmann, H. 1964b. Notes on the reality principle. In H. Hartmann, *Essays on ego psychology: Selected problems in psychoanalytic theory.* New York: International Universities Press. (Originally published 1956.)

Hartmann, H. 1964c. *Essays on ego psychology: Selected problems in psychoanalytic theory.* New York: International Universities Press.

Hatfield, E., G. W. Walster, and J. A. Piliavin. 1978. Equity theory and helping relationships. In L. Wispé (Ed.), *Altruism, sympathy, and helping: Psychological and sociological principles.* New York: Academic Press.

Hay, D. F. 1979. Cooperative interactions and sharing between very young children and their parents. *Developmental Psychology, 15,* 647–653.

Hebb, D. O. 1971. Comment on altruism: The comparative evidence. *Psychological Bulletin, 76,* 409–410.

Hendrick, I. 1942. Instinct and the ego during infancy. *The Psychoanalytic Quarterly, 11,* 33–58.

Hendrick, I. 1943a. Work and the pleasure principle. *The Psychoanalytic Quarterly, 12,* 311–329.

Hendrick, I. 1943b. The discussion of the "instinct to master." *The Psychoanalytic Quarterly, 12,* 561–565.

Hinde, R. A. 1970. *Animal behavior: A synthesis of ethology and comparative psychology.* (2nd ed.) New York: McGraw-Hill.

Hobbes, T. 1973. Self-love and society. In R. D. Milo (Ed.), *Egoism and altruism.* Belmont, Calif.: Wadsworth. (Originally published 1642.)

Hofer, M. A. 1975. Summing up. In *Parent-infant interaction. Ciba Foundation Symposium*. No. 33. Amsterdam: Associated Scientific Publishers.

Hoffman, M. L. 1975. Developmental synthesis of affect and cognition and its implications for altruistic motivation. *Developmental Psychology, 11,* 607–622.

Hoffman, M. L. 1977. Empathy, its development and prosocial implications. In H. E. Howe, Jr., and C. B. Keasey (Eds.), *Nebraska symposium on motivation, 1977: Social cognitive development*. Lincoln: University of Nebraska Press.

Hoffman, M. L. 1978. Toward a theory of empathic arousal and development. In M. Lewis and L. A. Rosenblum (Eds.), *The development of affect*. New York: Plenum.

Hoffman, M. L. 1981. Is altruism part of human nature? *Journal of Personality and Social Psychology, 40,* 121–137.

Hogan, R. 1975. Theoretical egocentrism and the problem of compliance. *American Psychologist, 30,* 533–540.

Hogan, R., J. A. Johnson, and N. P. Emler. 1978. A socioanalytic theory of moral development. In W. Damon (Ed.), *New directions for child development: Moral development*. No. 2. San Francisco: Jossey-Bass.

Holt, R. R. 1965. A review of some of Freud's biological assumptions and their influence on his theories. In N. S. Greenfield and W. C. Lewis (Eds.), *Psychoanalysis and current biological thought*. Madison: University of Wisconsin Press.

Holt, R. R. 1976. Drive or wish? A reconsideration of the psychoanalytic theory of motivation. In M. M. Gill and P. S. Holzman (Eds.), *Psychology versus metapsychology: Psychoanalytic essays in memory of George S. Klein. Psychological Issues*. No. 36. New York: International Universities Press.

Horney, K. 1937. *The neurotic personality of our time*. New York: Norton.

Horney, K. 1939. *New ways in psychoanalysis*. New York: Norton.

Horney, K. 1945. *Our inner conflicts*. New York: Norton.

Horney, K. 1950. *Neurosis and human growth: The struggle toward self-realization*. New York: Norton.

Hornstein, H. A. 1976. *Cruelty and kindness: A new look at aggression and altruism.* Englewood Cliffs, N.J.: Prentice-Hall.

Hull, C. L. 1943. *Principles of behavior.* New York: Appleton-Century-Crofts.

Hunt, J. McV. 1971a. Intrinsic motivation: Information and circumstance. In H. M. Schroder and P. Suedfeld (Eds.), *Personality theory and information processing.* New York: Ronald.

Hunt, J. McV. 1971b. Intrinsic motivation and psychological development. In H. M. Schroder and P. Suedfeld (Eds.), *Personality theory and information processing.* New York: Ronald.

Jones, E. 1955. *The life and work of Sigmund Freud.* Vol. 2: *Years of maturity, 1901–1919.* New York: Basic Books.

Jones, E. 1957. *The life and work of Sigmund Freud.* Vol. 3: *The last phase, 1919–1939.* New York: Basic Books.

Kanfer, F. H. 1979. Personal control, social control, and altruism: Can society survive the age of individualism? *American Psychologist, 34,* 231–239.

Kaswan, J. 1981. Manifest and latent functions of psychological services. *American Psychologist, 36,* 290–299.

Kauffmann, S. 1979. Exteriors. *The New Republic,* May 19, 22–23.

Kelley, H. H., and J. W. Thibaut. 1978. *Interpersonal relations: A theory of interdependence.* New York: Wiley.

Kessen, W. (Ed.) 1975. *Childhood in China.* New Haven, Conn.: Yale University Press.

Kirschenbaum, H. 1979. *On becoming Carl Rogers.* New York: Delacorte Press.

Klinger, E. 1977. *Meaning and void: Inner experience and the incentives in people's lives.* Minneapolis: University of Minnesota Press.

Koch, S. 1956. Behavior as "intrinsically" regulated: Work notes towards a pre-theory of phenomena called "motivational." In M. R. Jones (Ed.), *Nebraska symposium on motivation, 1956.* Lincoln: University of Nebraska Press.

Kohlberg, L. 1976. Moral stages and moralization: The cognitive-developmental approach. In T. Lickona (Ed.), *Moral development and behavior: Theory, research, and social issues.* New York: Holt, Rinehart and Winston.

Kohlberg, L. 1978. Revisions in the theory and practice of moral development. In W. Damon (Ed.), *New directions for child development: Moral development.* No. 2. San Francisco: Jossey-Bass.

Kondo, K. 1976. The origin of Morita therapy. In W. P. Lebra (Ed.), *Culture-bound syndromes, ethnopsychiatry, and alternate therapies.* Honolulu: University Press of Hawaii.

Krauthammer, C. 1979. When murder serves as terrorists' therapy. *The New York Times, The Week in Review,* April 15, 16E.

Krebs, D. L. 1975. Empathy and altruism. *Journal of Personality and Social Psychology, 32,* 1134–1146.

Laing, R. D. 1967. *The politics of experience.* New York: Ballantine Books.

Lasch, C. 1978. *The culture of narcissism: American life in an age of diminishing expectations.* New York: Norton.

Latané, B., and J. M. Darley. 1970. *The unresponsive bystander: Why doesn't he help?* New York: Appleton-Century-Crofts.

Leeper, R. W. 1948. A motivational theory of emotion to replace "emotion as disorganized response." *Psychological Review, 55,* 5–21.

Leeper, R. W. 1965. Some needed developments in the motivational theory of emotions. In D. Levine (Ed.), *Nebraska symposium on motivation, 1965.* Lincoln: University of Nebraska Press.

Levin, K. 1978. *Freud's early psychology of the neuroses: A historical perspective.* Pittsburgh: University of Pittsburgh Press.

Levinger, G. 1980. Toward the analysis of close relationships. *Journal of Experimental Social Psychology, 16,* 510–544.

Lin, Y. (Ed.) 1948. *The wisdom of Laotse.* New York: Random House.

London, P. 1970. The rescuers: Motivational hypotheses about Christians who saved Jews from the Nazis. In J. Macaulay and L. Berkowitz (Eds.), *Altruism and helping behavior: Social psychological studies of some antecedents and consequences.* New York: Academic Press.

Lowenfeld, H., and Y. Lowenfeld. 1972. Our permissive society and the superego: Some current thoughts about Freud's cultural concepts. In S. C. Post (Ed.), *Moral values and the super-*

ego concept in psychoanalysis. New York: International Universities Press.

Lubinski, D., A. Tellegen, and J. N. Butcher. 1981. The relationship between androgyny and subjective indicators of emotional well-being. *Journal of Personality and Social Psychology*, *40*, 722–730.

Maccoby, E. E. 1980. *Social development: Psychological growth and the parent-child relationship*. New York: Harcourt Brace Jovanovich.

MacIntyre, A. 1981. *After virtue: A study in moral theory.* Notre Dame, Ind.: University of Notre Dame Press.

Maddi, S. R. 1970. The search for meaning. In W. J. Arnold and M. M. Page (Eds.), *Nebraska symposium on motivation, 1970*. Lincoln: University of Nebraska Press.

Maddi, S. R. 1978. Rogers as revolutionary. (Review of *Carl Rogers on personal power: Inner strength and its revolutionary impact*, by C. R. Rogers.) *Contemporary Psychology*, *23*, 300–301.

Marin, P. 1975. The new narcissism. *Harper's Magazine*, October, 45–50, 55–56.

Martel, M. U. 1968. Age-sex roles in American magazine fiction (1890–1955). In B. L. Neugarten (Ed.), *Middle age and aging: A reader in social psychology*. Chicago: University of Chicago Press.

Martin, G. B., and R. D. Clark III. 1982. Distress crying in neonates: Species and peer specificity. *Developmental Psychology*, *18*, 3–9.

Maslow, A. H. 1954. *Motivation and personality*. New York: Harper & Row.

Maslow, A. H. 1959. Preface. In A. H. Maslow (Ed.), *New knowledge in human values*. New York: Harper & Row.

Maslow, A. H. 1964. *Religions, values, and peak-experiences*. Columbus: Ohio State University Press.

Maslow, A. H. 1968. *Toward a psychology of being*. (2nd ed.) New York: Van Nostrand.

Maslow, A. H. 1970. *Motivation and personality*. (2nd ed.) New York: Harper & Row.

Maslow, A. H. 1976. *The farther reaches of human nature.* New York: Penguin.

Masserman, J. H., S. Wechkin, and W. Terris. 1964. "Altruistic" behavior in rhesus monkeys. *American Journal of Psychiatry, 121,* 584–585.

Matthews, K. A., C. D. Batson, J. Horn, and R. H. Rosenman. 1981. "Principles in his nature which interest him in the fortune of others . . .": The heritability of empathic concern for others. *Journal of Personality, 49,* 237–247.

May, R. 1958a. The origins and significance of the existential movement in psychology. In R. May, E. Angel, and H. F. Ellenberger (Eds.), *Existence: A new dimension in psychiatry and psychology.* New York: Simon and Schuster.

May, R. 1958b. Contributions of existential psychotherapy. In R. May, E. Angel, and H. F. Ellenberger (Eds.), *Existence: A new dimension in psychiatry and psychology.* New York: Simon and Schuster.

McClelland, D. C. 1975. *Power: The inner experience.* New York: Irvington.

McClelland, D. C. 1978. Managing motivation to expand human freedom. *American Psychologist, 33,* 201–210.

McClelland, D. C., and D. G. Winter. 1971. *Motivating economic achievement.* New York: Free Press.

McDougall, W. 1908. *An introduction to social psychology.* London: Methuen.

McDougall, W. 1923. *Outline of psychology.* New York: Scribner's.

Menninger, K. 1978. *Whatever became of sin?* New York: Bantam Books.

Milo, R. D. (Ed.) 1973. *Egoism and altruism.* Belmont, Calif.: Wadsworth.

Montgomery, K. C. 1954. The role of the exploratory drive in learning. *Journal of Comparative and Physiological Psychology, 47,* 60–64.

Morgan, C. T. 1943. *Physiological psychology.* New York: McGraw-Hill.

Mowrer, O. H. 1961. *The crisis in psychiatry and religion.* New York: Van Nostrand.

Mowrer, O. H. 1964. *The new group therapy.* New York: Van Nostrand.

Mowrer, O. H. 1972. Conscience and the unconscious. In R. C. Johnson, P. R. Dokecki, and O. H. Mowrer (Eds.), *Conscience, contract, and social reality: Theory and research in behavioral science.* New York: Holt, Rinehart and Winston.

Munro, D. J. 1977. *The concept of man in contemporary China.* Ann Arbor: University of Michigan Press.

Murase, T. 1976. Naikan therapy. In W. P. Lebra (Ed.), *Culture-bound syndromes, ethnopsychiatry, and alternate therapies.* Honolulu: University Press of Hawaii.

Murphy, G. 1947. *Personality: A biosocial approach to origins and structure.* New York: Harper & Row.

Mussen, P., and N. Eisenberg-Berg. 1977. *Roots of caring, sharing, and helping: The development of prosocial behavior in children.* San Francisco: W. H. Freeman and Company.

Myerhoff, B. 1978. *Number our days.* New York: Dutton.

Myers, A. K., and N. E. Miller. 1954. Failure to find a learned drive based on hunger; evidence for learning motivated by "exploration." *Journal of Comparative and Physiological Psychology, 47,* 428–436.

Nietzsche, F. 1910. The genealogy of morals. In O. Levy (Ed.), *The complete works of Friedrich Nietzsche.* Vol. 13. London: Allen & Unwin. (Originally published 1887.)

Oldenquist, A. 1979. Moral education without moral education. *Harvard Educational Review, 49,* 240–247.

Parloff, M. B., I. E. Waskow, and B. E. Wolfe. 1978. Research on therapist variables in relation to process and outcome. In S. L. Garfield and A. E. Bergin (Eds.), *Handbook of psychotherapy and behavior change: An empirical analysis.* (2nd ed.) New York: Wiley.

Parr, S. R. 1977. All's not well aboard the "indomitable." *The Chronicle of Higher Education,* October 3, 40.

Perls, F., R. E. Hefferline, and P. Goodman. 1951. *Gestalt therapy: Excitement and growth in the human personality.* New York: Dell.

Perry, T. D. 1976. *Moral reasoning and truth.* Oxford, England: Clarendon Press.

Piaget, J. 1952. *The origins of intelligence in children.* New York: International Universities Press.

Piliavin, I. M., J. Rodin, and J. A. Piliavin. 1969. Good Samaritanism: An underground phenomenon? *Journal of Personality and Social Psychology, 13,* 289–299.

Piliavin, J. A., J. F. Dovidio, S. L. Gaertner, and R. D. Clark III. 1981. *Emergency intervention.* New York: Academic Press.

Pirsig, R. 1974. *Zen and the art of motorcycle maintenance.* New York: Morrow.

Putnam, H. 1978. *Meaning and the moral sciences.* London: Routledge and Kegan Paul.

Rawls, J. 1971. *A theory of justice.* Cambridge, Mass.: Harvard University Press.

Reynolds, D. K. 1976. *Morita psychotherapy.* Berkeley: University of California Press.

Reynolds, D. K. 1980. *The quiet therapies: Japanese pathways to personal growth.* Honolulu: University Press of Hawaii.

Rheingold, H. L., and D. F. Hay. 1978. Prosocial behavior of the very young. In G. S. Stent (Ed.), *Morality as a biological phenomenon.* Berlin, West Germany: Abakon Verlagsgesellschaft. (Report of the Dahlem Workshop on Biology and Morals, 1977.)

Rheingold, H. L., D. F. Hay, and M. J. West. 1976. Sharing in the second year of life. *Child Development, 47,* 1148–1158.

Richter, C. P. 1927. Animal behavior and internal drives. *The Quarterly Review of Biology, 2,* 307–343.

Ridley, M., and R. Dawkins. 1981. The natural selection of altruism. In J. P. Rushton and R. M. Sorrentino (Eds.), *Altruism and helping behavior: Social, personality, and developmental perspectives.* Hillsdale, N. J.: Erlbaum.

Rieff, P. 1959. *Freud: The mind of the moralist.* New York: Viking Press.

Rogers, C. R. 1951. *Client-centered therapy: Its current practice, implications, and theory.* Boston: Houghton Mifflin.

Rogers, C. R. 1957. The necessary and sufficient conditions of therapeutic personality change. *Journal of Consulting Psychology, 21,* 95–103.

Rogers, C. R. 1959. A theory of therapy, personality, and inter-personal relationships, as developed in the client-centered framework. In S. Koch (Ed.), *Psychology: A study of a science.* Vol. 3: *Formulations of the person and the social context.* New York: McGraw-Hill.

Rogers, C. R. 1961. *On becoming a person.* Boston: Houghton Mifflin.

Rogers, C. R. 1967. Carl R. Rogers. In E. G. Boring and G. Lindzey (Eds.), *A history of psychology in autobiography.* Vol. 5. New York: Appleton-Century-Crofts.

Rogers, C. R. 1969. *Freedom to learn: A view of what education might become.* Columbus, Ohio: Merrill.

Rogers, C. R. 1970. *Carl Rogers on encounter groups.* New York: Harper & Row.

Rogers, C. R. 1971. Toward a modern approach to values: The valuing process in the mature person. In C. R. Rogers and B. Stevens (Eds.), *Person to person: The problem of being human.* New York: Pocket Books. (Originally published in *Journal of Abnormal and Social Psychology,* 1964, *68,* 160–167.)

Rogers, C. R. 1972. *Becoming partners: Marriage and its alternatives.* New York: Dell.

Rogers, C. R. 1977. *Carl Rogers on personal power: Inner strength and its revolutionary impact.* New York: Delacorte Press.

Rosenhan, D. 1970. The natural socialization of altruistic autonomy. In J. Macaulay and L. Berkowitz (Eds.), *Altruism and helping behavior: Social psychological studies of some antecedents and consequences.* New York: Academic Press.

Roszak, T. 1978. *Person/planet: The creative disintegration of industrial society.* New York: Anchor Press/Doubleday.

Rusbult, C. E. 1980. Commitment and satisfaction in romantic associations: A test of the investment model. *Journal of Experimental Social Psychology, 16,* 172–186.

Rushton, J. P. 1980. *Altruism, socialization, and society.* Englewood Cliffs, N. J.: Prentice-Hall.

Rushton, J. P., and R. M. Sorrentino (Eds.) 1981. *Altruism and helping behavior: Social, personality, and developmental perspectives.* Hillsdale, N. J.: Erlbaum.

Sagi, A., and M. L. Hoffman. 1976. Empathic distress in the newborn. *Developmental Psychology, 12,* 175–176.

Sampson, E. E. 1977. Psychology and the American ideal. *Journal of Personality and Social Psychology, 35,* 767–782.

Sampson, E. E. 1978. Scientific paradigms and social values: Wanted—a scientific revolution. *Journal of Personality and Social Psychology, 36,* 1332–1343.

Sartre, J.-P. 1948. *Existentialism and humanism.* London: Methuen.

Sasaki, Y. 1976. Nonmedical healing in contemporary Japan: A psychiatric study. In W. P. Lebra (Ed.), *Culture-bound syndromes, ethnopsychiatry, and alternate therapies.* Honolulu: University Press of Hawaii.

Schachter, S. 1959. *The psychology of affiliation: Experimental studies of the sources of gregariousness.* Stanford, Calif.: Stanford University Press.

Schopler, J. 1970. An attribution analysis of some determinants of reciprocating a benefit. In J. Macaulay and L. Berkowitz (Eds.), *Altruism and helping behavior: Social psychological studies of some antecedents and consequences.* New York: Academic Press.

Sennett, R. 1980. *Authority.* New York: Knopf.

Sheffield, F. D., and T. B. Roby. 1950. Reward value of a nonnutritive sweet taste. *Journal of Comparative and Physiological Psychology, 43,* 471–481.

Sheffield, F. D., J. J. Wulff, and R. Backer. 1951. Reward value of copulation without sex drive reduction. *Journal of Comparative and Physiological Psychology, 44,* 3–8.

Shotland, R. L., and T. L. Huston. 1979. Emergencies: What are they and do they influence bystanders to intervene? *Journal of Personality and Social Psychology, 37,* 1822–1834.

Simonton, D. K. 1980. Thematic fame, melodic originality, and musical zeitgeist: A biographical and transhistorical content analysis. *Journal of Personality and Social Psychology, 38,* 972–983.

Simpson, E. L. 1976. A holistic approach to moral development and behavior. In T. Lickona (Ed.), *Moral development and behavior: Theory, research, and social issues.* New York: Holt, Rinehart, and Winston.

Singer, P. 1979. *Practical ethics.* Cambridge, England: Cambridge University Press.

Singer, P. 1981. *The expanding circle: Ethics and sociobiology.* New York: Farrar, Straus & Giroux.

Smith, M. B. 1961. "Mental health" reconsidered: A special case of the problem of values in psychology. *American Psychologist, 16,* 299–306.

Smith, M. B. 1978. Encounter groups and humanistic psychology. In K. W. Back (Ed.), *In search for community: Encounter groups and social change.* Boulder, Colo.: Westview Press.

Smith, M. B. 1980. Attitudes, values, and selfhood. In H. E. Howe, Jr., and M. M. Page (Eds.), *Nebraska symposium on motivation, 1979: Beliefs, attitudes, and values.* Lincoln: University of Nebraska Press.

Staub, E. 1978. *Positive social behavior and morality.* Vol. 1: *Social and personal influences.* New York: Academic Press.

Staub, E. 1979. *Positive social behavior and morality.* Vol. 2: *Socialization and development.* New York: Academic Press.

Sullivan, H. S. 1947. *Conceptions of modern psychiatry: The first William Alanson White Memorial Lectures.* Washington, D.C.: William Alanson White Foundation.

Sullivan, H. S. 1953. *The interpersonal theory of psychiatry.* New York: Norton.

Sulloway, F. J. 1979. *Freud, biologist of the mind: Beyond the psychoanalytic legend.* New York: Basic Books.

Suomi, S. J., H. F. Harlow, and C. J. Domek. 1970. Effect of repetitive infant-infant separation of young monkeys. *Journal of Abnormal Psychology, 76,* 161–172.

Thom, G. 1979. *Bringing the left back home: A critique of American social criticism.* New Haven, Conn.: Yale University Press.

Titmuss, R. M. 1971. *The gift relationship: From human blood to social policy.* New York: Pantheon.

Tomkins, S. S. 1962. *Affect, imagery, consciousness.* Vol. 1: *The positive affects.* New York: Springer.

Trevarthen, C. 1979. Communication and cooperation in early infancy: A description of primary intersubjectivity. In M. Bul-

Iowa (Ed.), *Before speech: The beginning of interpersonal communication.* Cambridge, England: Cambridge University Press.

Trivers, R. L. 1971. The evolution of reciprocal altruism. *The Quarterly Review of Biology, 46,* 35–57.

Turnbull, C. M. 1972. *The mountain people.* New York: Simon and Schuster.

Vaillant, G. E. 1977. *Adaptation to life.* Boston: Little, Brown.

Veroff, J., and J. B. Veroff. 1980. *Social incentives: A life-span developmental approach.* New York: Academic Press.

Vitz, P. C. 1977. *Psychology as religion: The cult of self-worship.* Grand Rapids, Mich.: Eerdmans.

Wallach, M. A. 1967. Creativity and the expression of possibilities. In J. Kagan (Ed.), *Creativity and learning.* Boston: Houghton Mifflin.

Waller, W. W. 1930. *The old love and the new: Divorce and readjustment.* Philadelphia: Liveright.

Warden, C. J. 1931. *Animal motivation: Experimental studies on the albino rat.* New York: Columbia University Press.

Warnock, M. 1970. *Existentialism.* Oxford, England: Oxford University Press.

Waterman, A. S. 1981. Individualism and interdependence. *American Psychologist, 36,* 762–773.

White, G. L. 1980. Physical attractiveness and courtship progress. *Journal of Personality and Social Psychology, 39,* 660–668.

White, R. W. 1959. Motivation reconsidered: The concept of competence. *Psychological Review, 66,* 297–333.

Wilson, E. O. 1978. *On human nature.* Cambridge, Mass.: Harvard University Press.

Wispé, L. (Ed.) 1978. *Altruism, sympathy, and helping: Psychological and sociological principles.* New York: Academic Press.

Wispé, L. G., and J. N. Thompson, Jr. (Eds.) 1976. The war between the words: Biological versus social evolution and some related issues. *American Psychologist, 31,* 341–384.

Woodworth, R. S. 1918. *Dynamic psychology.* New York: Columbia University Press.

Yalom, I. D. 1980. *Existential psychotherapy.* New York: Basic Books.

Young, P. T. 1952. The role of hedonic processes in the organization of behavior. *Psychological Review, 59,* 249–262.

Young, P. T. 1959. The role of affective processes in learning and motivation. *Psychological Review, 66,* 104–125.

Index of Names

Adamson, L., 226n
Adler, A., 61–63, 110, 132,
    233, 234, 254–256, 259n,
    274
Ainsworth, M. D. S., 226n
Albee, G. W., 232, 259n
Allen, W., 9, 10
Allport, G. W., 61–63, 78n,
    231, 259n
Als, H., 226n
Anderson, P. A., 239, 259n
Angyal, A., 247, 259n, 273
Ansbacher, H. L., 259n
Ansbacher, R. R., 259n
Appley, M. H., 225n
Aristotle, 273
Arkin, R. M., 26, 30n
Aronfreed, J., 26, 30n, 190,
    195n, 203, 225n, 271, 274n
Aronson, E., 174, 194n
Asch, S. E., 62, 63, 78n, 266,
    274n

Backer, R., 78n, 225n
Bambrough, R., 269, 274n
Bandura, A., 181–183, 191,
    193, 195n, 198, 202, 203,
    271, 274n
Barlow, J. A., 252, 259n
Bar-Tal, D., 194n
Batson, C. D., 225n, 226n
Baumrind, D., 188, 189, 194,
    195n, 263, 274n
Bell, S. M., 226n
Bem, S. L., 29n
Benedict, R., 135
Berger, P. L., 22, 30n
Bergin, A. E., 30n, 230, 259n,
    274
Bernard, J., 258n
Bernard, L. L., 225n
Berne, E., 128, 150n
Bertram, B. C. R., 78n
Bexton, W. H., 60n, 211, 225n
Bockoven, J. S., 259n

Bogart, H., 9, 10
Bolles, R. C., 225n
Borke, H., 29n
Bowlby, J., 225n
Brazelton, T. B., 226n
Brown, G. W., 248, 259n
Brown, R., 22–24, 28, 30n
Bryer, K. B., 29n
Butcher, J. N., 248, 259n
Butler, J., 29n
Butler, R. A., 67, 78n, 211, 225n

Cagan, E., 15, 18, 29n, 30n
Cairns, R. B., 71, 78n
Campbell, D. T., 20, 21, 30n, 60n, 197, 225n, 226n, 261, 274n
Cannon, W. B., 225n
Carper, J. W., 225n
Carson, R. C., 30n
Clark, A. W., 253, 259n
Clark, R. D., III, 30n, 78n
Cofer, C. N., 225n
Coke, J. S., 225n
Coles, R., 174, 194n
Crandall, J. E., 255, 256, 259n

Damon, W., 192, 195n
Darley, J. M., 23, 30n
Darwin, C., 50, 51, 207
Dashiell, J. F., 208, 225n
Davies, N. B., 60n, 226n
Dawes, R. M., 176, 194n
Dawkins, R., 60n, 74, 78n, 226n
de Castillejo, I. C., 29n
de Charms, R., 213, 214, 225n
Deci, E. L., 213, 214, 225n
Dewsbury, D. A., 60n, 225n

Domek, C. J., 71, 78n, 212, 225n
Dovidio, J. F., 30n

Eckerman, C. O., 73, 78n
Eibl-Eibesfeldt, I., 70, 73, 78n
Eisenberg-Berg, N., 194n, 195n
Eisenberger, R., 78n
Emde, R. N., 224, 226n
Emler, N. P., 188, 195n, 263, 274n
Erhard, W., 13, 17
Erickson, M. H., 236–238, 241, 245–247
Erikson, E. H., 260, 274n

Fairbairn, W. R. D., 80, 108n
Fellini, F., 168, 247
Fellner, C. H., 29n
Fenichel, O., 66, 78n
Fisher, A., 210, 225n
Fliess, W., 43
Frank, J. D., 244, 259n
Frankl, V. E., 231, 234–236, 239–241, 250, 253, 254, 259n, 274
Franklin, B., 232
Freud, S., 18, 31–34, 36, 37, 39–44, 44n, 45n–60, 60n–64, 66–68, 70, 75–77, 79, 80, 83, 89, 96, 98, 99, 109, 110, 114, 115, 117–120, 125–129, 135, 149, 151, 152, 156, 157, 169–171, 174, 193, 194, 197–199, 202, 206, 207, 209, 210, 214, 228, 233, 261, 262
Fried, C., 274n

Fromm, E., 18, 79, 80, 99–
    108, 108n–111, 113, 114,
    119, 122, 123, 127–129,
    131, 133, 136, 151, 152,
    154, 156, 158, 163, 186,
    196, 230
Fussell, P., 8, 29n

Gaensbauer, T. J., 224, 226n
Gaertner, S. L., 30n
Galassi, J. P., 261, 274n
Galassi, M. D., 261, 274n
Garfield, S. L., 233, 259n
Geisheker, E., 195n
Glasser, W., 239, 242, 246,
    259n
Goebbels, J., 102
Goldstein, K., 133, 150n
Goodman, P., 150n
Goodwin, R. N., 11, 29n
Gordon, T., 29n
Gottman, J., 180, 195n

Haley, J., 236, 259n
Hallie, P. P., 7, 8, 29n
Harlow, H. F., 67, 70, 71, 78n,
    211, 212, 225n
Harlow, M. K., 67, 78n, 225n
Harmon, R. J., 224, 226n
Harris, T., 248, 259n
Harrison, A. A., 24–26, 30n
Hartmann, H., 63, 64, 66, 76,
    78n, 211, 225n
Hatfield, E., 27, 30n
Hay, D. F., 29n, 60n, 73, 78n
Hebb, D. O., 74, 78n
Hefferline, R. E., 150n
Hendrick, I., 64, 66, 78n
Heron, W., 60n, 211, 225n
Herrnstein, R. J., 22–24, 28,
    30n

Hinde, R. A., 225n
Hitler, A., 6, 102, 108n, 110
Hobbes, T., 10, 11, 29n
Hofer, M. A., 226n
Hoffman, M. L., 78n, 225n,
    226n
Hogan, R., 18, 30n, 188, 193–
    195n, 263, 274n
Holt, R. R., 51, 57, 60n
Horn, J., 226n
Horney, K., 79, 80, 90, 91, 94–
    99, 108n–114, 119, 121,
    123, 126n, 127, 129, 131,
    133, 136, 143, 151, 152,
    158, 163, 186, 196
Hornstein, H. A., 194n
Hull, C. L., 225n
Hunt, J. McV., 225n
Huston, T. L., 27, 30n

Johnson, D. L., 71, 78n
Johnson, J. A., 188, 195n, 263,
    274n
Jones, E., 43, 45n, 60n
Jung, C. G., 61–63, 110

Kanfer, F. H., 19, 20, 23, 30n,
    261, 274n
Kaswan, J., 251, 259n
Katz, E. L., 224, 226n
Kauffmann, S., 10, 29n
Kelley, H. H., 176, 177, 180,
    183, 189, 191, 193, 194n,
    198, 199, 202, 262, 274n
Kessen, W., 259n
Kierkegaard, S., 143
Kirschenbaum, H., 150n
Klinger, E., 258n
Koch, S., 225n
Kohlberg, L., 186–188, 194,
    195n, 197

Kondo, K., 259n
Krauthammer, C., 16, 30n
Krebs, D. L., 225n
Krebs, J. R., 60n, 226n
Kutz, S. L., 73, 78n

Laing, R. D., 128, 150n
Lao-tzu, 139
Lasch, C., 14, 16, 29n
Latané, B., 23, 30n
Leeper, R. W., 217, 225n
Levin, K., 60n
Levinger, G., 179, 194n
Lin, Y., 150n
London, P., 29n
Lowenfeld, H., 228, 258n
Lowenfeld, Y., 228, 258n
Lubinski, D., 248, 259n
Luckmann, T., 22, 30n
Luther, M., 149

McClelland, D. C., 30n, 215,
    216, 225n
Maccoby, E. E., 189–193,
    195n, 199, 203, 214, 225n,
    271, 274n
McDougall, W., 205, 206, 208,
    219, 225n
MacIntyre, A., 274n
Maddi, S. R., 162, 172n, 258n
Marin, P., 13, 29n
Markman, H., 180, 195n
Marshall, J. R., 29n
Martel, M. U., 258n
Martin, G. B., 78n
Marx, K., 128, 189
Maslow, A. H., 18, 127, 129–
    140, 143, 150n–172n, 186–
    188, 194, 196, 197, 213,
    216, 230, 260, 261
Masserman, J. H., 74, 78n

Matthews, K. A., 226n
May, R., 128, 150n
Menninger, K., 231, 252, 259n
Meyer, D. R., 67, 78n, 225n
Miller, N. E., 67, 78n
Milo, R. D., 225n
Montgomery, K. C., 67, 78n,
    211, 225n
Morgan, C. T., 225n
Morita, S., 240–243, 255–257
Mowrer, O. H., 231, 239, 242,
    244, 252, 258n, 259n
Munro, D. J., 249, 251, 259n
Murase, T., 259n
Murphy, G., 64, 78n
Mussen, P., 194n
Myerhoff, B., 3, 29n
Myers, A. K., 67, 78n

Nietzsche, F. W., 53, 54, 60n,
    110
Notarius, C., 180, 195n

Oldenquist, A., 187, 195n

Parloff, M. B., 150n
Parr, S. R., 29n
Paul, Saint, 47
Pavlov, I. P., 205
Perls, F., 150n
Perry, T. D., 274n
Piaget, J., 65, 78n, 211
Piliavin, I. M., 24, 27, 30n
Piliavin, J. A., 24, 27, 30n
Pirsig, R., 95, 108n
Putnam, H., 274n

Rank, O., 110
Rawls, J., 247–249, 259n, 274,
    274n
Reynolds, D. K., 259n

Rheingold, H. L., 60n, 73, 78n
Richter, C. P., 225n
Ridley, M., 226n
Rieff, P., 43, 45n
Roby, T. B., 53, 60n, 78n, 211, 225n
Rodin, J., 24, 27, 30n
Rogers, C. R., 18, 127, 130, 140–143, 145–150, 150n–152, 154–172n, 186, 194, 196, 197, 213, 216, 260, 261
Rosenhan, D., 6, 29n
Rosenman, R. H., 226n
Roszak, T., 174, 194n
Rousseau, J. J., 54, 110
Rusbult, C. E., 179, 194n
Rushton, J. P., 183–185, 191, 193, 194n, 195n, 197, 198, 202, 261, 274n

Sagi, A., 78n
Sampson, E. E., 12, 21, 29n, 30n, 247, 259n
Sartre, J.-P., 268, 269, 274n
Sasaki, Y., 259n
Schachter, S., 215, 225n
Schopler, J., 26, 30n
Scott, T. H., 60n, 211, 225n
Sennett, R., 172n
Sheffield, F. D., 53, 60n, 68, 69, 78n, 210, 211, 225n
Shotland, R. L., 27, 30n
Simonton, D. K., 195n
Simpson, E. L., 187, 195n
Singer, P., 266, 267, 270, 274n
Smith, M. B., 13, 29n, 258n, 259n
Sorrentino, R. M., 194n
Staub, E., 178, 194n
Stayton, D. J., 226n

Sullivan, H. S., 79–83, 85–90, 97, 103, 108n–114, 119, 126n, 127, 129, 132, 133, 143, 151, 152, 158
Sulloway, F. J., 45n, 53, 60n
Suomi, S. J., 71, 78n, 212, 225n

Tellegen, A., 248, 259n
Terris, W., 74, 78n
Thibaut, J. W., 176, 177, 180, 183, 189, 191, 193, 194n, 198, 199, 202, 262, 274n
Thom, G., 259n
Thompson, J. N., Jr., 226n
Thorpe, J. K., 224, 226n
Titchener, E. B., 205
Titmuss, R. M., 4, 29n
Tomkins, S. S., 219, 225n
Trevarthen, C., 226n
Trivers, R. L., 78n
Tronick, E., 226n
Turnbull, C. M., 266, 267, 274n

Vaillant, G. E., 30n
Veroff, J., 215, 225n
Veroff, J. B., 215, 225n
Vitz, P. C., 19, 20, 30n

Wallach, M. A., 126n
Waller, W. W., 14, 29n
Walster, G. W., 27, 30n
Warden, C. J., 225n
Warnock, M., 150n
Waskow, I. E., 150n
Waterman, A. S., 261, 274n
Watson, J. B., 206
Wechkin, S., 74, 78n
Wells, H. G., 103
Wertheimer, M., 135

West, M. J., 73, 78n
Whatley, J. L., 73, 78n
White, G. L., 176, 194n
White, R. W., 63–66, 76, 78n, 190, 195n, 213, 225n
Wilson, E. O., 226n
Winter, D. G., 30n
Wise, S., 226n
Wispé, L. G., 175, 194n, 225n, 226n
Wolfe, B. E., 150n

Woodworth, R. S., 206, 207, 220, 225n
Wulff, J. J., 78n, 225n
Wundt, W., 205

Yalom, I. D., 229, 230, 238–240, 244, 245, 258n, 259n
Young, P. T., 217, 225n

Zimmermann, R. R., 70, 78n, 212, 225n

Index of Topics

Abortion, 268
Activity level, 207, 211, 219
Affective responsiveness to
external stimuli, 217–225,
272–273
Affiliation, need for approval
as causing, 188–189, 194,
215, 271
Alienation, Marx's concept of,
128
Altruism:
biology of, 54–55, 74–77,
221–225, 272–273
social learning analysis of,
183–185
Amish, 2–3
Androgyny, psychological,
12–13, 247–248
Animals:
apparent social concern in,
74–77

attachment in, 70–72, 74–
77, 212
Anomie (feelings of meaninglessness), 77–78, 124, 139,
227–229, 245, 254
Appetite:
eating as motivated by, 52–
53, 69, 210–211, 218, 219
sexual motivation as, 52,
68–69, 210
Approval, need for, as causing affiliation, 188–189,
194, 215, 271
Arbitrariness of values (radical
subjectivism), arguments
against, 265–270
Assertiveness, 17–18, 260–261
Attachment:
in animals, 70–72, 74–77, 212
Maccoby on, 189–190, 214
Veroff and Veroff on, 215

"Attacks" of morality, Freud on, 48

Biology:
   current evolutionary theory in, 54–55, 74–77, 221–225, 272–273
   early motivation theories and, 207–210, 217, 271, 272
   influence on Freud of, 50–53, 55, 60
Blood donors, 4–5
Boy Scouts, 7–8, 16–17
Brotherly love, Freud on, 41, 47

Chambonnais, 7–9
China, People's Republic of, 162, 249–252
Competence:
   development of, 66–69, 72, 211–212
   motivation for, 63, 66, 69, 76–77, 79, 190, 213–214, 271
Compulsions, treatment for, 236–237
Conditionality in relationships, 176–181, 183, 262
Confucianism, 249, 252
Consciousness raising about shared values, 252, 254–255, 258
Curiosity behavior (development of competence), 66–69, 72, 211–212

Dating, marketplace analysis of, 24–25, 176

Depression, treatment for, 242, 244–249, 251, 253–254

Eating as motivated by appetite, 52–53, 69, 210–211, 218, 219
Effectance (competence) motivation, 63, 66, 69, 76–77, 79, 190, 213–214, 271
Egoism, trivial and nontrivial senses of, 200–204, 271
Empathy (sympathy), Aronfreed–Maccoby view of, 26, 190–191, 203–204, 271–272
Encounter (therapeutic and training) groups, 13, 129, 132, 148, 154–155, 174, 244–245
Ethical considerations, rationality of, 273–274
Ethics and science, 264–265
Euthanasia (mercy killings), 266
Evolution and altruism, 54–55, 74–77, 221–225, 272–273
Existentialism, 127–128, 264, 268–269
Exploration behavior (development of competence), 66–69, 72, 211–212

Freedom, Fromm's conception of, 100–104, 110
Functional autonomy of motives, 61–63

Genetics and altruism, 54–55, 74–77, 221–225, 272–273
Gestalt therapy, 128

Groups, therapeutic and
training, 13, 129, 132,
148, 154–155, 174, 244–
245

Healing rituals, 244
Hierarchy of needs, 130–135,
154, 157
Homonomy, trend toward,
247

Identity, need for, as explanation, 260
Ideology, in psychology, 1, 11,
28, 227
Ik, 266–267
Infants and young children:
appeal of, 223–224
social concern in, 2, 49, 72–
73, 76–77, 224
Insomnia, treatment for, 233–
234, 236, 239
Intrinsic motivation, 213–214
Invention of values (radical
subjectivism), arguments
against, 265–270

Kidney donors, 5

Laws, scientific, 21–22

Malevolent transformation,
85–86
Manipulation behavior (development of competence),
66–69, 72, 211–212
Marriage:
interaction in, 180–181
marketplace analysis of, 24–
25, 176
Rogers on, 159–160

Meaninglessness, feelings of,
77–78, 124, 139, 227–229,
245, 254
Mercy killings, 266
Metamotivation, 138–139,
216–217
Moral development, 186–188,
191, 194
Moral treatment, 255

Naikan therapy, 257–258
Narcissism, 40
Natural selection and altru-
ism, 54–55, 74–77, 221–
225, 272–273
Nazis, 6–7, 102, 254
Needs, hierarchy of, 130–135,
154, 157
Neurotic trends, 91–94, 113,
121
Nose example in Morita psy-
chotherapy, 243

Object relations, 80
Obsessions, treatment for,
236, 240–241
Oedipus complex, 36–37, 40–
41, 42
Orchestra example, 168, 247
Organismic valuing process,
144–146, 155

Peak experiences, 139, 153
People's Republic of China,
162, 249–252
Peremptory quality of motivations, 56–57
Persistence, egoistic account
of, 21
Personal causation, motive
for, as explanation, 213–
214

Phobias, treatment for, 234,
236–238, 242–243, 255
Pleasure principle, 35
Power, need for, as explanation, 216, 271
Psychological values, dominance of, 117, 164, 170
Purpose, problem of, 205–
207, 219–220, 270–272

Radical subjectivism, arguments against, 265–270
Rationality of ethical considerations, 273–274
Reality principle, 35, 119
Reciprocal altruism, 75
Reciprocation of help, 26–27
Reciprocity (conditionality) in
relationships, 176–181,
183, 262
Religion, 6–9, 19–20, 47, 193,
230–232, 244, 252–253,
260, 264

Science, ethics and, 264–265
Scientific laws, 21–22
Self-determination, need for,
as explanation, 213–214,
271
Self-expression, terrorist attacks as, 16–17
Self-help (therapeutic and
training) groups, 13, 129,
132, 148, 154–155, 174,
244–245
Self-punishment, social learning analysis of, 182–183
Self-system, in Sullivan's theory, 83–84, 88
Seventh Day Adventists, 6

Sexual motivation as appetite,
52, 68–69, 210
Sexual problems, treatment
for, 235–236
Shoulds, tyranny of, 95–97,
99, 112–113, 121, 151,
187, 260–261
Sleeplessness (insomnia),
treatment for, 233–234,
236, 239
Social approval, need for, as
causing affiliation, 188–
189, 194, 215, 271
Social concern:
apparent, in animals, 74–77
current evolutionary theory
in biology, 54–55, 74–77,
221–225, 272–273
in infants and young children, 2, 24, 72–73, 76–77,
224
Social difficulties, treatment
for, 235, 237–238, 244–
245
Social exchange (conditionality in relationships), 176–
181, 183, 262
Social interest, Adler's concept of, 254–256
Social learning theory, 181–
186, 187, 191, 193, 262,
271
Striving, egoistic account of,
21, 217
Subjectivism, radical, arguments against, 265–270
Sublimation, 37–38, 43, 62–
63, 110, 114–115, 151–
152, 156–157, 169, 197,
208, 261
Subway study, 24, 27

Sympathy, Aronfreed–Maccoby view of, 26, 190–191, 203–204, 271–272
Syphilitic's dread of infecting others, 42

Taoism, 139
Terrorist attacks as self-expression, 16–17
Training and therapeutic groups, 13, 129, 132, 148, 154–155, 174, 244–245

Tyranny of shoulds, 95–97, 99, 112–113, 121, 151, 187, 260–261

Unconditional positive regard, 142, 145, 147, 155

Values as invented (radical subjectivism), arguments against, 265–270